WITH ONE HAND TIED BEHIND MY BRAIN

with one hand tied behind my brain

A MEMOIR OF LIFE AFTER
STROKE

AVREL SEALE

TCU Press

Fort Worth, Texas

Library of Congress Cataloging-in-Publication Data

Names: Seale, Avrel, 1967–author.
Title: With one hand tied behind my brain : a memoir of life after stroke / Avrel Seale.
Description: Fort Worth, Texas : TCU Press, [2020] | Summary: "Most would not expect a book about a stroke to be entertaining, but this memoir will force you to laugh through a tragedy, then cry, then laugh again. Avrel Seale was fifty, did not smoke or drink, had low blood pressure, and had hiked more than two hundred miles the year a stroke nearly ended his life. In an instant, he was teleported into the body of an old man-unbalanced, shaky, spastic, and half-paralyzed. Overnight, he was plunged into a world of brain surgeons, nurses, insurance case managers, and an abundance of therapists. Beginning three weeks before his stroke to set the stage, Seale leads us through the harrowing day of his stroke and emergency brain surgery with minute-by-minute intensity. We then follow him through ICU, a rehab hospital, and a neuro-recovery group-living center, where we meet a memorable cast of other stroke survivors and also those recovering from auto accidents and gunshots. Finally home, Seale leads us through a new life of firsts, including returning to work, to driving, to playing guitar, to camping, and even to writing a book-all with one hand. What emerges from his humor ("elegant but dev-astating") is a revealing critique of the hospital experience, the insurance industry, and rehab culture. And his nothing-off-the-table quest for recovery shows both the sobering struggles and inspiring possibilities of life after a stroke in twenty-first century America. — AVREL SEALE lives in Austin with his wife, Kirstin, and three sons. He has been a newspaper reporter and columnist and has spent much of his career at the University of Texas at Austin, as editor of its alumni magazine, speechwriter for its president, and as a writer for its news, marketing, and development offices"—Provided by publisher.
Identifiers: LCCN 2020034078 (print) | LCCN 2020034079 (ebook) | ISBN 9780875657646 (trade paperback) | ISBN 9780875657677 (ebook)
Subjects: LCSH: Seale, Avrel, 1967- | Cerebrovascular disease—Patients—Texas—Biography. | LCGFT: Autobiographies.
Classification: LCC RC388.5 .S433 2020 (print) | LCC RC388.5 (ebook) | DDC 616.8/10092 [B]—dc23
LC record available at https://lccn.loc.gov/2020034078
LC ebook record available at https://lccn.loc.gov/2020034079

TCU Box 298300
Fort Worth, Texas 76129
817.257.7822
www.prs.tcu.edu
To order books: 1.800.826.8911
All rights reserved.

Contact Info
The author can be reached at AvrelSeale.wordpress.com.

For Kirstin
"All I Ever Need Is You"

Contents

Part Four

"I feel funny inside ... it must be love! No—wait, it's a stroke."
—Abe Simpson, *The Simpsons*

Introduction

On Friday morning, January 19, 2018, I left for work and didn't sleep in my own bed again for ten weeks. For three months, I didn't wear underwear—not bragging, just stating a fact. I was two-handed and learned to do almost everything with one. I was right-handed in a world built for right-handedness and learned to do almost everything with my left. I learned how to drive using only my left foot and left hand after thirty-five years of driving the other way.

Without any prior interest in the Americans with Disabilities Act, I became an expert in wheelchair ramps and curb cuts, handrails and bathroom grab bars.

I learned a lot about the brain that year. For instance, some people are incapable of miming activities with their face. If I told you to pretend to blow out a candle, and you couldn't do it, you would have what's called buccofacial apraxia, and that's a thing. *I* can mime blowing out a candle, but some people cannot. Didn't know that before last year.

I learned that sometimes you have to learn how to walk before you can crawl.

I learned a thing or two about faith, about living in the moment and working for the future all at once. And about frustration and despair and grief—and hope, and joy. I learned about apple cider vinegar and Prozac and Botox. Massage and acupuncture.

I found out who my real friends were, and there were more of them than I would have guessed.

I found out how much my wife, Kirstin, really loved me, and how much I loved her, and what that whole "in sickness and in health" line actually meant. I found out what our three growing boys were actually capable of.

To say stroke doesn't discriminate is not entirely true, because many causes are preventable. It certainly discriminates against smokers, doubling their chances. It discriminates against the out of shape, though not all of them. In America, the persistence of smoking and obesity in the South has led researchers to refer to the region as the Stroke Belt. Beyond preventable factors, it discriminates against men, and against black people, who are twice as likely as white folks to have strokes.

But I was fifty years old, did not smoke or drink, had low blood pressure, and had hiked more than two hundred miles the year a stroke nearly ended my life. Spoiler alert: it didn't. But it did change that life, changed it good.

In an instant, I was teleported into the body of a doddering old man, shaky, unbalanced, spastic, half-paralyzed, and so weak I was unable even to sit up for more than a few minutes at a time. Overnight, I was plunged into a world of brain surgeons, nurses, medical techs, hospital administrators, case managers, insurance companies, and lots and lots of therapists—forty-one of them at last count. Terms entering my vernacular included CVA, AVM, PRN, balance billing, subrogation, and pre-auth and re-auth.

I saw from the inside as never before and hopefully never again the American health care "system," which, as the sarcasm quotes suggest, is not a system at all, but more accurately a *sector* composed of related businesses that are either incredibly profitable or else in danger of disappearing.

At each step of recovery, I was passed off to a new team of therapists with a new program, and all institutional knowledge of me would vanish instantly. There would be a new clipboard holding a clean stack of intake forms, fresh and warm off the copier, forms with dozens of tiny blanks for me to fill in with my non-dominant hand. These forms, often photocopies of photocopies, asked all of the same questions I had answered dozens of times before: First and foremost, what was my twelve-digit insurance ID number? Then and only then did we proceed: What was my birthdate? What was my injury, and the date of my injury? Was I allergic to any medications?

These forms were followed by well-intentioned interviews with enthusiastic fresh faces: How did I pronounce my name, and where did *that* come from?! Did I have any feeling in my leg? Had there been any changes in my vision? How much return had I gotten in my right arm? Was I able to curl my right toes up? These intake interviews were necessary, of course, because it seemed no one ever shared my medical information with those at the next stop on my journey, no matter how many forms I signed granting them permission to do exactly that.

I wanted to hack into all seven hundred television channels at the same time, like a Bond villain, and announce to all the world that, for the very last time, there had been *no changes in my vision since the stroke*, and the next person who asked me that would be severely caned.

But while stroke does discriminate, it is also a great equalizer. Without warning, it can bring low the religious—Pope Benedict XVI—and the atheist, Richard Dawkins. It smites the powerful, like Joe Kennedy at seventy-three, and the penniless, like the guy I sometimes see at the bus stop, moving exactly like me. It can rob an actor of speech, like it did Kirk Douglas at seventy-nine, and confine a Broadway legend like Tim Curry to a wheelchair at sixty-seven. It afflicts heroes of highbrow art, like Marian Anderson, Richard Attenborough, and Ray Bradbury, and of popular entertainment, like Loretta Lynn at eighty-five, Bob Barker at seventy-nine, Dick Clark at seventy-five, Rick James at fifty, and guitar legend Django Reinhardt, killed by a stroke at forty-three.

Some survivors have been purveyors of innocence, like A. A. Milne; some, purveyors of debauchery, like Hugh Hefner; and some, purveyors of obscenity, like Larry Flynt. Of course, the old, but also the young, like TV stars Frankie Muniz at twenty-six and Aubrey Plaza at twenty. It is only the famous we hear about. But of the world's 7.5 billion people, 15 million suffer a stroke each year (0.2 percent). Of these 15 million a year, a third of them die during the stroke, like Django and actor Luke Perry. Fifty-nine percent of folks who have my particular kind of stroke—an intracranial hemorrhage— die within a year. And of those who do survive their stroke, 25-40 percent lose a significant portion of their ability to use language, that loss known as "aphasia." Aphasia is primarily the result of left-brain stroke, and since strokes are fairly evenly split between left-brain and right-brain, between 50 and 80 percent of left-brain strokes (as mine was) result in aphasia.

I won't say that I was spared my life and my language so I could write this book; I am not quite that much of a mystic nor, hopefully, narcissist. What I will say is that because I survived with my language center largely intact, I now have an uncommon opportunity. I don't consider this book a deep dive into health care policy, but if I can help shine a light on some of its most obvious shortcomings, then maybe people smarter than me can figure out how to actually fix it.

But maybe, too, I can give stroke survivors and the folks who care for them a voice, survivors who might have lost their language, or do not have the bandwidth to deal with a stroke and make notes for a book at the same time, or just don't have enough gas left in the tank after this kind of injury. That I am still relatively young, have some energy and ambition, and yet also have had a fairly comprehensive medical catastrophe—that combination must be good for something.

Part One

Wade (right) and me at Kelly Pond in Sam Houston National Forest, January 1, 2018.

With Andrew and Cameron the Monday before the stroke at a Martin Luther King Jr. Day work project.

Last photo of me on the eve of the stroke, buying Ian a bike on his eleventh birthday.

CHAPTER 1

If We Could Stand the Weather

*Apoplexy chiefly attacks individuals of middle or of advanced age; and it
has been observed, that persons of a corpulent habit, and those having a
short neck and large head, and who lead an inactive and sedentary life,
or make use of a full, rich diet, are more liable to it than those of different
habits. Men are much more liable than women to apoplexy.*

—*Vitalogy, 1904*

As dawn broke over New Year's Day 2018, a light dusting of rare snow
covered my windshield. It snows about every eight years in Austin, but
it had snowed twice this year already. Strangeness abounded.

Wade pulled up to the house and parked under the basketball hoop in
the cul-de-sac. He threw his duffle bag into the backseat of my truck and
helped me load my three-foot plywood chuck box into the bed. When the
wipers had pushed the snow crystals off my windshield, we headed east. It
was three hours from Austin to Sam Houston National Forest. The forecast
for the night of January 1 in Montgomery, Texas, the nearest town to where
we would be camping, was twenty-one degrees. We drove deep into the forest
and camped on the banks of Kelly's Pond. This calls for a little explanation.

Over the last several years, Wade and I, who had been friends thirty-five
years, since high school, had established a tradition of camping on or as
close as possible to New Year's, no matter what the elements had in store
for us. Three years earlier, we had backpacked twenty-six miles around
Lake Georgetown, just north of Austin, much of it in freezing weather, and
had hammock-camped under tarps in a spectacular electrical storm and
downpour. A photo shows the two of us at the trailhead under a cold, gray

sky, loaded down with gear and covered head-to-toe in matching bright-blue rain suits, two enormous, terrifying Smurfs.

The following year, we had come to this same national forest and camped when it was in the mid-thirties. Being an adult leader in Boy Scouts had hardened me, and I had learned a saying in that culture: "There is no such thing as bad weather, only poor equipment choices." Each passing New Year's campout Wade and I went on seemed to test that aphorism more severely.

We had never really articulated it, but I believe we thought that if we could camp at New Year's no matter what the weather was, we could handle anything else life threw at us that year. Indeed, we survived the night on Kelly's Pond and headed back west to Central Texas Tuesday morning.

By Wednesday, I was back at work at the University of Texas at Austin, where I had spent most of my career in different roles as a writer and editor, seventeen years as editor of the university's alumni magazine, then four years as the president's speechwriter. I now worked in the university's central communications office as a sort of all-purpose writer for the UT brand.

Friday, January 5, was still cool but not cold. It had warmed up a lot since New Year's Day, into the forties. I got to work at eight and downed a cup of coffee quickly before setting out for the opposite corner of campus, a brisk mile-and-a-half walk that took just more than thirty minutes. My boss, Teresa, and I were meeting that morning at UT's medical school to conduct a messaging workshop. In the last four years, the school had been built from the ground up. Following a contentious election, the voters of Travis County had empowered the health district to levy a modest tax on county residents to fund a new medical school at Texas's flagship university. It was the first medical school to be built at a major university in nearly fifty years. Every medical school requires a teaching hospital, and the locally dominant Seton Healthcare had agreed to build a brand-new such hospital adjacent to the med school.

The medical school was named for UT alumnus, personal computer mogul, and billionaire benefactor Michael Dell. The university's president hired the founding dean when I had been his speechwriter. The dean's specialty was stroke. This resonated with me, because, of all the major categories of catastrophic diseases and injuries, the one I knew the most about was stroke. Oh—I knew something about ulcerative colitis, which my mother had survived after a long and scary bout in her forties and for which she had made several high-stakes trips from the South Texas border to the Mayo Clinic in Minnesota when I was a UT student. And I knew way too much about Parkinson's, to which my father had succumbed almost four years earlier after it had ravaged his neuromuscular system for two decades.

I did not know a lot about cancer, even after funerals of grandparents and gone-too-soon coworkers and increasingly common scares among my own cohort. Nor did I know much about heart disease beyond what you might find on a ninth-grade quiz.

But stroke—stroke I knew a lot about. My father-in-law had a stroke just six months into his retirement, and Kirstin had been neck-deep in the details of that stroke for the past five years. She had been at his side in and out of multiple rehab hospitals, at doctor visits without number, through assisted-living centers, screening and hiring caregivers, dealing with insurance headaches, rehab, ankle braces, arm slings, wheelchairs, shower benches, handicap parking permits, driver's license woes. For her, it had become an unpaid but very-much-full-time job, one she was willing and even eager to do because of her abundance of love and sense of responsibility. Still, dealing with this stuff was no one's first choice of a pastime. I had a front-row seat on his medical catastrophe, but Kirstin—she had been on the stage.

The purpose of my cross-campus hike that cool January morning was to meet with Dean Clay Johnston and a team of about fifteen of his lieutenants. We needed them to help the central administration put a finer point on what the Dell Medical School was all about.

Since the dean had arrived in Austin from San Francisco, he had given hundreds of public talks in which he pointed out the things in the medical field that needed to be improved, nay, revolutionized—the reversed incentives, the way in which the system treats patients in the aggregate as commodities, the things done purely out of tradition for no good reason. One of his classic examples, which always got a knowing chuckle out of the audience, was the hospital gown. "Why is the opening always in the back," he mused with Seinfeld-like observationalism, "when nearly all of the interest, medically speaking, *is in the front*?"

Since arriving at Texas, the dean had been preaching the gospel of "patient-centered care," something that sounded so common-sense and obvious I was amazed it needed articulating. It seemed to belong in the same category as "the customer's always right" and "an object in motion tends to stay in motion unless acted on by some force." How could it have ever been that a patient was not at the center of their care? Still, in this sector, "patient-centered care" seemed to pass for a revolutionary concept.

Occasionally during the workshop with the dean and his top brass, my eyes wandered out the seventh-story window and across Red River Street to the teaching hospital, Dell Seton.

One of the most striking features of my life, at least to me, is what a clear and obvious product I am of both of my parents. If you know someone's parents, sometimes you can look at them and see they are a mix of both. "He's got his mother's eyes and his father's nose." Facially, I don't strongly resemble either of my parents, but my psyche is an exacting portmanteau of the two—I am a psychogenetic chimera.

Each of my parents had a dominant passion in life that expressed itself in an artistic form. My mother's passion is writing. She is a short-story specialist and essayist and at seventy-two was named Poet Laureate of Texas. My father was a prolific composer, a professor of music, and the longtime director of the regional symphony in South Texas, where they raised me.

My two older brothers both inherited the artist's soul, but in them it was manifested visually. Ansen had a long career in photography before branching out into mixed-media public art. Erren had an intense career in graphic design, then opened a store selling home furnishings, which became heir to his aesthetic gifts.

But me? I was half Mom, half Dad—no question about it. I wrote my first book in eighth grade, a fan-fiction novella set in Narnia. The next year I picked up a guitar and started jamming with friends. Ever since, these twin passions of writing and music have vied for dominance in my life, with neither of them able to push the other aside.

By 2018, I had accrued a twenty-eight-year career in writing—journalism and marketing—and all the while had been deeply involved in music—writing, performing, recording. The brain is divided into halves, after all, and at times it felt like my mother and father had each taken a hemisphere and were engaged in an eternal tug-of-war. Write! Play! No, write books! No, write music!

I suppose I had doubled down on writing, as it was both my vocation and avocation. The ultimate busman's holiday, I had written nine books in parallel to my day jobs. The first eight I published myself. But just two months earlier, after twelve years of trying, I succeeded in getting my first book published by someone else. Getting that book published should have been an exhilarating time of celebration, but in fact, it was the most frightening thing I had ever done. It was a time of profound trepidation, and signing that publishing contract was an unnerving leap of faith. I say this because I worked at a Tier One national research university, and my book was on a paranormal subject. It was a nonfiction book about the mystery of sasquatches—bigfoots. And now you understand the trepidation.

After many years of quiet interest in the subject, I had gone on a one-hundred-mile solo hike in East Texas in search of evidence that might corroborate the dozens of strange accounts coming out of those woods. What I found became my book *Monster Hike*. I had to write it. As I often tell people who are "considering writing something," a true writer writes because they cannot *not* write. I am incapable of not writing books, all the time. It is what I do. It's my default setting. I don't know what "writer's block" even means. If I finish a book and don't have another idea queued up and ready to go, it takes about two weeks before anxiety and depression set in. The writing gene surely came from my mother, but I think the *project* gene, the deep need to constantly have an audacious goal before me, is as much from my father, whose collected works, now housed at the university where he taught, require thirty-five linear feet of shelf space and include three ballets, two operas, a film score, and 120 other compositions for just about every conceivable grouping of instruments and voices.

But none of my previous books had posed this dilemma for me. I had never even once considered whether to put my name on something or to publish it anonymously. I thought long and hard about whether to go public, to "come out." I was the primary breadwinner for my family, for three boys, the oldest of which was already getting emails from colleges. To willingly associate myself with a fringe topic like bigfoot, one which overwhelmingly elicited laughter and eye-rolling, was to endanger my career, our chief means of support. It could have been the greatest "unforced error" of my life.

But at excruciating length, I concluded my soul could never really be at peace until it was published, by someone else or by me. Perhaps most importantly, I wanted to model courage for my sons, intellectual courage. That seemed more important than modeling safety and conformity. And although it would be many years before they could understand the risk I took in doing this, I hoped one day they would look back on the act with some degree of pride—that they would know Dad had done at least one brave thing in his life.

I gave the manuscript to Kirstin, who didn't object. I also let my bosses read it as a heads-up. To my surprise, I found a willing publisher almost immediately, and by mid-November—almost exactly a year since I had finished the hike—the book was out.

Write! Play! Write books! No, write music! David McLeod and I had been friends since first grade, when our parents met at First Presbyterian Church of McAllen, Texas. At fifteen, we formed the aforementioned band, he on bass, me on guitar. We gigged extensively in the early nineties after college. And though day jobs, marriages, and moves would cause us to hit the pause button multiple times, we never really stopped, and eventually we wound up living just a few miles apart in Austin. For the last several years, we had been gigging as a duo in Austin under the name Moondog. And after thirty-five years of playing together, we were releasing our first album.

As I sat at work and answered email, I listened through the new mixes of songs David and I had recorded in Dripping Springs, west of Austin, about six weeks earlier. We only had to get the mixes finalized and mastered, then push them to iTunes or Spotify or some such service I did not really understand because I had never moved beyond listening to music on CDs. I had missed the MP3 platform altogether and was vaguely aware that now, with a certain kind of Orwellian speaker-microphone combo sold by Amazon, you could just say the name of a song or album and "Alexa" would play it forthwith. I was only fifty, and yet already I felt I was living in a civilization that had passed me by. Anyway, writing and recording the songs with David had been the realization of a lifelong dream for us both, and it was better late than never.

The week of January 15 was par for the course. It was the height of cedar season in Central Texas, which meant debilitating allergies for me and most people I knew. We managed the best we could, mitigating the stinging eyes, runny nose, and sneezing fits with over-the-counter antihistamines, nasal mists, neti pots, and, when we were completely off the rails, cortisone shots. The university and the public schools were closed that Monday for MLK Day, so Kirstin found a nearby work project by which we could honor Dr. King's memory. Armed with a purse pack of tissues, Zyrtec, and Flonase, we headed undaunted into a cedar forest and joined about twenty others to spend three hours spreading mulch on a hiking trail at a county park.

Thursday was our youngest son's birthday. Ian was turning eleven and was the only one left who was actually a child. As he had outgrown his bike once again, we piled into my truck after I got home from work and went to Academy Sports + Outdoors to pick out his next trusty steed. With that box checked, we returned home and celebrated with a chocolate cake and eleven candles. Gainful employment, a short work week, a new bike, chocolate cake, a book published, a record ready to drop. I must say life was pretty good.

Friday, January 19, began like most other winter days—our house, cool and still, gradually grinding into motion. From our walk-in closet, I extracted a pink Oxford shirt that I had inherited when my father passed on four years earlier. I was four inches taller than him, so the shirt sleeves were a little short, but I liked wearing it anyhow—a little piece of him with me. This was followed by khakis, brown leather shoes, and my small oval-rim silver glasses.

Two of our three boys were up and eating cereal and fixing their lunches. I fed Gracie, our lab-boxer-pit mix, hollered goodbye to Kirstin, took the protein shake off the counter, and climbed into my pickup.

Each morning, I would drive fifteen minutes toward work, leave my truck at the park-and-ride, and get on a bus for the remaining forty-five-minute ride to campus. I got off at a 7-Eleven, made my way the two remaining blocks to work, and flashed my wallet in front of a sensor so my ID card would unlock the building, as it was still five minutes until eight.

The morning was not too remarkable and consisted of one small meeting to start messaging work for the university's college of engineering.

At lunch, Teresa took me and her other direct reports to Hopfields, a French-inspired eatery a few blocks north of campus, for a belated thank-you lunch that had gotten pushed since before the holidays. Returning from that, I answered a few emails and quit a little early for the day to prepare for a podcast interview in support of *Monster Hike*.

At 2:35, I sent Teresa one last email for the day. Since I worked in a public space that was not good for prolonged phone or Skype interviews, my plan was to seal myself up in the supply room off the main office for the hour-long interview.

This required several trips between my desk and the supply room to transport my laptop and all its cords and dongles, my microphone and headphones, a glass of water and a copy of the book in case I was asked to read a passage. As I was making my final trip between my cubicle and the supply room, my right hip began to buckle strangely with each step.

CHAPTER 2

Texas Flood

Hemorrhagic or sanguineous apoplexy . . . consists in the rupture of a vessel, and extravasation of blood and the substance of the brain, or outside the nervous masses. The symptoms are usually sudden, and its development most rapid. . . . It is seldom that a physician can be procured in time to save life in apoplexy.

—*Vitalogy, 1904*

I don't recall precisely what I thought in the moment my hip started buckling with each step, but it was probably something like, "Whatever this is, I don't have time for it." My Skype interview was just over twenty minutes away. The buckling worsened as I walked back toward my cubicle. I knew something was not right, so purposefully stayed outside my cube so that if I collapsed I would be noticed. Within seconds, I was on my knees.

Immediately, a coworker saw me on the floor and asked if I was all right. Soon, I turned and sat on the floor in the aisle, continuing to try to answer questions from a growing number of concerned colleagues about what it was I was feeling. Light-headed? Not really. Faint? Dizzy? No. No.

At 2:40, I pulled out my phone and searched for an email from the woman with whom I had the three o'clock interview. I hit reply and handed the phone to my boss, Teresa. "Can you please write this woman and tell her I won't be able to make our call? A medical reason." Teresa did as I asked. As that was happening, one of our art directors was dialing 911. Another art director went downstairs to the front door to await the ambulance and bring the EMTs to me.

Within two minutes, I could no longer move my right leg. Then I looked at my right arm and something terrifying happened. It's hard to explain, but it didn't seem like *my* arm. It was like an out-of-body experience but only in relation to one part of my body. Then I tried to move my arm and could not.

I knew all too well what was happening. I was having a stroke.

All my thoughts turned at once to Kirstin. I simply could not believe she, after five years of dealing with her father's stroke nonstop, was being made to walk this path again. Lightning had struck her twice. It was not lost on me that the name of the podcast I had been preparing to record was *Shattered Reality.*

The EMS crew arrived within four minutes of my slow-motion collapse. As this happened, my coworkers fell back to their cubicles and prairie-dogged from less conspicuous positions, giving the first responders room to maneuver.

I began to breathe heavily and to weep, and though the EMS crew was moving as fast as humanly possible, I nonetheless implored them between red-faced sobs to "Please hurry!" as if that might somehow help. They carried me out of the room backwards on a stretcher, through the university's visitor center with which we shared the building, down a winding staircase, and out the front door.

As they prepared to load me into the ambulance, they asked me where I wanted to go. I thought this odd—to ask a person who is having a stroke where they want to go.

"Seton," I said between gasping and sobbing. I knew it was "in-network" because all three of my sons had been born there. This was the second thing that seemed fundamentally wrong—that a person having a stroke would have to actively think about which hospitals were in-network and which might be out-of-network. Moreover, I knew it was close because I passed it every day on the bus ride to work.

From there it was all sound and light and confusion—sirens wailing through the intersections. I wept for Kirstin, but my second thought all the while was, *damn* this is going to be expensive.

By that time, *Shattered Reality* was being recorded for broadcast that night. "Today is our sixty-first show, so we're breaking records and milestones," said Fahrusha, the host. "It's our first show of the new year, and unfortunately we also had an upset today—that's a first, too. We do hope Mr. Seale feels better, but unfortunately he has a medical emergency, and he's not available at this particular time."

Teresa followed the ambulance to the hospital and began posting updates to our office's online Slack channel: *Avrel is in emergency. Kirstin is with him. I'm in waiting room. Will keep you guys updated. Prayers that this is nothing.*

In five minutes, we had arrived at the ER at Seton Main, and I was rolling through the hallways on a gurney, disoriented by turns this way and that and the slow strobe of fluorescent lights passing overhead.

I was so happy to see Kirstin's face and hear her sweet, strong voice, but was confused by the fact she was already there. Teresa had called her before I had even been loaded into the ambulance, and because Kirstin was already in her car and driving, she simply made a U-turn and started to the hospital, driving as fast as I had driven each time she had gone into labor and I had taken her to the same place.

She had been driving from her office to pick up Andrew, our fifteen-year-old, from school and take him to an appointment. She texted him: "I can't pick you up today. I'll call and tell you what's going on when all three of you are home." Then Kirstin called her mother, who lived one block from us, and told her I was having a stroke and that she should go to our house and meet the boys when they got home from school.

At the hospital, nameless, faceless people stripped me of my clothes and somehow got me into one of the backless gowns the dean had used as an example of what's wrong with health care. I have no clear memory of when or how this happened, but I do remember a lot of team lifts to get my deadweight from one surface to another. This was done with blankets that had eight matching-colored handles, four down each side. "Red on this one?" one would ask.

"No, yellow for this one, red to get him back," the other tech would reply. Then I would feel the lift and the transfer.

The next order of business was a CT scan. This confirmed what I had known since 2:45—that I had had a stroke on the left side of my brain that had paralyzed my right leg and arm.

Teresa [3:24 PM] Avrel has had a stroke. Left side of the brain.
Teresa [3:44 PM] If you are so inclined, I'd like to ask the team to please PRAY.
Teresa [3:50 PM] It was a hemorrhagic stroke. I will keep updating here.

Back at the office, my coworkers were Googling "hemorrhagic stroke" and finding passages like this one: "[One] study documented death rates after an intracerebral bleed of 31% at 7 days, 59% at one year, 82% at 10 years and more than 90% at 16 years. Clearly this is a serious and frequently fatal condition."

Kirstin met me back in the ER, where I was still crying, buffeted by waves of raw despair about the future. She took my hand. "This is not like other strokes in our life," she said in a low voice, knowing exactly what I was thinking. "You've got this. We've got this. We've got this . . ."

> *Teresa [4:01 PM] He's being taken to Seton by Dell Med.*
> *Teresa [4:08 PM] They need to slow the bleeding in the brain and Dell Seton has better facilities for this. I'm headed there. Is Avrel's phone there?? Can someone bring it down to me in a few minutes with his bag and laptop?*
> *Jennifer [4:09 PM] The EMS guys grabbed his phone and took it with them*
> *Teresa [4:09 PM] Please get his laptop from the supply closet.*
> *Leslie [4:10 PM] His backpack and jacket are here.*
> *Teresa [4:10 PM] Ok, I will tell Kirstin. Please pack up his other stuff. I'll text when I'm close to the office. Kirstin found his phone. Thanks guys. I'll come up to get his stuff and debrief you.*

I was again on the move, this time to Dell Seton, the sister hospital connected to the med school some thirty blocks away, which had a more advanced neurological center. I was loaded back into the ambulance.

Even in my confused and grieving state, with half my brain filling with blood, questions about the health care system were presenting themselves to me so rapidly I could not capture them all. It was clear to me and everyone else in the office that I was having a stroke. If Dell Seton was the best place for stroke victims, why was I not taken there in the first place but rather asked where I wanted to go? This seemed like a pretty simple problem to solve. We can put a man on the moon, but first responders ask patients with critical and easily diagnosable injuries where they would like to go, as if they all would know which nearby hospital is strongest in which specialty: "Well, St. David's has an excellent cardio team, and the department head there graduated first in his class from Harvard. But this is clearly a stroke, and, as everyone knows, the neuro team at Dell Seton has superior imaging technology and a more robust rotation of surgeons on call."

Kirstin rode in the front of the ambulance, but I was not aware she was with me. From the passenger seat, she called our boys at home. With sirens wailing as we slowly swiveled through intersections gridlocked by five o'clock traffic, Kirstin used her calmest, strongest voice to tell the boys to put her on speaker so that she could talk to all three of them at once. "Dad is very sick," she announced, "but he's going to be okay, and we're on our way to the hospital. Neenee will be there in a few minutes, and she will spend the night with you."

We pulled into the ambulance bay. I felt the cool outside air, and then we were in another hallway. I was immediately rolled into another windowless room where four people team-lifted me from the gurney to another CT scanner.

Within fifteen minutes of arriving, I had a seizure and remember nothing else. According to Kirstin, I went gray, eyes glassy and lifeless. I was wheeled into surgery prep.

Teresa [5:39 PM] Avrel has had a post-stroke seizure. Kirstin says it's busy in the ER. Neurologist is there. Will keep updating.

I was intubated, which proved tricky given the way my large tonsils crowded access to my windpipe.

Teresa [6:00 PM] Avrel has been intubated because he cannot breathe on his own. There are eleven people working on him. Please pray. Kirstin's mom is with the boys. Their friends just arrived at the hospital.

At 6:05, Kirstin gathered herself and sent a group text to my mother and two brothers. This, she remembers, was the hardest. As the daughter of a stroke survivor, as a mother herself, and as the mother of three brothers no less, she knew better than just about anyone what it would feel like to receive this text:

Hi. Avrel is in the hospital. He had a large hemorrhagic stroke on the left side of his brain this afternoon. He is having a CT scan now. May have surgery later today. I will keep you posted. Love you all.

As soon as that text reached McAllen, my brother Erren began coordinating with our mother to come to Austin. Erren and his husband, Fernando, owned and operated a store selling home decor and folk art. Having just locked the store door at six and waiting to ring up the last customer, he printed out a sign for the glass door saying "Closed until Tuesday for family emergency." A few hours of packing and other preparation, and by nine, Erren, Fernando, my mother, and her significant other, John, were speeding through the black of the King Ranch to see however much of me was left.

When my oldest brother, Ansen, got Kirstin's text, he was en route from Houston, where he had been making an art proposal, back to his home in San Antonio. He redirected his phone to navigate him to Austin instead.

Back at the hospital, the neurosurgeon explained to Kirstin that, according to the most recent CT scan, the bleeding had spread. Their best chance to stop it and the attendant swelling of the brain was surgery. Did she want them to perform surgery?

Yes, she replied, in parentheses wondering if there were people who, given the option, chose *not* to have surgery. Apparently so, according to the surgeon. Many did not.

> *Teresa [6:32 PM] Avrel needs brain surgery. They will start within the hour.*
> *Teresa [6:37 PM] They're moving him into surgery now.*

It had been exactly four hours since the stroke.

Kirstin was asked to step out of the room because the next step was a sterile procedure, the insertion of the central line, an IV that is placed not in the arms (those I had already) but in the neck. The central line is used to deliver drugs that are too strong for the smaller veins in the arms to be trusted with. Instead, drugs are inserted about three inches above the heart, where the veins are so large and tough that they can handle these caustic potions.

They wheeled me out to surgery. When the prep room was empty, Kirstin stepped back in, raised her phone, which had not left her hand since she got out of the car at the first hospital, and took a remarkable picture. In it, the room is empty except for three rolling stands on which hang IV bags and various electrical monitors. The white linoleum floor is strewn with twenty-eight pieces of trash in the visible frame. It looks like an explosion of medical waste—plastic cups, Band-Aid wrappers, blue rubber gloves, plastic tubes, plastic bags, straps, papers—like the aftermath of a hurricane that had hit a hospital.

Teresa [8:00 PM] Avrel is in surgery. No updates except that the surgeon is doing something to deal with the 4.7 cm hemorrhage in the brain. Surgeon said going in may reveal why this happened. He will be moved to ICU after the surgery.

Teresa [8:05 PM] Brothers are arriving soon, so I am leaving soon. I have Kirstin's friend's number and she is going to keep me updated. I'll keep updating here.

Teresa [8:09 PM] [pray emoji]

News of my stroke moved out first in nodes and then in concentric waves from those nodes—from Teresa to Kirstin to her mom and best friends to my close friends. Kirstin worked the phone continuously for what seemed like days. She called David's house. His wife, Lisa, picked up the phone, and Kirstin told her. David was in the bathroom caulking the bathtub, and pretty much went to pieces. Teresa's boss and my friend Gary, who had gone to the hospital too and driven Kirstin's car to Dell Seton so Kirstin could ride in the ambulance, called a mutual friend of ours who was at happy hour. He also called the dean of the medical school to ensure I was getting the best surgeon they had. And so it went hour after hour, the news rippling out in nodes and waves, nodes and waves.

Teresa [10:01 PM] Avrel is out of surgery and doing okay. He will remain intubated and asleep tonight in the ICU. He is at risk of brain bleeding again, so they will watch him closely. He is also at risk for pneumonia. I will let you know if I hear anything else tonight.

I was at risk of pneumonia because I had thrown up during the seizure, presumably the Pascal Burger from Hopfields's French-inspired lunch menu—camembert, cornichons, whole-grain mustard, caramelized onions on a brioche bun, and pommes frites with aioli. If it was to be my last meal, not a bad one.

CHAPTER 3

Life by the Drop

After a Fit— Should the patient recover from the fit, great and unremitting care must be observed to prevent another attack. The diet should be light, but nourishing; milk, light puddings, cooked vegetables, fish, etc., are extremely valuable; a full animal diet should not be allowed till all fear of a relapse is past; and stimulants should almost invariably be avoided. The cause of the disease should as far as possible be avoided or modified. If much depression exists a little light wine may be used.

—Vitalogy, 1904

A slow fade from black. A new room. Hazy shapes moving in low light, blurred by a medicated stupor and my glasses who knows where. Familiar voices murmuring in soft tones.

It is sometime in the nine o'clock hour Friday night. Kirstin moves to my side, and I feel her hand on my shoulder. Among the familiar voices, I hear David, friend of forty-three years and bandmate. I see him low, as if sitting or kneeling, to my left. He is hunched and crying, perhaps sad, perhaps grateful I am still alive, perhaps both. I hear Wade's voice, the first time since our New Year's campout.

Others float in and out of my consciousness as they move through the ICU waiting room.

Ed Cavazos and I had been friends since high school in McAllen. His wife, Elaine, had become one of Kirstin's best friends. Like K, Elaine was a cool customer in the face of crisis, a trait that served her well as a mother of four and a professor of social work. Elaine had been the first of our friends to the hospital and quickly made herself indispensable as a point person. Ed soon joined her.

I had met Dave Harmon in McAllen too, where we were both newspaper reporters fresh out of college. After I had moved back to Austin, Dave and David moved into a trailer together in McAllen. All of my closest friends, most of whom I met in McAllen and now lived in Austin, formed a sort of "mystic rose," a circle of points in which all points connect directly to all other points. They are true friends with each other with or without me. Many gathered that night, seeing which way the coin would fall—heads or tails. They would continue being friends, but would it be with or without me in the circle?

Every hour, around the clock, I am awakened by three quick soft knocks on my door. A white-coated doctor, a neurologist, is rounding for "neuro checks."

"I just need to ask you a few questions, okay?"

"Mmm-kay."

"Can you tell me your name?"

"Ay-vruh See..."

"Good. What day is it today?"

"Frideh? Maybe Saturdeh."

"That's right. It's Friday. What is your birthday?"

"Januareh twenty-fith, ninetee sixty-sevuh."

"Where are you?"

"Seton—I mean Dell Seton." They probably would have accepted "the hospital."

"Do you know why you're here?"

"Stroke."

"Who is the president?"

Now—I am sure knowing who the president of the United States is has been a touchstone of reality for American medicine for 240 years. To not know that would mean you were a hermit living off the grid or else had taken leave of your faculties completely. But suddenly, I was not so sure. I momentarily wondered if I was even right, or if the last two years had been a cheap plot device, one which, now that I was waking up in a hospital, would prove to have been a bizarre dream in which a TV game show host became the leader of the free world. I said who I thought it was, and I was right.

According to others who witnessed me, I spoke in one- or two-phrase whispers, so soft that all other conversation in the room would have to cease and bodies would have to bend down to hear me, like in the old E.F. Hutton commercials. At one point, Erren noticed a pained or annoyed expression on my face, and when he asked what it was, all I said was, "Infernal . . . beeping."

It was a complaint about the nearly continuous beeping coming from the nurses' station in the hallway. He liked my choice of *infernal*, and it gave him and Kirstin greater confidence that somewhere beneath the stroke and beneath the drugs, I was still "in there."

Teresa [12:43 AM] Avrel is awake and the report is that he looks good, he's a little alert, and the nurse was very positive about his ability to follow commands. He is paralyzed on the right side but they are saying it's early. The CT scan was clear—no blood in the brain. They will continue to check that over the next few days. That's all I know right now.

As soon as I came to after surgery, my life became a never-ending parade of people I had never met before—nurses, techs, orderlies, housekeepers, rehab doctors, neurosurgeons, neurologists, therapists. First among these were the nurses. I don't know if I idealized them as angels after a fashion or in my medicated state saw them through a gauzy veil, but nearly to a one they exhibited a kind of genetic perfection at which I marveled. Straight teeth and clear skin, shiny hair, and kind, serene faces.

I have never been good with names, and during these early days in ICU, I relied on a mnemonic system of Disney princesses and actresses to refer to them when talking with Kirstin or Elaine. There was Moana, a beautiful angel with straight black hair, clear plastic-frame glasses, and a radiant, compassionate smile. There was Amy Adams, the strawberry blonde, who insisted her name was Lana every time I called her Amy. There was "the Pixar nurse," whose thick purple headband and black plastic frames suggested one of the girls in *Despicable Me*. Each successive nurse became the center of my universe, the most important person in the world at that moment, the one who could cause pain or relieve it, the one who could reposition me, the one who, with a word or a look, could control my emotions and control my outlook on a highly uncertain future.

The dream starts near midnight. I am in the desert, in a valley, a wilderness, a starless night, when out of nowhere, the lightning begins. The lightning shoots through my leg. I am aware that there is work being done on my leg, but I am not allowed to go into the workshop. I am not allowed to see it. The work being done is beyond me. I am not allowed to see this power. It is a mash-up of every manifestation of God to have entered my consciousness— the power of the burning bush, a baptism by blinding veins of fire flashing at fifty-three thousand degrees. It is the Night of Power in the cave of Muhammad. It is a mystery of connecting synapses I cannot comprehend but of which I am the beneficiary. The dream lasts only a few minutes, until the following night, when work resumes. With every lightning bolt, there is a corresponding spasm running through my right leg.

Awake again. I notice my right leg is colder than my left—the lower down the leg, the chillier. I move my left leg against my right to warm it up. Aside from being cold, my right leg feels heavy whenever I maneuver my left leg under it. Crushingly heavy deadweight. For those who have never seen me in shorts, let me explain that my legs are not impressive, except perhaps in their length. During a camping trip the previous summer, a fellow Scout dad had taken to calling me "chicken legs." (He was a little short on diplomacy.) They certainly didn't feel like chicken legs now. When I would roll to my side, my left leg would feel as if it had a dead anaconda on top of it. This was my first realization of how heavy bone and a little muscle actually is when it is not supporting itself.

I noticed almost immediately that I was able to flex my arm and my leg every time I yawned. This was comforting in a way, because it proved that the limbs still worked, that they weren't gone, that they weren't dead. I wasn't paralyzed. All the muscles were still there. The problem, of course, was getting the signal from the brain to the muscle. Impressive movements would accompany every sneeze, yawn, and stretch after waking up. The first ten times it happened, it had the feel of a miracle. (*Amahl and the Night Visitors* . . . *"He walks!"*) I later learned this was called "flexor synergy." Then, the yawn would subside, and I would try to will my arm to stay up, but I could not. Slowly it would fall to the bed, and the sad reality would rush in, backfilling the void left by retreating hope.

Teresa [7:03 AM] Avrel was stable and responded to all the nurses' commands during the night. I've told the family they have an army of people ready to do anything to help. Avrel's condition is very serious and still dangerous, so they've asked for no visitors. I'll let you know if we need to mobilize in other ways to help. Thanks, team, for rallying in support of dear Avrel. This is unreal.

Teresa [10:50 AM] All the doctors have been by the room now and they all think Ave is doing well. They have started weaning him off the ventilator to see if he can tolerate breathing on his own. He's been a champ at it so far. They will do this for two hours and then decide if he can protect his airway (meaning not choke or aspirate). There is a respiratory therapist explaining things to him and Kirstin. He will be in the ICU for 7-10 days, then to a regular hospital floor, and then to rehab. They referred to it as a marathon.

Teresa [12:20 PM] Great news! Avrel is off the ventilator and breathing on his own and able to talk. The family is going to set up a page on CaringBridge for updates. I'll post the link here as soon as I get it. But I'll keep updating if I hear anything else before then.

Teresa [4:46 PM] Avrel's CaringBridge site is now up and family friend Elaine has made the first journal entry. It's a recap of the last 26 hours. There appears to be further improvement as she writes that he may be in ICU a much shorter period than we heard earlier today. Loving all the good news! It is looking like Avrel's language centers are intact!

During these first days, pain was a constant topic of conversation, with me frequently being asked to rate my pain on a scale from one to ten. There were some headaches—to be expected as they had drilled a hole in my head and put tubes and all manner of other alien substances in there just hours earlier. Alas, even in good times, I was no stranger to headaches, but these hospital headaches were easily swatted away with medical-grade pain relievers.

More unusual for me were body aches and chills. Every time we discussed pain, I complained of a fever, but my temperature, which was being monitored continuously, was normal. Aches and pains from the stroke and the surgery were creating a sort of phantom fever.

Saturday afternoon, twenty-four hours since the stroke, I attempted my first real conversation. I had a question for Kirstin. I asked her if I had had surgery. One would have thought the forty staples in my head would have offered a clue, but I was still in the fog of war.

Sunday morning, I awoke to the impulse to chant a verse of scripture from my religion, the Bahá'í Faith, both as a way to get my voice back and as a reminder of the preciousness of life. I chanted it over and over again: "Bring thyself to account each day ere thou art summoned to a reckoning," I slurred. "Bring thyself to account each day ere thou art summoned to a reckoning ..." The rest of the verse, which I knew well the gist of but could not accurately recite, went, "for death, unheralded, shall come upon thee, and thou shalt be called to give account for thy deeds." I had never come so close to death, and the verse had special potency to me that day.

I was vaguely aware of Kirstin, busily but quietly going between different parts of the room and softly into the hallway to take a phone call or ask a nurse for something, and softly back in, always taking care of the next piece of business. The blood pressure cuff, which never left my arm, automatically kicked on and off every three minutes or so. The index finger of my left hand was in a plastic clip, like a gentle clothes pin, that made my finger glow with red light, an evil E.T. This "pulse ox" measured the oxygen level in my blood.

That afternoon, I transferred to a wheelchair and was asked for the first of dozens of times to "scoop my foot," that is to say, to lift my right foot off the ground by bringing my left foot in behind it, sweeping my foot off its feet, as it were.

With my left foot holding up my right leg off the ground, a tech rolled me out to an elevator, and I was taken down into a basement lab full of heavy doors and radiation warning signs. It was time for my swallow test, specifically, a video fluoroscopic swallowing exam. There seemed to be more people standing around than I expected. As I sat sideways in front of an x-ray video camera, I was given a series of substances to swallow. The first was a cup of barium, which coated my throat and esophagus. Next, we started the test with a cookie, then moved to a cracker (Hey! I like this test!), then to a small plastic cup of nectar. I thought next might be a Jell-O shot, but no. The liquids progressed from thick to thin.

Henceforth, I was frequently admonished to tuck my chin every time I swallowed food or drink. "Chin-tuck! Chin-tuck!"

On Monday, day three, I began clear liquids like broth, a mushy popsicle, apple juice, and tea. I remained on a "puree diet," which featured a substance known as "thinned chicken." Only occasionally these days will I ask Kirstin when thinned chicken will be on the menu at home.

One part of the puree diet I was fully on board with was ice cream. It was probably Monday night that my dinner was first accompanied by the customary small round container of chocolate ice cream. I vividly recall the moment the open container appeared before me. I grabbed it with my left hand as I had a thousand times before—and then waited, as if something else was going to happen to get the ice cream to my mouth. I sat for probably ten seconds before fully realizing my dilemma. I looked at the plastic spoon, then down at the ice cream, then back at the spoon. "Hmm." It was the first confounding moment in a new lifetime of confounding moments. Eventually I set the container back on the bed table, picked up the spoon with my left hand, and began stabbing the dessert with the spoon, the whole container coming up off the table every time the spoon gained purchase. (Note to hospitals with stroke survivors: ice-cream sandwiches.)

It was also about this time I had another CT scan and an MRI. The CT scan was a nonevent, quiet and over in less than a minute. It confirmed that there was no new blood in my brain. Where the scan during the stroke had shown a bright white blotch where the bleeding was, now there was black, a mass of dead brain cells bigger than a golf ball.

The MRI, by contrast, was, with no exaggeration, one of the worst experiences of my life, and that includes the stroke. I had never really known the difference between a CT scan and an MRI, and when I thought about them at all, I would constantly confuse them. Never again.

The first thing they did after getting me on the table was press my head into a plastic cage, the front of which smushed in my nose in such a way as to prevent my head from moving in the slightest. Next, the tech asked me what kind of music I liked. Cool, I thought, this will be a breeze—even fun. I told him I'd take some Jerry Reed. In a couple of minutes, he returned and had dialed in a song I knew but will now never listen to the same way. It was one of Reed's lesser novelty hits called "The Preacher and the Bear," a cover of an older song from the forties. One of Jerry's "talking blues" numbers, it told the tale of a holy man breaking the Sabbath by hunting on a Sunday morning. When he came across said bear, he implored God to deliver him like He did Daniel from the lions' den. Meanwhile, I was imploring the Lord to deliver me from this godforsaken contraption that was like something from a torture-porn movie.

As the tinny lo-fi version of the song came through the earbuds, my head cage and I were moved into the MRI tube, where the music was now layered by a deafening clapping sound multiple times every second. How anyone could have thought that music would lessen the awfulness of this excruciating clacking, I had no idea. Seconds passed like minutes, minutes like hours. Panic rose in my chest. The room was empty, but I called out to anyone who might be able to hear me. "I need out! . . . I need out!"

Presently the tech came back into the room and scolded me. "Sir," he said pissily, "if this is going to work, you're going to *have* to be still!"

"I'm panicking." I protested that it seemed to be taking much longer than the five minutes advertised. What fresh hell was this? If this was part of the cure, then I would take the disease!

The technician sent for medication to take the edge off, which arrived after five or ten minutes and which they pumped into me intravenously. This virtually put me to sleep, and I certainly wish they had rendered this aid before I started. The second time I opted not for Jerry Reed or any other sort of music that would be overlaid by a deafening clacking noise, but for ear plugs.

Each day they disconnected another apparatus from me, each a victory, each a step back from the ledge of mortality. First was the breathing tube. Next was the "central line," which delivered medicine directly above my heart so that the veins and capillaries that were smaller would not burn up. The catheter stayed in place for six days. When it was finally time for me to try to go to the restroom, they provided me a bedside toilet with a seat apparently designed for a six-year-old. *How is a grown man supposed to simultaneously poop and pee in something the diameter of a crochet hoop?* I wondered.

Next to come out was the drain tube from the back of my head. Once out, this required a staple to close the gap—the forty-first staple. The tech explained that numbing the area would require two shots that would sting, and that I could avoid this by simply taking a staple to the head un-numbed. I opted for the latter and winced as she shot a staple into my scalp. The staple gun, fresh out of the package, after one use—one staple—then became medical waste. She emptied the magazine by shooting the remaining nineteen staples into the trash can. ("Why does health care cost so much?!") She offered to give me the gun if I wanted it. I pictured the cluttered state of my workbench in the garage, and I passed.

When I occasionally scratched the crown of my head, there was now a strange hollow sound just slightly different than before, lower in pitch, and I could tell someone had been in there.

Virtually the moment I was free of all those restraints, rehab began. I give great credit to the hospital for recognizing the importance of getting straight to it and not letting me rot in a bed for several weeks before getting down to work.

The physical therapist put me through some rudimentary tasks. Could I shrug my right shoulder? Good! Could I touch my nose with my left hand? Stick out my tongue? Raise my eyebrows? Then the grand finale—could I try to stand?

First, I sat up, then got my feet off the bed. With a large male tech spotting me on my right side, somehow, I got to standing, then pivoted and faced a six-foot mirror they had rolled into the room and positioned on the opposite side of the bed. Now, I beheld myself fully for the first time.

I was on the right side of the dirt, but that's about as much as could be said for me. My future career as a model had been cast into grave doubt. Not only had my hair not been washed or combed since Friday morning, it was stained orange with iodine across the top of my head where my incision was, reminiscent of the Sex Pistols' Johnny Rotten or perhaps a scarlet-crested partridge. In the middle of my forehead, a scab, like a Hindu's bindi, showed where I had been lightly impaled by the apparatus that immobilized my head during surgery. My right eyelid was slightly droopy, but my eyes were quickly drawn to the more noticeable defect at my mouth, which slouched down on the right side. Below that, my right shoulder sank a full two inches below my left. So I guess what I'm saying is that the image in the mirror looked like Johnny Rotten had aged very badly, gotten a bindi for some odd reason, and then commissioned Salvador Dalí to paint him in a hospital gown. It was not a look I strive to repeat.

When I tried to stand on my own, I was shocked. My eyes were telling me that I was standing straight (I should say "being held up straight"), but my brain was telling me that I was standing at forty-five degrees to the floor. I was about to learn a new word: proprioception.

Proprioception is sometimes called the sixth sense, and it is the sense that tells your brain where your body parts are relative to each other, which is why most of us can close our eyes, then touch our nose, or stand with our feet together, or perform a thousand other tasks. It was first described in the 1500s as "muscle sense," a pretty good name, but it was not until the last century that the interface between the brain and muscles was even vaguely understood. This network of "proprioceptors" is in our muscles and joints, and I had never heard of them or thought anything about them for fifty years. Talk about not valuing something until it's gone.

Wednesday, I took what had become known in previous weeks as the "Trump cognitive test," which the president had been given by his doctor and then used to brag about his fitness for the Oval Office. Among other basic tasks, he and I had both correctly identified line drawings of a rhinoceros, a camel, and a lion. Situation Room, here I come.

Teresa [10:08 AM] Avrel called me! It was quite emotional. He thanked us for acting so quickly and promised he will be back. He sounded different, but really good.

When it came time for them to move me out of the bed for the first time, the nurses employed a crane-like contraption fixed to the ceiling, carrying me in a sling like a helicopter transporting a beluga whale. I sat in a chair for about thirty minutes, which seemed like a big enough accomplishment at the time.

One of the internal medicine doctors, whom I took an immediate liking to, partly because he casually and continuously drank Muscle Milk as he did his rounds, asked if I "had been taking the Browns to the Super Bowl." Alas, I had not. When Kirstin began asking detailed clinical questions about my case, as she did of each doctor who came to the room, Dr. Muscle Milk asked with a smile, "And exactly what kind of medical professional are you?" Her dad's stroke had basically bestowed on her a master's degree's worth of knowledge, albeit expertise for which she did not get paid.

Kirstin and a nurse asked me if I wanted to go look out a window around the corner from my room. I agreed that would be nice. They spotted me as I transferred into the wheelchair, and we left the room. A few feet away, a ceiling-to-floor window revealed Red River Street, and I could see the medical school's administrative building in front of me, the building where I had met the dean and worked on the school's messaging exactly two weeks before my stroke.

Down to my left was "the Drum," UT's giant circular basketball arena. So many memories. I was in high school the first time I was in the Drum. It was spring break of 1983, and I had traveled from my home in McAllen to see the band Yes. Three years later, as I reported to college, it became the scene of a dreadful ritual known as adds and drops, its circular lobby the perfect embodiment of a process that seemed endless. But there were more good times to be had there too, concerts by Rush, Van Halen, Chicago, Foreigner, Journey, Ozzy Osbourne, Triumph. I had walked across the stage there and received my degree from the College of Communication. When I returned to UT as editor of the alumni magazine, I had heard the Dalai Lama there. I had heard Willie Nelson playing at the funeral of Coach Darrell Royal.

Then came marriage and kids, and a whole new slate of special events. Just the previous year I had taken my fourteen-year-old there for his very first concert, James Taylor. He fell sound asleep somewhere between "Fire and Rain" and "Steamroller Blues," another expensive nap.

Of course, there was plenty of basketball there too, and not just the Longhorns. I had bought tickets to take my younger two sons to see the Harlem Globetrotters there the next week. Kirstin would take them instead, and I was glad. She deserved some happy and normal-feeling time after a week of stress and adrenaline and life-and-death decisions. Now, after forty years, the Drum was slated to be razed to make room for the expansion of the medical school.

Below me, across the street, was a large brass sculpture of a conch shell. The nurse said the cops had to regularly ask homeless people to climb out of the conch shell. There was no sleeping in the conch shell, no camping in the conch shell. Move along.

I continued to make steady progress, and on day five I was moved out of ICU and "onto the floor," which I learned was a euphemism for any hospital room that was not the ER or ICU. (When the boys were born, I had spent a few nights in the hospital with Kirstin actually "on the floor." This was not that.)

It was about then my cell phone rang. A pleasant woman from my insurance company was calling. Allison explained she had been assigned to be my "telephonic caseworker."

The next day, we got word that my next move would be to a small rehab hospital also run by Seton. I was basically ready to make the move. We just had to get authorization from the insurance company. As the discharge date drew near, we called my insurance company to figure out what our status was and when we would be moved out. I had not experienced what some have called "ICU psychosis," a real phenomenon in which the patient tears out tubes and IVs, accuses the staff of conspiring against him, and basically just goes crazy, but nevertheless we had been in ICU for six days and naturally were eager to take the next step.

One would have thought that the insurance company also would be eager to move us out of intensive care, as this was the most expensive room in downtown Austin by several orders of magnitude, but there was only mysterious silence on the other end as our insurance caseworker struggled to see the correct screen. Perhaps someone was updating it right now, she said. This might explain the delay.

Just then, two rehab doctors walked in while we were on speaker phone with insurance and jumped into the conversation, asking with a touch of swagger if it would help matters if there were doctors in the room. I'll be doggone if the tone of the conversation didn't change immediately for the better. One of the doctors left his cell number for a call back, and before we knew it, we had a scheduled departure time of 4:45 that afternoon.

CHAPTER 4

Family Matters

The main cause of apoplexy, doubtless, is disease of blood vessels. . . .
The gradual degeneration or ossification of arteries common to old age
renders them inelastic, and as the blood is forced on them by the action
of the heart, they give way. Hemorrhage within the cranium is sometimes
caused by the bursting of aneurysms involving the arteries of the brain.
. . . Apoplexy . . . often is the result of hereditary tendencies.

—*Vitalogy, 1904*

In the scramble to pinpoint the cause of the stroke, I had been asked multiple times in the first few weeks if anyone in my family had had a stroke, to which I replied no. Parents? No. Grandparents? No. Brothers? Nope. Aunts or uncles? Not that I could recall.

I had always been a genealogy buff, the keeper of family stories, but it did not occur to me until days later, scrolling back through my pedigree, that my great-grandfather had suffered a stroke. He had died later at fifty-two. I had just turned fifty-one.

But everyone has eight great-grandparents (ideally), and we all probably have at least one who had a stroke—diagnosed, undiagnosed, recorded, unrecorded. I just happened to know an inordinate amount of family history; I doubted that this alone constituted "a family history of stroke."

Somewhere, I had a picture of Horace Bradford Seale (1877-1929) at about my age sitting on his porch in Athens, Texas, in a wheelchair, the old wood and wicker kind. Perhaps, in an incredibly unlucky draw, I had inherited some weak plumbing from him. I don't know when exactly he had the stroke, but being only fifty-two when he died, he likely was younger at his stroke than I was at mine.

The story goes that when he started feeling puny (as they would have said back then), he boarded a train in Athens, southeast of Dallas, to Mineral

Wells, west of Fort Worth. It was there in 1877, the year Horace was born, that J. A. Lynch, who had settled the area, purportedly cured his rheumatism with the "foul-tasting" water. By 1920, likely around the time my great-grandfather arrived, some four hundred mineral wells had been dug with specially constructed bathhouses around them, and the town was a thriving tourist destination, "The South's Greatest Health Resort," they bragged, in defiance of the much better known Hot Springs, Arkansas.

When he arrived back in Athens, my great-grandmother Linnie there to greet him, two men carried him off the train on a stretcher. He never walked again, living out however many years he had left in a wheelchair after the fashion of FDR's—wood frame, wicker back and seat, wooden leg rests, large wheels in front, small wheels in back.

Though we don't know the nature of his stroke for sure, the story, describing a gradual onset before paralysis, suggests an ischemic stroke, one caused by a clot, not a bleed, like mine. The only thing I can say definitively was that, also unlike mine, his was a right-brain stroke. The lone post-stroke photo of him shows a dropped left shoulder and a clenched but swollen left hand.

All this started me wondering what kind of treatment stroke patients had available to them a century ago. On my shelf at home, I found a 969-page tome called *Vitalogy*. First published in 1904, it was a compendium of practically everything known about the human body by Western medicine at that time—a highly entertaining mash-up of scientific knowledge, folk remedies, and completely baseless opinions stated with absolute certainty. The authors are given as George P. Wood and E. H. Ruddock, though Ruddock is said to have died in 1875.

I opened the huge, black, leather-bound book and began looking for a chapter on stroke. Initially that search was in vain, because the word "stroke" was not even used then. The medical term for a stroke was an "apoplectic fit" or "apoplexia." "This disease is characterized by the abrupt loss, more or less complete, of consciousness, from extravasation of blood (hemorrhage) within the cranial cavity," the book read.

As I learned, *apoplexia* is the Greek term for being struck down violently, as in taking a blow to the head in battle. So "stroke" is simply the direct English translation of this from Greek. Hippocrates, the father of medicine, appears to have been the first to describe the condition, some 2,400 years ago.

Before him, we can only guess at what folks thought this was or did about it, but we do know that people have been doing craniotomies for at least five thousand years. It's true. Skulls have been found with clean holes, "burr holes," remarkably the same size and position as mine (search up "trephined skulls" or "trepanning"), and we know that the patients survived the procedure because the edges of the holes show definite signs of healing. We do not know if they were actually stopping a hemorrhage or releasing evil spirits—perhaps they're one and the same. Whichever it was, more than 1,500 "trephined" skulls from the Neolithic Age have been discovered throughout the world.

But back to more recent history, *Vitalogy* describes two kinds of stroke: "1. Congestive apoplexy is an overloaded condition of the vessels of the brain, and at the same time small blood points occur all over the surface of the brain substance. 2. Hemorrhagic or sanguineous apoplexy is the most frequent, and consists in the rupture of a vessel, and extravasation of blood and the substance of the brain, or outside the nervous masses. The symptoms are usually sudden, and its development most rapid."

Though the authors were right about there being two kinds, it is quite untrue that hemorrhagic strokes are more frequent; to the contrary, 87 percent of all strokes are clots, or "ischemic." A mere 13 percent are bleeds, like mine. It wasn't until 1928 that strokes were officially divided into two types and the umbrella term "cerebral vascular accident" (CVA) was adopted to stand for both.

Vitalogy then walks us through "Modes of Attack and Warnings":

Apoplexy may come on suddenly or gradually. The patient may be suddenly struck falling, at once bereft of motion and consciousness. . . . More frequently however, apoplexy is indicated by well-marked premonitions, which are, chiefly, headache; giddiness, particularly on stooping; fullness and pulsation of the blood-vessels of the head; epistaxis; retinal hemorrhage; sleepiness, with heavy snoring breathing; transient blindness, loss of memory; considerable difference in the sizes of the pupils of the eye; deafness or noises in the ears; nausea, vomiting, numbness, or tingling in the hands or feet; unsteady gait; partial paralysis, sometimes involving the muscles of the face, sometimes those of a limb; the patient becomes comatose, and drowsiness gradually increases to perfect coma or stupor. . . . This complaint may be distinguished . . . from intoxication, by the impossibility of temporarily arousing the patient by shouting or any other means, and absence of alcoholic smell.

My stroke seemed a strange hybrid composed of symptoms cherry-picked from this list. The paralysis was almost immediate, but I did not lose consciousness for about three hours. Reflecting the times, *Vitalogy* contains a great passage on what to do if the process of having an apoplectic fit is gradual:

> **Preventative and Accessory Measures**—Undeviating temperance in eating and drinking. Physical and mental exertion and excesses of every nature, fits of passion or excitement, sudden changes of temperature, overheated rooms, warm baths, wet feet, etc., must be uniformly avoided. Errors in diet, exposure to a hot sun, violent emotions, etc., may excite the gravest symptoms in persons predisposed to apoplexy, and may possibly cause a recurrence of the attack.
>
> The neck should be free from all tight cravats; the feet should be kept warm; exposures to cold, and especially to cold feet, are dangerous. Sour stomach should always be cured, if possible, as soon as known to exist, which can be done with a few doses of magnesia. The hours of sleep should be regulated not to exceed 8 or 9, and the bed should be a hard mattress, using only a small pillow that the head may be kept low. Whenever there is giddiness of the head, cold water, poured on the head and along the spinal column, will be found a very salutary measure. Pure air in the rooms is indispensable. Direct exposure to the sun's rays should be invariably shunned. Sudden turning of the head, to look upward or sideways, should also be carefully avoided, as well as straining at stool. For at least two hours previous to retiring to bed, no food must be allowed to enter the stomach.

On my follow-up trip to see my brain surgeon, I asked about possible causes. I told him that the one risk factor whose box I checked was high cholesterol. It had been high since the first time I ever measured it, really high. I had always intended to do something about it on the next doctor's visit, but it had been high for years and years.

I wanted there to be a rhyme or reason for this calamity, even if it was my own fault. Despite having led a moderately . . . festive life, I do have a certain Calvinistic streak when it comes to people taking personal responsibility for their own lot, and I was already resigned to the fact that somehow this was traceable to cheeseburgers and fries, neglecting kale, not being a jogger, and all that. Once, at the grocery store and parched, I grabbed a bottle from the store refrigerator of what I thought was a frappuccino, mocha something or other, opened it while still shopping and enjoyed most of the bottle before getting home. Now at home, I marveled at how rich it was and took a closer look at the bottle. Turns out, I had not been enjoying a frappuccino, but rather had just drunk nearly twenty ounces of coffee creamer, straight from the bottle. I paused to reflect on what I must have looked like to others in the store, especially the cashier, who had the most time to study me. I chuckled at the thought, then took the last sip. Waste naught, want naught. Point being, I've been far from a dietary saint and was ready to accept this as a consequence.

The surgeon's answer was swift and unvarnished: No, a hemorrhagic stroke would not happen because of high cholesterol. That was not a thing.

In an instant, I was plunged back into the mystery of what had caused this. Mystery notwithstanding, I needed to get my cholesterol down anyway, because the very last thing any of us needed was for me to have a heart attack too. My father had had quadruple bypass surgery with 95 percent blockage at the age of seventy, and he ate relatively well. But I supposed there was some comfort in the knowledge that I was still blameless so far as anyone knew. I guess January 19, 2018, just had not been my day.

Around five months post-stroke, I started through the three-inch-thick binder that Kirstin had compiled, making notes during doctor visits starting on the afternoon of January 19. As I say, in searching for the cause of the stroke, I had been asked numerous times if there was a history of stroke in my family. There had not been, except for Horace. So I had answered no, and the congenital cause box always went unchecked. Then I read in Kirstin's handwriting "prob vascular malformation—cause stroke." On page 7 of Kirstin's notes, she wrote, "looks consistent w/AVM . . . One blood vessel was larger than expected this far away from heart. No cause for concern as of now. :-)"

AVM stands for arteriovenous malformation. My mother has an AVM. In fact, about five years earlier, she was troubleshooting a whooshing sound in her ear that she could not get rid of. She came to Austin for a cerebral angiogram, and I took her to the hospital and stayed with her while she recovered. They injected her with dye and scanned her head for signs of an aneurysm. The images showed an AVM high in the back of her brain. At the time, I took in that information in almost a passing way, its only relevance being that this strange tangle of vessels might or might not have been responsible for the whooshing sound that kept her awake in an otherwise silent house. It never occurred to me that it could be hereditary, that I should add it to the list of things that might be coming my way, like her ulcerative colitis, like Dad's Parkinson's or quadruple bypass.

It was highly likely that an AVM had caused my stroke, but not one health care provider had ever asked me if there was a history of AVM in my family; they only asked if there was a history of stroke. But just because Mom has an AVM didn't mean I inherited it from her or that I inherited it at all. Almost all AVMs form in utero, so I was almost certainly born with this. The risk of a brain AVM bleeding hovers around 2 percent each year. A 2 percent chance every year. I was due, plain and simple. The fifty-year warranty on my upstairs plumbing had expired.

A neurologist at Dell Seton told me that after a stroke, my chances of having another stroke basically returned to normal, not to zero, of course, but to that of the general population. An AVM was the "probable" cause. Without a definite cause, though, it became something of a sword of Damocles. I thought again of the verse "Bring thyself to account each day ere thou art summoned to a reckoning, for death will come upon thee unheralded and thou wilt be called to account for thy deeds."

I thought about my father a lot during these days. He had died three and a half years earlier and was the only person whose final breath I ever had witnessed. Parkinson's had ravaged his body for more than twenty years. I had the distinct feeling that I had exchanged bodies with him in an instant, that the first day of my stroke was like the last day of his life. I had been teleported instantly into the body of an unbalanced, shaky old man. I spilled food all over myself when I tried to eat with my left hand. I was scared of falling. Doctors and nurses who saw Kirstin in my room asked me what my "daughter's" name was. I had become my father in an instant.

The critical difference was that, while he had gotten weaker every day, I was slowly getting stronger. I lived my life now as a mirror image to his heartbreaking degeneration. Could I get another twenty-eight years out of this body as he had his?

Thirteen weeks after the stroke, on the second Sunday in April, Mom and her gentleman friend, John, arrived at our home for a visit. John watched a golf tournament on TV. Mom and I sat on the porch in the sun in matching white rocking chairs.

"I wanted to give you all space," she explained forcefully in the North Texas accent she had never lost, "but I want you to know that I'm thinking about you every day." Her voice wavered with emotion. She continued. "After I got back home from here the first time, I went to the cemetery to tell Dad what happened. I said, 'You need to know something about Avrel.'" That trip to the cemetery must have given her a better vantage point to commune with him, to reflect on the life they had brought into the world together, when she was a twenty-seven-year-old English teacher and he a thirty-year-old band director.

"The first thought I had when I heard," she said, "was, 'Why couldn't it have been me instead of you? I've lived a rich, full life; you're right in the middle of yours. Why couldn't it have been me?'"

I knew just how she felt, and I was filled with the terrifying thought that, if she had passed the AVM to me, I might have passed it to one or more of my precious boys, a sort of time bomb the detonation of which no one could predict. No parent I know would not take a bullet to save their child, not step in front of a speeding train if it meant their child would be spared. Maybe that was some sort of reflection of God's love for each of us.

But it does not work that way, does it? We cannot prevent bad things in life from happening to our children by somehow attracting those monsters to ourselves, like a visitor to Jurassic Park running in front of a T. rex, shouting and waving their arms to lure the predator away from their family.

All we can do is model resilience. That's all I could do, so that if, God forbid, one of them does meet with a catastrophe, they might remember how their old man was—how he got back up and got back to work. How, when the stroke tried to take away his right hand, he gave it the finger with his left.

Before I left Dell Seton, I had a memorable conversation with the chair of the neurology department, David Paydarfar. I recognized him immediately when he entered my room from a brochure or annual report or some sort of collateral I had worked on recently.

Alone in the room with Kirstin and me, with no interns, nurses, or other assistants tagging along, he greatly impressed me with his thoughtful take on my situation. It's natural to want to know why things happen, he commiserated. We might find out, but we also might never. The bleeding destroyed the evidence. "It's like a burglar who sets fire to the home to cover up the evidence. The arson destroys the scene of the crime," he said.

What still remained to be seen was what exactly the burglar had stolen.

The Song *(2015, three years prior)*

My father lies upon his bed in afternoon sun
Hands on stomach, fingers splayed as if still holding the oboe
Eyes closed, chest rattling his coda of half notes and half rests.
A year on, and my son sits in his cafeteria,
Holds the euphonium, exhales his first note.
Is that his own breath in that brass,
Or is he some new mouthpiece of my father,
Invisibly tweaking his embouchure
Adjusting his posture
Dilating his airway
That the Song might go on
Another verse if not forever?
And does my son hear the ancestral call
Of Wagner, fox hunt, shofar, didgeridoo
Back and back and back to the first
Who stood clad in the ram's hide on a hilltop
And blew through something louder than his throat,
That the stars might know
We are here.

CHAPTER 5

Lookin' Out the Window

Remedies—The patient should be immediately removed to a pleasant, airy, and cool place, and placed in a recumbent position, to favor a return of blood from the brain. All compression should be removed from the neck, and all types of bandages or ligatures. The feet and legs must be immediately immersed in very warm water, in which lye or ashes has been added. . . . The feet and legs should remain in the water 15 or 20 minutes, and friction be applied to them. The whole surface must also be bathed with a mild tincture of cayenne pepper, applied very warm. If the tincture is not at hand, put dry cayenne on a flannel cloth and rub the patient's body with it, and put mustard poultices at pit of stomach and back of neck.
—Vitalogy, 1904

I *think I'll look out the window today.* I actually had that thought—*I think I'll look out the window today.*

Wow. It was a shock to the system to catch myself setting "looking out the window" as a goal. It reminded me of when Andrew was a toddler and Cameron was a baby. When we were on road trips and couldn't see Cameron's eyes because he was in a rear-facing car seat, we would ask Andrew, "Is Cameron asleep?"

"No," Andrew would reply, "he's looking." Hence the binary system was established: asleep or looking.

I had my choice of three windows out of which to look when my eyes thirsted for scenes of life beyond the rehab hospital, which was often. The window in my room looked west, giving me the occasional sunset, but it most often just framed the Texas School for the Blind and Visually Impaired, surrounded by bare trees under a gray February sky. Down the hall to my right was a floor-to-ceiling window that looked south across Forty-Fifth

Street and thence toward a large nondescript building housing some state agency or other.

My favorite window was down the hall to my left. Through it, rain or shine, I could watch construction workers building an upscale apartment. Steel frame, studs to support interior walls, Sheetrock, insulated siding, stonework, glasswork, level by level and layer on layer, it would go up as I watched it a few minutes each day, occasionally parking my wheelchair for an hour or more as I visited with family members or friends. I came to regard the construction project as a metaphor for the rebuilding of my neuromuscular system, and I also wondered if I would leave the rehab hospital before the workers finished the building.

A few days earlier I had arrived here from the hospital. It was surreal to feel the cool January air on my face as I was wheeled out of Dell Seton after six days in ICU and loaded into a van with a hydraulic lift. I was sure I had never been in a building for six consecutive days before without leaving. Charles, my doughy, round-shouldered driver, made no attempt at conversation and was only too happy just to get me to my destination in one piece. Riding in the cargo hold, with my wheelchair strapped to the floor, I felt every crack and pothole of those downtown Austin streets, but at length, we were making our way north along Lamar toward the rehab hospital. From the back of the van I asked him if this was the beginning of his shift or the end of the shift, trying desperately to make conversation to take my mind off the vertigo I was experiencing as we swerved and dipped. He volunteered that it was the beginning of his shift, and that work usually wasn't too bad because he could get a lot of sleep at the dispatch station.

When we finally had crept through the five o'clock traffic and arrived at the small, three-story rehab hospital, Charles dutifully lowered me with the hydraulic platform and unstrapped my safety buckles. I was again braced by the cool air and, with my left arm, began to wheel myself toward the hospital entrance with purpose, leaving him behind to fuss with the van.

I had been to this place several times, bringing my children to visit their grandfather, Kirstin's dad, after his stroke. I, of course, had no inkling then that this place might be my own home for weeks on end. It was surreal to say the very least. Inside, Charles signed a form testifying to the fact that he had delivered me, like 190 pounds of Omaha Steaks, then joylessly turned on his heel and headed to his next pickup, or maybe back to the dispatch station for a nap.

My room was on the third and top floor. Beyond my bed, a narrow alcove ran past the bathroom to a window. The alcove was just large enough for the hospital cot that Kirstin slept on night after night, as her mom or my mom stayed at our house with the boys, making sure they were fed and watered. It was a blessing that we lived within easy biking distance of all three of their schools, a fact that made them largely self-sufficient most days. They got themselves up in the mornings, fed themselves, and did their own laundry. We had trained these routines into them years earlier, and boy was that paying dividends now.

I had signed an agreement to abide by the hospital's rules about transfers, and that meant calling for a tech every time I needed to transfer from my bed to anywhere else. My status was celebrated with a festive yellow wristband proclaiming FALL RISK in all caps. One visiting friend remarked that it should have read FLIGHT RISK. At any rate, I could not get out of bed without calling a tech. Sometimes they were there within seconds; other times they might have been tied up with someone else and be the better part of ten minutes. Knowing there could be a delay, at the first hint of an urge to use the restroom, I hit my nurse call button, setting off infernal beeping in the hallway.

Once the nurse or tech arrived, they lowered the bed to make it level with the wheelchair. This was followed by a discussion of which way I should turn and a final check that the brakes were set. There were two schools of thought about transfers. The first was the scooch, which held to the axiom that the shortest distance between two points is a straight line. The other was to have me stand, pivot, then slowly sit, not plop, as plopping is a cardinal sin of transfers. When I rose to standing, most techs would steady me with a three-inch-wide cinching device called a gait belt. Others would grab me by the back of my underwear and give me a wedgie in order to control me.

I felt for these techs—who were overwhelmingly women and nevertheless had to control a top-heavy man who was six foot two and nearly two hundred pounds. It was a strange sensation to be handled thus and so often by women. When I called a nurse, I never knew who I might get, and we might not even have been past introductions before we were locked in an awkward embrace, like middle schoolers slow-dancing, me smelling her shampoo, her smelling my lack of it. One tech had perfume so strong I had to gasp in short breaths every time she was near. She gasped a lot too, huffing and puffing, laboring with every motion when she transferred me to the toilet or back to the bed in a way that made me feel like a burden. "Straight your body!" she would pant desperately in her thick Mexican accent. "Straight your body!"

Once I had successfully made that transfer, I would use my left foot to scoop my right leg before we turned to make the seven-foot journey to the bathroom. Kirstin or my brother Erren, who had made the six-hour trip from South Texas for the second time in as many weeks to stay by my side, would get off the cot and lift it onto its side so that the bathroom door would open wide enough for the wheelchair.

When the nurse and I jointly had wrestled the wheelchair over the threshold and into the bathroom, it was time for transfer number two, as it were, and the whole process was repeated: angling the chair just so, locking the wheels, standing just long enough to pull down my shorts before gingerly sitting.

Inside of a week I had utterly lost track of how many people had seen me bottomless. I was so unperturbed by the act that I had to stop myself from casually dropping trou in front of family and friends.

After a week of being cathed, I was thrilled to finally be able to urinate on my own. When I did, I had to go in what was called "the hat." I was fond of hats and had a great many of them at home, but I thought this must be the most unfortunate hat in all of hatdom. It's hard to identify just what kind of a hat it resembled, but imagine a pilgrim with a really small head, who, instead of wearing a black felt hat of the kind you're picturing, had a hat of white plastic, and then developed a truly terrible habit of taking his hat off, turning it upside down, and urinating in it five times a day. It fit at the front of the toilet bowl, in the general vicinity of a seated man's urinary equipment, above the waterline but underneath the seat. In the main part of the hat, hash marks showed how many CCs I had pee-peed. I became expert at predicting which line I would fill the cup to. "This is going to be 450," or "Let's go 375 on this one." I was usually within 50 CCs one way or the other.

Relieved as I was to go on my own, I was sorely disappointed upon learning I had to undergo a sonogram after I got back in bed every time I urinated so they could determine that I had voided my bladder adequately. Anything more than a hundred CCs left in the bladder and they would cath me again. There was, and they did. It was odd in the extreme to be getting a sonogram, as the last of these I had witnessed was during Kirstin's third pregnancy. I will never forget how cold the gel was when it hit my skin below my navel. I thought perhaps they were using a gel form of nitrogen. The rule was that I had to have three consecutive scans of less than 100 CCs before they would stop cathing me. One nurse would get a 0 reading, another one would get 150. The next one would be back to 19, the next 164. At last I got three in a row, a hat trick, if you will, and was not cathed again from that day to this one.

I always sat on the toilet, even if just to pee. The one exception to this came late one night when a kind but otherwise unimpressive tech thought I might just stand to go and save us both the hassle of getting me down and getting me back up. Being game for anything and probably thinking this would represent progress if I did it successfully, I gave it the college try. She stood about two feet away as I took aim. Suddenly, I felt my body turning and my head, still with staples holding my incision together, pitch forward. All I could do was inhale as deeply as I could in preparation for impact, wherever that came. The nurse, five foot ten and of athletic build, grabbed me in the nick of time and, with nervous laughter meant to smooth over what was nearly a grave mistake that would have required a lot of paperwork, helped me turn and sit.

One of the first complaints I had when I reached the rehab hospital was a developing armpit rash from the lack of air circulation. A little powder and propping my arm up with a pillow while in bed cured this. What was not so easily batted away was the enchanting experience known as jock itch, an entirely new condition for me. I addressed it by asking Kirstin to bring the Gold Bond powder from home, the bottle I had hauled through the mountains of New Mexico for thirteen days the previous summer but never once needed. It helped but did not cure. The nurse recommended I switch to prescription-strength Nystatin ointment, and I eagerly agreed. I used said ointment for about twenty-four hours before realizing it was making my condition much worse. Apparently, Augmentin was not the only medication to which I had an allergy. I now added Nystatin to the list, primarily because it turned my penis purple but also because, disturbingly, it transformed it into the shape of a mushroom. Thankfully I was already married, because I suspected neither one of these characteristics was especially useful in attracting a mate.

One nurse remarked that I was among the least medicated people he had ever seen there. Erren, who stayed with me on the cot for three nights, and I joked that I should have gotten a sash for the fictitious rehab hospital homecoming dance that read "LEAST MEDICATED."

Here, at Central Texas Rehab, I would make the acquaintance of an endless succession of nurses and techs. Everyone has known nurses, but perhaps some readers have avoided hospitalization and therefore might be unfamiliar with the role of a tech.

The medical professions are like nothing so much as a caste system. At the top are the doctors and the executives—call them the brahmins. At one hospital along my journey, I was told by a reliable source that the doctors had their own dining room, sparing them the indignity of having to eat in the presence of those who did not graduate from medical school. Not only that, they didn't even deign to eat the same fare, but had their own chef. ("Why oh why does health care cost so much?!") Although this is bound to be common (the hospital in question was one of a corporate chain of more than one hundred hospitals) the therapist who told me this only learned of it when a doctor invited her to a lunch meeting. After he spilled the beans, she asked if they were going to that dining room. "Ummmm, no," he chuckled.

Below the doctors/brahmins are the therapists. I had more than forty of them across the three major categories of therapy during the first nine months of my recovery: physical, occupational, and speech. Interestingly, several of them independently told me that most universities that currently offer master's degrees in therapy are doing away with those and that future therapists would mostly be called doctors. They would not be paid like doctors, mind you, so long as the law of supply and demand remained in effect, but they would have the title. As the physical therapist who told me this dragged me around the surface of the therapy pool, her take was that it was simply an upsell within higher education: she would have to pay more for a doctorate than she did for her master's because it would require three years instead of two, but the hospital where she worked would not pay her a dime more. She'd have the title though.

Below them, the nurses, who could dispense medicine, of which more later.

Below them, the techs, who took vital signs and helped people on and off the toilet and in and out of the shower.

Below them was housekeeping. In our caste scheme, these would be known as untouchables, but in health care there is far too much untouchability to be contained in just one caste.

Among the apparently infinite reservoir of nurses and techs, whose castes I couldn't always keep straight, there was the loud and jolly Jamaican Nigerian.

There was the Iranian, the Filipino, the Vietnamese, the Chinese, and lots of Mexicans and Central Americans. Nothing would devastate health care more than a clampdown on immigration.

Some nurses would infantilize me, lots of "baby this" and "baby that." Sometimes this banter would take on a strange sexualized quality—darling, sweetheart, honey—any one of which probably would have been a fireable offense if the genders had been switched. But I much preferred these terms of endearment to cold indifference. Some nurses were absolute angels in human form; others didn't give a tinker's damn about me—at least not that they let on. Some greeted me without so much as a grunt, treating me as nothing more than a task, a box to check. One gave no greeting, not even eye contact. She did and said only as much as necessary not to be fired that very night. There were also the nurses who assumed that in addition to having had a stroke, I also had gone deaf. "SIR, I NEED TO TAKE YOUR VITALS, SIR!"

The thing that distinguished a good nurse was the ability to see my real needs, to see beyond the protocol. I became quite frustrated at having to explain my situation over and over and over again. Incredibly, one nurse asked me if one side of my body was weaker than the other. "Do you know what a stroke is?" I wanted to ask her. "Don't you people write this stuff down? And if not, what is all that incessant tapping on the computer you do? Are you playing a video game?" But I held my tongue and simply replied, "Yes, one side is weaker."

My favorite nurse was Richard, about my age, from Lake Charles, Louisiana. He got me. He spoke to me first instead of to Kirstin. He treated me with the utmost respect and kindness, as his intellectual equal.

But for too many, protocol was the alpha and the omega. There were only boxes to check, computer screens to log in and out of. The nurses' questions seemed to be arbitrary, and each nurse seemed to care about a different set, sometimes overlapping, sometimes not. For instance, it was three weeks into my stay at the rehab hospital when a nurse began asking me about the quantity and quality of my stools. This had never come up before. Something must have been said in an all-hands staff meeting, because suddenly, everyone was interested in my bowel movements, even though there had never been any cause for concern.

I was asked at least four times a day if I had had a bowel movement that day, no matter how many times the answer had been "yes." Again, I wondered if they were writing things down or perhaps just testing me—like an FBI investigator trying to catch me in a lie. "MISTER SEALE," they would shout, again assuming my deafness, "Mr. Seale, have you had a bowel movement today?!" they would call out loudly, the door to my room open so that all might hear. One nurse, who never bothered learning my name, and therefore only called me "sir," stopped me in the hallway on my way back to the room and loudly asked, "Sir, did you have a bowel movement today?!"

"Yes," I said softly.

"What size would you say it was—small, medium, or large?" the interrogation continued.

"Medium, I guess," I mumbled.

"Would you say it was soft, hard, or somewhere in between?"

How much detail did she need? I took a dump, okay?! Everybody calm down! Perhaps we could just discuss it over the hospital intercom for maximum humiliation. Hospital life desensitizes you to all things formerly personal and dignified. Just as I had to stop myself from dropping trou in front of family and friends, I also had to censor my commentary about my bowel movements once I left the confines of the rehab hospital. "Hey everybody. Good to see you. How is everybody today? I just had a *large* bowel movement that was *quite firm*. Like a nine out of ten. Anyone else? Show of hands!"

Interruptions were a constant of hospital life, whether the interruptions were of conversations or of sleep. Throughout the day, at random intervals, healing rest was continually interrupted. Knock knock knock... "Housekeeping!" Knock knock knock... "Food Services—we need to get your menu choices for tomorrow." Knock knock knock... "Internal Medicine." Knock knock knock... "Hi there. I'm the counselor." Knock knock knock... "Hello, it's the rehab doctors, just checking up on you." Knock knock knock... "I need to get your vitals." Knock knock knock... "Have you had a bowel movement today?"

At one point, I was woken up at five a.m. for a blood draw. When I asked why it was necessary to do it at five in the morning, the answer I got was not that blood was any different at five in the morning (I had not been asked to fast), or that it had to be done before breakfast, or that there was any other medically compelling reason to do it at five in the morning. The answer I got was that it was done at five in the morning because a hospital driver arrived at seven a.m. to pick up the labs for the day. Aha! This is what the medical school dean was talking about! The patient was *not* at the center of their care. The *system* was at the center. The convenience of the doctors, the convenience of the hospital, the efficiency of the wheels and cogs of this gigantic complex.

There was always a flurry of activity between six-thirty and seven a.m., a rush to get things done, to get people on and off the toilet, to get them dressed, to get them ready for breakfast. The reason? Shift change. Numerous boxes had to be checked by both nurses and techs before they could go home, and the night shift ended at seven a.m. The system was at the center of the care.

Nurses and techs classify patients by the level of assistance that they need, or rather with the level of liability the facility is comfortable with. There is max assist, moderate assist, min assist, contact guard, and standby. I gleaned this not from any kind of comprehensive explanation, but by eavesdropping on conversations in the hallway. "He's max assist times two." "She's a min assist." "He's a contact guard."

As you slowly improved, you gained "clearance" to do certain things yourself. This process began with my being cleared to transfer from my bed to my wheelchair and from my wheelchair to the toilet with the assistance of Kirstin instead of a staff member. I cannot describe the feeling of freedom this alone bestowed. It was freedom for me—I no longer needed to hit the call button for every change of venue. But of course, it represented new responsibility for Kirstin. "Honey—" I would groan at three in the morning, "I'm sorry, but I need the bathroom." I would hear a deep breath from the alcove, then she would rise to sitting, get her bearings, then get up and wrangle all the covers and mattress pad and pillow, turn the cot on edge, push the wheelchair to me, and lock the wheels.

My room was right outside of a nursing station, and every time anyone called for anything in this hall, the beeping would begin—about once every other second. The cruelest part of this arrangement is that the nursing station where the beeping occurred was not even staffed. Kirstin became aware that there was a "silence" button on the phone that was beeping and henceforth took it upon herself whenever she felt like it to walk into the hall and silence the beeping.

I'm not going to lie—there are many parts of hospital life I could get used to and did.

There was the afternoon nap, frequent interruptions notwithstanding, that I became exceedingly accustomed to.

There was the bed itself, in which one could achieve an infinite number of angles through the operation of multiple switches. Kirstin had dispatched my friends David and Wade to a Target to get an "egg crate" pad that augmented its already considerable comfort. After a rehab session, when I would return to the bed, it was so comfortable it was as if I was being cradled in the hand of the Lord Himself.

There was having my meals brought right to me. For a man of simple tastes, the flavor and texture were more than adequate and far exceeded hospital food's reputation. The only thing I found wanting was the quantity, and I had to ask them several times to bring me more when they would show up with what I began referring to as "old lady portions."

There was this relatively new thing Ed and Elaine had bought for me called a smart speaker. They gifted me with it so that I might "drop in" and talk to the kids or Kirstin at home without even having to call them. This I attempted several times with mixed results, and I found FaceTime calls more satisfying. Rather, the real treasure here turned out to be the Spotify account attached to the smart speaker. Suddenly, I had instant access to albums I had not heard in years, like the first record I ever bought: "Alexa, play the album *Frampton Comes Alive*," and just like that, here it came. I strained my memory in an attempt to see how deep her reservoir was. "Alexa, play Andy Gibb. . . Alexa, play Alabama. ... Charlie Daniels ... Tommy Emmanuel, the album *Guitars and Other Cathedrals* by Adrian Legg, the album *Stampede* by the Doobie Brothers ... the album *Aja* by Steely Dan." Most mornings, before breakfast, I got things going with Vulfpeck's "Mr. Finish Line" or a shuffle of Stevie Wonder, and the nurses and techs coming in and out of the room would marvel both at the voice commands and at the sound quality emanating from a speaker barely larger than a soda can. I didn't yet even realize it could do basic things like tell me the time or the weather, let alone quiz me on trivia.

I also had my laptop that now lived on the rolling table I ate from, and at times I made attempts to glance through my personal email. One day early on, I got an email from my mother-in-law with a link to a video. It was a TED Talk by a stroke survivor who was also a neuroscientist. Jill Bolte Taylor had written a book about her experience called *My Stroke of Insight*. "You might have already seen this," my mother-in-law wrote. "Pretty fascinating." Actually, I had seen it several years earlier but had forgotten the details. In the twenty-minute video, the animated speaker with long silver hair laid out her thesis that because her stroke was left-brain, this periodically disabled her sense of individuality and as a result, plunged her into the knowledge that she was one with everything around her, including all the people in the world. Despite also having had a left-brain stroke, I did not enjoy a similar spiritual insight. Perhaps I simply did not bleed in the same areas. Perhaps it was because I already believed that humanity was one thing. In any event, the insights I gained from the stroke seemed considerably less profound—along the lines of "well, *this* sucks."

In addition to my laptop, there was the TV to distract me. Watching TV in bed was something Kirstin and I had agreed to ban from daily life before we even started having kids, not wanting the device to be quite so ever-present in our lives—the first thing we saw in the morning, the last thing we saw at night. But man, oh man was it nice to have that escape now. And there was plenty of mind candy in those weeks. There was the Super Bowl, a win by the Eagles over the Patriots with Justin Timberlake at halftime dancing away in a deer shirt and a camo suit. Each night for weeks, I fell asleep to the Winter Olympics in South Korea, as commentators picked apart the latest backside 1080 or McTwist by up-and-coming snowboard phenoms and whether they could remain at the top of the leaderboard as Shaun White, the aging lion of the sport at thirty-one, prepared to put down what could be his last Olympic run!

Setting aside the fact that these athletes were at most half my age, I had never been Olympics material. But that was not to say I had not been active.

CHAPTER 6

Things That I Used to Do

I wanted my right leg back for all sorts of self-evident reasons. Being bound to a wheelchair necessitates all kinds of infrastructure changes, accommodations, vehicles, slows everything down. And like it or not, it turns you into an object of pity for those who dare to make eye contact. No matter how emotionally neutral the look may seem, it is always complicated by the perception of the beholder.

Something else I never really thought about before—it makes you shorter than everyone else. Every time I stood up in ICU or in the rehab hospital, there was a shocked reaction as I generally towered over the nurse, the therapist, or whoever was helping me. "Oh my gosh! You're so tall!" I never knew quite what the right response was to this. "Yes, well, you see, I'm standing up now, whereas a few moments ago, I was seated in a chair."

Another thing I learned was how annoying it was for someone to enter a room and stand behind you while having a conversation if you're in a wheelchair. I'm sure I did the very same thing before I was in a chair, but never again will I talk over someone's head from behind their back.

The ultimate aspiration in the leg department was to be able to hike again. I had hiked more than two hundred miles total in the year prior to my stroke. In eight days, I had hiked one hundred miles in East Texas, which formed the basis of my book *Monster Hike*. A few months later, I had hiked seventy-five miles in the Rockies in New Mexico with Andrew and his Boy Scout crew at Philmont Scout Ranch, a humongous property that hosts some thirty thousand Boy Scouts every summer. The training or "shakedown" hikes before that brought my total to more than two hundred miles. When I could hike again, not just walk down a smooth and level hallway but really hike, I would know I had recovered, that I was back.

The arm and hand constituted an altogether different set of goals (though, as I was to learn, walking has much more to do with one's arms than I ever suspected).

One of the great loves of my life was the guitar, which I played for hours at a time or until something pressing took me away from it. Playing it was my default setting. I began playing in high school, and in the intervening thirty-five years, five players had an outsized influence on what and how I played: Stevie Ray Vaughan, Eric Johnson, Adrian Legg, Tommy Emmanuel, and Jerry Reed.

For the four years prior to my stroke, I had concentrated almost all my effort on the instrumentals of Jerry Reed and had slowly brought them to performance level. I felt a special connection to his 1967 signature instrumental "The Claw," maybe because that was the year of my birth. Reed called it the claw because of the way he used his right hand—his picking hand: a thumb pick, his middle finger, and his ring finger formed a claw. After the stroke, the claw had a completely different meaning to me because it was the shape my right hand was often clenched into.

I dreamed about being able to move my fingers the way I used to, the way I just had on our recordings—thumb pick and fingers flying in complicated patterns of sixteenth notes, banjo rolls, and boom-chuck, boom-chuck patterns popularized by Merle Travis and Chet Atkins. When I say I dreamed of this, I'm not saying simply that I pined for it; I had dreams that I was using my picking hand for the first time, and it was like a miracle for which I was ecstatically grateful. Then I would wake up, and my claw would be lying lifelessly at my side, still waiting, and waiting, and waiting.

I had asked Kirstin to bring my nylon-string acoustic guitar to the hospital. It now leaned silently against the corner; when I mustered the courage to try, I could not even get my fingers within striking distance of the strings. This was far and away the biggest hole in my life. Hike, camp, work with my hands, play guitar. As Guitar Slim and Stevie Ray Vaughan once sang, these were "things that I used to do."

But of course, few activities are just a leg thing or just an arm thing. When I hiked, I used my arms to steady myself with trekking poles, and to adjust a heavy pack, and to help get over fallen logs and under low-hanging branches. And I played guitar best when standing and adjusted my sound with a combination of effects pedals I controlled with my feet.

And beyond those specialties there was an array of things I enjoyed doing that just used every part of my body and that I doubted I would fully get back. Perhaps my finest hour as a father was the hour I put the finishing touches on a raft I had led the boys in building and launched into the Colorado River below Austin for a two-day adventure.

I was inspired to build it when I stumbled on a YouTube video of a similar vessel. The eight-by-sixteen-foot raft was built of four four-by-eight-foot plywood frames that each held an array of ten Sterilite plastic bins. The four units were laid side by side and joined together by sixteen-foot steel fence rails. Each unit had two long doors on the deck that gave us access to all forty bins. The top edges of the bins rode above the waterline, so in addition to keeping the raft afloat, the bins also provided a huge amount of storage for anything that would fit in them—sleeping bags, food, backpacks, dry bags, fishing tackle, the marine battery that powered the trolling motor, etc.

On each corner of the raft we used large lag bolts to brace four-foot posts, with eye screws that held hammocks. For the middle of the raft, we built a hefty plywood chuck box that held our cast iron skillet and Dutch oven and spatulas and charcoal and mess kits and first aid.

During spring break two years before my stroke—with Wade and his youngest son, my three boys, myself, and a prayer—we set out to float, pole, and paddle fourteen miles along the scenic, mostly lazily winding Colorado. Near sundown we reached the large island in the river on which we had planned to camp. We dragged the raft ashore at the head of the island, off-loaded the chuck box and set it up on its removable legs so it sat three feet off the ground, and unlatched its side doors, which swung down to ninety degrees to serve as food-prep surfaces. The Dutch oven came out along with the charcoal chimney, and we dispatched the boys to explore the long, densely treed island. They brought back wood for a campfire. It was only two days and a night, but the episode lives in my memory as the pinnacle of whatever abilities and virtues I ever brought to fatherhood. However, that was just one of a long line of building projects I did with and for the boys, like the log cabin-style fort I built from landscaping timbers, the sixty-foot zip line, the block-and-tackle elevator, the Cubmobile, the tennis ball-slinging trebuchet, and so on.

Even on that January morning before the stroke brought me low, I was thinking ahead to spring break, just starting to dust off river maps and take a mental inventory of the raft's components. This was me at my best with the boys, and now I had no idea, none, if those days were on pause for a year, or five, or if they were behind me forever.

The raft also illustrates my penchant for doing things the hard way. Many years earlier, when I would go deer hunting, I did not use a rifle, but rather a bow. And I did not use a compound bow but rather used a traditional bow. For what was the purpose of using a bow, and then upgrading it with technology to something almost as easy and accurate as a gun? And it was not just any kind of traditional bow, but, of course, the most primitive kind, a longbow. My longbow required nearly sixty pounds of force to draw. I could no more do that now than levitate.

While many people craved the latest in high-tech gadgetry, I loved learning about the primitive in any pursuit, the earliest building blocks of technology. Nothing engendered my respect as much as woodworker Roy Underhill taking thirty minutes of PBS broadcast time and creating a rocking chair with just a few hand tools that hadn't changed much in the last thousand years. His show, *The Woodwright's Shop*, filled me with quixotic ambitions to build my own foot-powered lathe.

I regularly trawled through antique stores with the boys in tow to find the woodwright's tools. The ax that would fell the tree. The saw that would square the ends. The two-handed drawknife that would strip the bark. Standing the wood on end, I would hold the blade of the froe along its top end and, with a club, beat the blade into the grain, then split the piece down its length with an incredibly satisfying crackle. I could then plane it smooth and use an auger to hand-drill large holes that could hold stool legs, which I would taper with a hatchet before pounding into place.

All this made me feel rooted to the past. I enjoyed trying to make Christmas presents for the boys when they were young. A Jacob's ladder. A do-nothing machine. A nutcracker I turned on the spring-pole lathe that sort of resembled a soldier but turned out to be simply a club with which the boys could gleefully smash pecans like cavemen.

Now, I could not so much as support a hammer with my right hand, let alone control it. I pictured my workbench in the garage, strewn with tools, and wondered if they would stay right there, frozen in time, until one day, perhaps decades from now, when Kirstin would prevail on the boys to go through them, take what they wanted, and sort the rest for an estate sale.

My point in all of this is that I used to dream big dreams and, when those dreams were relatively safe, I would try to bring the boys along, to teach them what it was to be proudly unconventional, to work from sunup to sundown for a quixotic goal, to be just a little wild in this ultra-tame world, to swim in a river, to lie under the stars, to fall asleep from exhaustion to the yips and howls of coyotes. Was rafting on pause for a year, or five, or was it behind me forever? Would the boys even be game for such a trip anymore by the time I was able to take them again?

For Time Is Short (written 2015, three years prior)

And now, my sons,
Let us speak of weighty things,
For time is short.
Let us not speak of weather, but climate.
Let us not speak of fish, but whales.
Nor of celebrity, nor sport, nor even bodily health.
Let us speak of history, or better, mystery.
Let us speak of prophets and their promises.
Let us speak of what we see in clouds,
For these are visions, and visions are the future.
Time is short so let us turn from screens that filter reality,
And instead hurry to the forest to hear the owls echoing at dusk
And see the night wood sparkle with fireflies,
A galaxy writ low and close
That we might fly through it
With our feet on the ground.
Time is short so let us climb the nearest mountain,
Not the highest,
And speak of nothing.
Our footfalls crunching out our purpose and meaning are enough.
Let us float down the widening river and submit to its pace
And surrender to its wisdom.
Time is short, so behold the arc of history,
Then seize your segment of it, and twist.
Do not be passive or soft or incurious,
But keep a fierce heart within a hardened chest,
And a restless mind within a bowed head,
That you might matter beyond your suburb,
And at the end of days the Maker might say
We were worth the effort.
My sons, let us speak of weighty things,
For I am dying.

As are you.
As are we all.
Oh my sons, time is short,
So let us live.
And when we speak,
Then let it be of the only wisdom:
Let it be of love.

CHAPTER 7

Slight Return

Moderate exercise of the muscles is a remedial agent of high value; it tends to promote a more active circulation through the entire system, and, consequently, to diminish the pressure on blood vessels which a little extra force might cause to give way. If active exercise cannot be taken, frictions performed by a second person, by means of a bath of strong mustard water, should be administered, followed by a thorough rubbing, all over the body, but especially the spine and extremities. Use Turkish towels or flesh brushes.

—Vitalogy, 1904

"**H**e's a diner!" The first morning of therapy, I was hurried out of bed by a panicked tech. "He's a diner!" she panted to the nurse who was taking my vitals. Needless to say, I didn't know what the hell was going on.

The significance of this diner status was that I was due in the dining room in five minutes for breakfast so that my speech therapist, who also did therapy related to swallowing, could observe me swallowing my food. Whether I was listed in the system as a "diner" or as someone who could eat in his room was a matter of mystery and guesswork for the next several days. I never knew if I was going to be a diner or not until moments before, and regardless of that status, there was always a rush to take my vitals and get me dressed for the day due to the shift change at seven o'clock.

My first day as a "diner," I wheeled myself, pushing the wheel with my left hand and paddling against the linoleum with my left foot, down the hall and around the corner to the small community dining room. I sat across a round table from a woman who looked to be in her late fifties or early sixties and whose daughter, a teacher in Dripping Springs west of Austin, had come to be with her since it was Saturday. A whole team of people was coaxing the patient to eat. "Mrs. Willard, you have to eat," said the speech therapist, Ellen.

Ellen was a tall brunette with a smart bob and smiling eyes. This is all I can describe of her because, like everyone else on the staff, she wore a face mask for the duration of flu season, which almost perfectly overlapped my tenure there. "Our goal for today is for you to eat half of your oatmeal," Ellen patiently explained to the ornery woman. This naturally made me wonder why she had not been served half the amount with the goal of eating it all.

"Too cold!" Mrs. Willard shouted in a country accent, even as she sat in her wheelchair wrapped in a thick hospital blanket from her neck to her feet. "Come on, Mom," said her daughter gently. "It'll help you get your strength back."

"Tew cowuld!" she shouted again.

The third diner at the table was Mrs. Zamora, an elderly woman with kind, gentle eyes, making glacial progress on her scrambled eggs. "*Mastica bien tu comida,* Mrs. Zamora," said Ellen in the best accent that college Spanish could bestow, before turning her attention back to Mrs. Willard. Mr. Seale was clearly the least of her problems this morning. I devoured my scrambled eggs and hash browns, washed them down with coffee, juice, and water— chin obediently tucked, and wheeled away from the sad scene in six minutes flat.

The diner experience, and much else here, gave me the sensation of being teleported, perhaps by the Ghost of Christmas Future, into a nursing home. To be fair, there were no patients taking wheelchair naps in public areas, and no stench of urine, all too common at such facilities. But as I wheeled down the hallway and saw one bedridden octogenarian after another through open doors, and heard them shouting to long-suffering family members over blaring TVs, there was a crushing sadness that hung in the air, the flowers and balloon bouquets and get-well cards notwithstanding. Overnight, I had become old.

Now and then, I would catch a glimmer of a thirty-something, and occasionally even a teen—the girl with the dark-rimmed glasses, shaved head, and jarring cranial scar. But such sights did not raise my spirits: "Hey, I guess I'm *not* in an old folks' home after all!"; they were only sad exceptions that proved the rule, other souls made old before their time. Thirty going on seventy. Seventeen going on sixty-five.

The whole point of this hospital was rehabilitation, and for three exhausting hours a day, I gratefully received it. There were three categories of neural rehab, and I began my stay devoting an hour to each every day. There was an hour for speech and cognition. (To avoid stigma, this was abbreviated as "speech.") There was an hour of physical therapy and an hour of occupational therapy, the latter categories being shortened to PT and OT.

Speech and cognitive therapy were administered by Ellen, whose acquaintance I had made during breakfast. I now had her undivided attention. She asked me to read newspaper articles and regurgitate the details of them. She had me play games on an iPad that measured my spatial reasoning. For memorization, she suggested five organizational tools, including repetition, grouping, association, writing things down, and visualization.

I volunteered to her that I occasionally used visualization to help memorize prayers. One prayer in particular comprised a seemingly random list of settings, but I had managed to memorize the list by creating a movie in my head, one in which I was flying through and over the objects and features I was listing: "Blessed is the spot, and the house, and the place, and the city, and the heart, and the mountain, and the refuge, and the cave, and the valley, and the land, and the sea, and the island, and the meadow, where mention of God hath been made and His praise glorified." The same technique I sometimes used to memorize lyrics.

Ellen showed me a list of nine animals and asked me to use grouping or categories to memorize them: lion, zebra, giraffe, cat, dog, hamster, chicken, cow, and horse. She assured me there was no right or wrong method. Immediately, I grouped zebra, giraffe, horse, and cow into one group— ungulates, or hooved animals. Then I grouped the lion and the house cat into the category "cats." The chicken was a category all to itself—birds. Finally, the hamster and the dog got lumped into "other mammals." Twenty minutes later, I successfully remembered all of the animals, but Ellen said she had never seen these categories used before. When I asked what categories were common, she replied with a professionalism that masked nearly all of her amusement that, normally, people grouped zebras, giraffes, and lions under "wild animals"; horses, cows, and chickens under "farm animals"; and cats, dogs, and hamsters they classified as "pets." That struck me as quite anthropocentric, but we moved on.

In one session, we went into an office with a large black panel studded with a circular array of green and red lights. "Every time you see a green light come on, name as many states as you can." Not to boast, but I pretty much crushed this one.

The next task, explained Ellen, would be to name states but also cities within those states. When a green light came on, I would name a state, and for every red light that came on after it, I would name a city within that state. We would start with Texas. These were timed tests, and as soon as Ellen said "Go," I was off to the races: "Austin, Dallas, Houston." Sitting in my wheelchair, I slapped at the red lights after each city: "Fort Worth," slap, "San Antonio," slap. "El Paso," slap, "Waco," slap. Then a green light came on again, and it was time to switch states. Just moving geographically across the border, I called out, "Oklahoma!" This was fun! "Oklahoma City . . . Tulsa . . . Enid—" The red lights persisted. "—umm Ardmore . . . Lawton . . . uhhh—Shawnee," more red lights, one after the other, "Idabel . . . Poteau, umm, Vance Air Force Base—does that count as a city?" More red lights. "—How many cities in Oklahoma do most people know?" I asked desperately. Ellen, realizing the flaw in her game, broke down laughing and let me off the hook. I enjoyed moments that revealed the humanity and experimentation behind a therapist's thinking, even in failure, episodes that revealed a therapist's autonomy and the fact they were engaged and not just a slave to a script.

I met a physical therapist a month later who shared with me his favorite memories of "therapy fails." One of his worst ideas was the time he had a client who would not look up when walking. So the therapist fashioned a collar for him out of cardboard, a huge disc designed to prevent him from seeing his feet. You can imagine the consequences if someone wearing a large, stiff cardboard disc around his neck fell. He described another episode when he had tied a rope to one of his patient's feet and told him he was going to try to trip him as he walked. He succeeded, he recalled with a belly laugh.

After a week, Ellen decided I no longer required her services. I had been evaluated to a fare thee well, and cognitively was performing as well as I probably would have pre-stroke. Stroke survivors, regardless of how slightly their cognitive abilities might have been affected, often describe a "fog" through which they must fight. I remember that fog, that light haze through which all things appear dreamy or gauzy. The struggle to find just the right word. And we don't know what we don't know. Surely there were subtleties and nuances that were lost along the way, but I was somewhere safely between super genius and village idiot.

I rather enjoyed the quizzes and challenges, but this dismissal from speech was a relief to me, of course, because it meant that, at least by these gross measures, I had not lost a noticeable number of my marbles in the flood. The irony in shortening "speech and cognition" to face-saving "speech" is that I probably would have really benefited from actual speech therapy. I had and still do have issues with lazy enunciation, and mild stuttering, and a generally weak tone. The more tired I am, the worse it gets. But all were in agreement that these problems were minor compared to the near paralysis of my right leg and arm. For those, I would need extensive PT and OT.

My first principal physical therapist was Heather. She had long dirty-blond hair, favored pink and burgundy scrubs, and had a chipper can-do attitude, as a therapist should. She was a native of Bastrop, about an hour away, and a horse lover who had participated in rodeos in high school in the goat-tying event. Wrestling ornery, hairy beasts that didn't want to be controlled to the ground and binding their feet must have been good training for her current line of work. Soon enough, she would bind my foot, not to its mate but rather wrap my toes with an Ace bandage and then raise my foot and wrap the same bandage around my calf (calf tying?) so my toes would clear the ground when I stepped.

It was time to get out of my wheelchair and try some walking. With my foot tied at a right angle to my shin, we started outside the gym in the hallway with a huge contraption known as a "LiteGait." This can best be pictured as a diaper suspended by four seat belts from a seven-foot-tall rolling frame. It allowed you the freedom to stumble but not to fall. "SaWEET!" Heather sang out as I took my first steps. I could not have gone more than thirty feet that first day, but it was enough to be upgraded the next day from the LiteGait to a wide quad cane, which was a relief, because the LiteGait would have been a hell of a thing to try to get around town in.

A quad cane is a cane with four small feet arranged in a rectangle so that the cane is always perpendicular to the ground and also stands up by itself. Concurrent with this graduation from LiteGait to cane was a graduation from an Ace bandage to an AFO. The AFO, or ankle-foot orthosis, was a rigid plastic brace that cradled my foot underneath and strapped around my calf and shin holding my foot rigidly at a right angle and preventing me turning my ankle. This was an off-the-shelf AFO, in contrast to the custom, hinged one I would get later.

The hallways were one hundred feet long. This made it easier to measure how far a patient had made it in a given day. I sometimes spotted therapists counting ceiling tiles to measure distances that were fractions of hallways. As I inched down the hallway with the quad cane in my left hand and a tech spotting my every step from behind, Heather would sit on a rolling stool and scooch along next to my right leg. There, she alternated between poking my hip to get my hip flexor to activate and spotting my right knee so that I didn't hyperextend it during my backstep. Away I went with my posse, which often included Kirstin shooting photos or video on her phone as she backpedaled in front of me like a docent—thirty feet the first day, seventy-five the next, 110 the next, and so on. At the end of four weeks of rehab, I was walking four hundred feet without having to sit. This took me about twenty minutes. Though it was progress, I could not help dwelling on the fact that just over a year earlier I had hiked a hundred miles—a hundred miles!—in eight days. And now, this.

Most of my time in PT as well as in OT was spent in one of two gyms that occupied identical spots on the second and third floors of the hospital. At any given time, there were two to four other patients in the gym with me, usually older, all with their own constellation of struggles and with varying degrees of sadness, anger, resignation, pain. Some were bitter and difficult. Others were as happy as clams, alive for another day, and moreover enjoying the attentions of an apparently endless procession of cute twenty-four-year-old female therapists.

One patient might be seated in a wheelchair using the hand cycle while being shocked with an "e-stim" unit. One might be navigating a short flight of wooden steps that had been assembled in the corner. Another might be sitting at a large table in the middle of the room and intermittently standing. One dominant memory of this stage of my rehab was being asked if I was in pain or if I was just exerting effort. Either this stuff was way harder for me than it was for most people, or I was trying a lot harder than most people. The way in which I would screw up my face would constantly elicit questions about pain or effort.

In the early days, Kirstin was basically living at the hospital with me, sitting next to me in rehab, documenting my rehab achievements with her phone camera, getting me water when I looked longingly at the sink. When she wasn't there, she was racing home to see to a thousand details of our life, paying bills, compiling lists of people we wanted to write thank-you notes to at some unknown point in the future, getting the must-do tasks at her part-time job done, and ordering rehab equipment from Amazon. When she discovered that e-stim units were available on Amazon, I showed up in the gym with my own battery-powered unit two days later. When I complained to the therapist that the Aircast she was putting my arm in made my hand sweaty and made me claustrophobic, Kirstin showed up a day later with a half-length Aircast ordered from Amazon. Occasionally we supported the local economy as well. When my occupational therapist used a vibrator to stimulate my forearm muscles and get movement in my hand, Kirstin was at the nearby Walgreens within thirty minutes buying a vibrator for me. When it looked like I might be going home soon and was still wheelchair-bound, she ordered "suitcase" wheelchair ramps that would get me in the front door. I would want for nothing so long as she and Amazon both existed.

One delightful and immensely helpful part of physical therapy was the pool, which I used three times at the rehab hospital. It was a tiny indoor pool that the staff struggled to keep warm enough as it was enclosed with a glass wall, and it was February. After donning a bathing suit and wheeling to the elevator, which deposited me on the ground floor, I rolled into the humid room and nervously along the pool deck until I reached a plastic seat mounted on a massive swinging arm. With lots of help, I was transferred into a chair, and they strapped me in before lowering me into the water, a somewhat terrifying sensation. It was like a dream in which I was Houdini but had no idea how I was going to get out of this. Once down, I unclicked the belt and floated to my feet as easy as could be. (Fat floats, you know.)

Now I was given all sorts of assignments. Christy, our assistant, would set a metronome to ticking, and I would try my best to walk in time. Step, tick, tick, tick. Step, tick, tick, tick. Stepping up a level and stepping down a level. Sidestepping one way, then back. We hit a beach ball to each other as the therapist looked at a live video feed on a poolside TV screen of my legs from an underwater camera.

My last day in the pool, I had a minor complaint about my back. I was prone to back irritability even before the stroke. Now, with all of the asymmetrical limping and lurching, frankly it was a miracle I was not in constant pain. My pool therapist knew just what to do: Watsu. For fifteen minutes, she held me in her arms, like a husband might carry a wife over the threshold of their new home, and gently moved me through the water. The physical sensation was soothing and relieved my pain. The psychological sensation was curious. This was not the natural order of things, a woman cradling a nearly two-hundred-pound man like a baby. I did not know quite what to make of that, but I was game for anything and put myself at the mercy of these patient and good-hearted people. Also, I mistakenly called it "Watto," which is not a Japanese-inspired form of water therapy, but rather the birdlike Toydarian junk dealer in *Star Wars*. Who can keep all these things straight?

As we passed the two-week mark at the rehab hospital in Austin, we began to prepare for a move to the countryside—the small town of Dripping Springs west of Austin. This is where the rehab doctors recommended I go to continue inpatient recovery. Monday came and went, and we received word that the move had been denied by my health insurance. It was a doctor on the insurance company's payroll who had never laid eyes on me, denying the recommendation of the rehab doctors who saw me every day. I didn't quite understand that. This impasse necessitated what is known as a peer-to-peer conference between my doctors and the insurance company doctor. After that meeting, I was told the denial would stand, and at that point the best option was for me to stay in the rehab hospital for one, two, maybe three more weeks.

The word on the street was that there just weren't as many of these rehab hospitals as there used to be. "It's just not profitable," the doctor told me. Those words landed with a thud and sit uncomfortably with me to this day. Was that the sole measure of whether something as important as this should exist?

Around this time Dave Harmon came to visit me. Dave and I met after college at the first real job for both of us, in the newsroom of the *Monitor* newspaper in McAllen. He had been the best man in my wedding, and we had stayed close through camping and through sharing in the joyous misery of each other's home improvement projects. He now headed the investigative unit of the *Texas Tribune* and had a refreshing and droll take on just about everything. I suspect that is why we had clicked all those years ago; neither of us was afraid to look at the big picture and come to unconventional conclusions if that's where the evidence pointed.

We sat with the light off, me in bed, he in a chair at my feet, the room lit only by however much of the dim gray light of a February morning made it through my window in the alcove. I was explaining the way that the insurance company had dragged its feet when it was time for me to leave ICU and come here. "It's kind of bullshit," I said, "this whole system." In retrospect, and relative to the things that were still to come, that frustration now seems quaint. "You wonder where all this will wind up," I said, "because it can't go on like this forever. Everyone recognizes that the system is broken. The money that we spend versus the outcomes we get just don't line up."

"Oh, it's absolutely bullshit," Dave commiserated in statement-of-fact way. "The whole concept of insurance is fascinating." Dave had had a long love affair with central Mexico, had recently bought a house in the scenic colonial mountain city of Guanajuato, and was just then having it renovated. "When you look at Mexico, there really is no health insurance or auto insurance. Something breaks, you get it fixed."

"Yeah," I said, "supply and demand. We talk a good game about free-market capitalism, but they're the ones who are really living it, right?"

"It's really a statement on our own cultural aversion to risk," Dave noted. In Mexico, the great majority takes its chances without health insurance, auto insurance, life insurance, and the result is that costs are transparent and real competition exists. Well sure, the snarky might answer, if you want care in *Mexico!* Good luck with that filthy surgical equipment in Tijuana or that doctor from a third-world medical school!

The truth though, as has been noted many times, is that we're not nearly as healthy as we should be based on how much we pay. And Mexico is not nearly as bad as such arguments would make it out to be. Dave and I had both lived in South Texas and watched as retirees from across the United States gleefully streamed across the border for bargain-basement meds and for dental work, gladly paying hundreds instead of tens of thousands of dollars and wrapping up their day with a salty margarita before heading north across the river to their RV parks in Donna or San Benito or Mission.

I was learning an astonishing fact: that my care was directed by a kind of doctor I didn't even know existed, a doctor imbedded inside my health insurance company. That is to say, all the ultimate decisions about my treatment—what was allowed and what was denied—were made by people who had never even laid eyes on me. Let's let that sink in for a moment. In fact, there was a perfect inverse correlation between a person's familiarity with me and their power to affect my treatment: therapists knew me best by far, and they had the least say in the duration or the tempo of my treatment.

I only discovered that the insurance company had an in-house physician when Dr. Li—a faceless, formless man—would deny covering the next step of recovery as "medically unnecessary." In my mind, Dr. Li was Sauron from the Lord of the Rings—sinister, lusting after ultimate power, ever at a distance yet able to track my every move. In reality, I guessed he was a perfectly affable man, a cog in a lucrative machine, putting bread on his own family's table (that bread being a Roquefort-and-almond sourdough and that table being a twelve-foot eighteenth-century Chippendale—mahogany with two walnut inlays: one, the winged caduceus medical symbol, the other, a dollar sign).

This relationship was not the law, of course; there was nothing legally prohibiting my going to any doctor I wanted and pursuing any kind of therapy. But economic laws are as binding as law itself where real life is concerned.

I don't have the answers to untangle this mess, but I do know we have cobbled together a way of doing things that has somehow managed to capture the worst of capitalism and of socialism. What we seem to have now is a sector with all of the infamous inequities of capitalism but none of the efficiencies of Adam Smith's "invisible hand." On the other side, we seem to have embraced the high societal costs of socialism and the impersonal Orwellian malaise you might expect of a socialist mega-state without enjoying any of the economies of scale one would assume such a system might produce.

Swirling in every layer of the mix is the omnipresent interloper, insurance. Insurance is most definitely a function of a free market, so why does it feel like socialism? It feels like big-government socialism because it is something we have no real say in. I have a say in where I work. *My employer* has a say in who my insurer is. And like everything else in our society, runaway conglomeration pretty much guarantees that in thirty years the "free market" will offer employers an array of options that include Package A or Package B. That's if antitrust laws still exist and have prevented an absolute monopoly. But let's back up a moment.

The cost of the first week of my stroke was a quarter of a million dollars. The reasons for this extreme cost are delineated in books much longer than this one. My layman's "hot take," perhaps too obvious to even commit to print, is that these costs are astronomical because insurance pays them. Stay with me.

We don't feel the true cost in a direct way because a third party is absorbing the lion's share of the blow. So my emergency room drugs cost $40,000 for one day much like the Pentagon infamously paid $700 for a hammer; no single customer in his right mind would pay $700 for a hammer, but if millions are paying a fraction of a penny for it, then this obscenity becomes lost in a sea of details too vast to track. Had I to pay for those ER drugs out of my pocket, it would have ruined my family. But because it was spread over 106 million customers and their employers, the impact in my case was blunted.

I suppose I should be thankful for that blunting, but deep in my gut I know the house always wins in the end. We and our employers all are paying exorbitant premiums to keep these plates spinning, to keep this ultra-complex apparatus running. Not only are we paying for the $700 hammer, we're hiring someone to sell it to us. The health insurance industry employs 460,000 people in America. Naturally, the executives that run these massive companies make fat stacks. In 2011, the CEO of BlueShield of California cleared $4.6 million.

I wondered if it was worth it, so I did some math. I haven't kept my paystubs over the last thirty years, but currently, a quarter of every dollar I earn goes directly from my employer to health insurance—it never even touches my bank account. I spent a year out of college in the gig economy, playing in a band and substitute teaching, but I've been in the workforce full-time for twenty-seven years. I built a spreadsheet estimating my cumulative cost of health-care insurance for those twenty-seven years, and it came to $449,625. So if you have a brain hemorrhage for which you spend a quarter of a million dollars in one week, and another quarter of a million dollars in the subsequent months, then yes, you come out ahead, barely, and so I suppose it's worth it.

But this is just begging the question—just accepting all of the assumptions inherent in the status quo. Why is health care so expensive to begin with? Why is it so expensive that the typical worker faces financial annihilation without this incredibly complicated apparatus called insurance standing in the breach?

Of the ten most lucrative careers in America, nine are in health care. Nine of the top ten. At the top is anesthesiologist. Let me hasten to say that the next time I need to be put under, I want my anesthesiologist to be well paid. I want them to be well trained, rested, and happy. But should they really rank above the person holding the knife?

The average annual salary for an American dermatologist at this writing is more than $400,000—average.

I understand that everything has proximal causes. Doctors have lots of student debt, so higher education has a degree of culpability. Lawsuits have necessitated a whole new layer of hidden costs in the form of malpractice insurance. That said, some statistics surely are just unjustifiable on their face. "Nine out of ten" is one such statistic.

But doctors look like Buddhist monks who have shunned all worldly possessions compared to pharmaceutical executives. The biggest line item on my more-than-$250,000 ICU bill was for what? Drugs. Currently, there are seven pharmaceutical company CEOs who make in excess of $20 million a year.

When I was a kid, my brothers and I would recite commercials for things like Mr. Microphone and Ginsu steak knives and the Ronco Pocket Fisherman. Now, my boys, the youngest of whom is eleven, can recite long passages from commercials for Ozempic, a diabetes injection pen, or Tremfya, for moderate to severe plaque psoriasis, or Viberzi, for moderate to severe irritable bowel syndrome. A few years ago, I saw a commercial during the Super Bowl aimed at those suffering from "opioid-induced constipation." A thirty-second Super Bowl commercial that year cost $5 million. That my kids can recite a commercial for opioid-induced constipation pills is surely one sign that The End is nigh. I suspect the end of civilization will feel not unlike moderate to severe bone-to-bone rheumatoid arthritis. Ask your doctor if Humira is right for you. If advertising is any indication of wealth, then big pharma is crushing pills in platinum mortars with diamond pestles.

CHAPTER 8

Empty Arms

Many medical authors regard common table salt as one of the best remedies known in a fit of apoplexy. Many thousands of lives might have been saved by simply knowing how to use salt in this disease.

—*Vitalogy, 1904*

Of the three branches of neuro-rehabilitation—speech therapy, physical therapy, and occupational therapy—occupational therapy is likely the least understood, owing to its vague and easily misconstrued name. Does it deal with getting you back to work? Well, yes. But OT also covers putting on socks, and navigating a kitchen with your new body, and building strength and coordination in your arm and hand. I found the difference between OT and PT to sometimes be indistinguishable and arbitrary, but in general, I came to regard PT as "leg stuff" and OT as "arm stuff," though both kinds of therapists would object to such oversimplification.

In the early days, I referred to my right hand in a variety of ways, usually meant to leaven the situation. One of these nicknames was "the monkey paw." This usually got a knowing laugh out of fellow strokees, as they each had one of their own. But Kirstin did not like the reference, not one bit, and she told me so. At first, I bristled. *It was my hand; why should I not be able to call it the monkey paw or anything else I pleased? It didn't work!* Then I would feel how she would stroke my hand softly, would look at it lovingly, sometimes even would speak directly to it with soft, supportive words of encouragement. It was the first time I had ever considered that I had been or could be disrespectful to a part of my own body. Soon enough, I realized she was right. I stopped trying so hard to be Mr. Irreverence, and limited myself to a value-neutral nickname for my right hand I had floated early on in the process that she seemed to like, "Pancho," because, well—you get it.

On about my third day in the rehab hospital, it became time for my OT evaluation. Sandy, a fit fifty with a frosted pixie, hit the doorway of my room like a hurricane comes ashore. She talked nonstop, interspersing instructions—"press here, now pull there, that's it"—with exclamations of "Praise God!" and addressing me as "precious man!" and giving advice to me, as Kirstin looked on, to "get your sweetheart to do this" and "get your sweetheart to do that." Sandy was at 125 percent with no filter but lots of contrition. When something would go wrong, such as her suddenly being in the wrong position to test something, she'd let loose "G . . . damn it! Sh—" She would stop herself in mid-word. "I'm so sorry. It's Lent, and you would never know I love Jesus." Five minutes later she would praise God again and then swear again and then apologize, and the whole thing would repeat about it being Lent and her loving Jesus, like a video loop, she pulling on my limbs, telling me to resist, telling me to shrug, massaging my shoulder, feeling for my shoulder blade.

When it was time for the therapy itself, she turned me over to Lisa, a no-nonsense young lady from Shreveport who was kind but not easily impressed. Whereas Heather was like a cheerleader—chipper and enthusiastic—Lisa worked with the quiet authority of a dog trainer who had encountered every conceivable deficit before and adjusted for it with zero drama or fanfare. Whereas Heather would sing out, "SaWEET!" Lisa would say, "Not bad." I appreciated their personalities equally.

In my new body, nothing came automatically as once nearly everything did. And the first things, the most urgent things, Lisa helped me learn were the basics of taking care of myself. In therapy parlance these fundamental tasks of independent life are known as "activities of daily living," inevitably shortened to ADLs, which I sometimes confused with bad cholesterol numbers. How do you take off your shirt when one shoulder, arm, and hand doesn't work? You use your good hand to unbutton the top two or three buttons, then grab the back of your collar and pull the entire shirt forward over your head. This is the one and only way it can be done. You can spend a thousand years trying alternatives and never succeed. A chimp will accidentally type out *Hamlet* before you get a shirt off any other way. Many ADLs shared this trait of single-solution efficacy.

Once my clothes were off, it was time for a shower. I learned that my rights at this hospital included the right to a shower every other day. This was a big deal, both something I looked forward to and a big undertaking. A shower had to be scheduled out several hours in advance to assure there would be a tech available to help me—this was unless the shower itself was part of OT, as it sometimes was.

Once my T-shirt, socks, and shoes were off, I would scoop my right foot with the left and scooch my wheelchair into the bathroom. The OT would start the hot water, then, with wheels locked, I would stand, drop my shorts, and quickly transfer to the plastic chair in the large walk-in shower. Averting her eyes as part of a dignity kabuki dance at which we both made an attempt, the OT or tech would step out of the bathroom but leave the door cracked so she could hear me. Every two minutes or so she would check in to see if I was still alive. "Yep! Almost done!" I would call back before filling my hand with soap from the pump and going again for my neck, armpits, and all parts located between my navel and knees.

When I could not in good conscience draw it out for one more delicious minute—either from guilt over the OT's time, guilt over the hot water supply for other patients, or guilt over the level of the lakes that supply Austin's water—I placed the handheld wand back into its holder, manned up, and turned the shower off, then pulled the shower call cord. I snatched the huge, thirsty towel that had been tucked into a grab bar just outside the curtain. Being a stingy user of towels my whole life, the liberal use of towels was something I could not get used to. In addition to this behemoth, well nigh the size of a camping tarp, there was always a fresh towel on the floor for my feet, and another on my wheelchair waiting to receive a wet behind.

When dry, it was time to get dressed. This long process would begin the same way, probably for the rest of my life. When I was safely seated again, Lisa told me to lift my right leg with my hand and cross it over my left knee. Then, with my left hand, I would find the waistband and gather my shorts in my palm until I found the right leg hole. At this point, I would pull the shorts over my foot to my knee, then uncross my legs so my left foot could step through its own hole. Then I would reach behind me, push up off the seat into standing, and pull my shorts up. Sitting back down, I would then take one sock with my left hand and insert all five fingers into its opening, then spread my fingers and rotate the sock until all my toes were inside it, at which point I could pull it into place, spinning it as needed to match it to my heel.

As long as my leg was still crossed, this would be a convenient time to get the shoe on as well. The days of putting both socks on and then my shoes were over, for minimizing this crossing and uncrossing of legs became the key to keeping the process of getting dressed to under half an hour. (For the first three months, putting on underwear seemed like manufacturing pointless work, and so I deemed the foundation garment entirely unnecessary and, in retrospect, probably something textile moguls and marketing executives had dreamed up and convinced folks they actually needed. But old habits die hard, and eventually I returned from commando to civilian.)

My shoes, which were the same shoes I had hiked one hundred miles in a year and a half earlier, had been restrung with bright white elastic shoelaces that allowed me to pull them on and push them off while remaining tied, for I could no more tie shoelaces now than summit Everest. But my vanity had not been affected by the stroke, and as I did not care for the look of these, Kirstin within a couple of weeks had gone on Amazon and ordered a set of Zubits to replace them. Zubits are powerful magnets through which regular shoelaces are threaded and then tied off; to put shoes on you squeeze the magnets together. A well-placed pry with an index finger breaks the bond to get the shoes off. Far from being an adaptation for stroke or one of the many "hemi" products for folks with one hand out of commission or gone altogether, these Zubits were a product my sons had introduced to the family several years earlier, and not a single therapist throughout my rehab had ever seen them.

With my bottom half shorted, socked, and shod, it was time for the shirt. I've already described getting a shirt off. The key to getting a shirt on is the same as getting shorts or pants on: you must start by getting the weak limb into its proper hole first; nothing else will work. For me, this meant getting my right arm all the way into my sleeve, then left arm, then head, followed by artful writhing to get all the fabric hanging in its proper place.

When it came time to brush my teeth, Lisa's pro-tip was to squirt the toothpaste directly into my mouth instead of putting the paste on the brush. This was genius! Why had I not been doing this for decades? Her other tip was to buy toothpaste with a flip-top instead of a screw-on cap. Seeing everything in this new light made me wonder why screw caps still even existed. Brushing teeth with one's nondominant hand was weird in the extreme, taking at least twice as long as it used to and requiring a cup to rinse my mouth instead of just using my hands. Try it tonight and see.

I shaved about every four days now. The process took about twenty-five minutes. It would have been less of a project had I done it every day, but somehow that seemed too daunting. It started with the long-hair trimmer on the electric razor. Then I moved to the electric razor's normal screen. Finally, I got the escapees with a wet razor. Being clean-shaven did make me feel more normal, less like a hobo.

If reading this description of ADLs has seemed exhausting or frustrating, now imagine doing it all with your nondominant hand.

When Lisa had taught me my ADLs like showering, dressing, and grooming, it was time to see how much strength I could get back in my shoulder, arm, and hand.

A key part of this therapy was electrical stimulation, "e-stim." The e-stim unit consisted of two sticky pads that could be connected to any surface of the skin, and connecting them at various points activated different muscles as the voltage found the shortest path from one electrode to the other. On the triceps and your arm automatically straightens. On your biceps and your arm curls. On the traps produces a shrug, quads will cause you to kick out, hamstrings to bend, and so on. For me, e-stim overwhelmingly went on the topside of my forearm and on my shin. Stimming my forearm made me raise my hand from a limp-wristed position into a fist. Placing the electrodes closer to my hand caused me to extend my fingers. The voltage would cycle on and off in distinct patterns. It would start with a constant stream . . . weeeeee . . . causing constant flexing of the targeted muscle, then would break into slow pulses . . . bump . . . bump . . . bump . . . bump . . . and then faster pulses . . . bump bump bump bump-bump-bumpbumpbumpbump . . . then off, and it would start over . . . weeeeeee. When Lisa was in OT school, she had learned the most important thing about e-stim was to dial the voltage down before turning it off. One time, she connected the electrodes and simply turned the power on. This resulted in her punching herself in the face and splitting her own lip.

Slowly, ever so gradually, I began to claw back my independence. A grounds pass issued by a doctor allowed me to go outside for the first time. On a mild late afternoon in February, with Erren, Kirstin, and Elaine, I wheeled to the sunny side of the building and sidled up to a picnic table to enjoy what had become the coin of the realm for me, a shake from Sonic. When just about anyone came to visit, they would text ahead, "Want anything?" The Sonic was nearby. A shake was simple, satisfying, and consumable.

The grounds pass was followed by quick trips away from the hospital. My first trip was with Kirstin to the credit union. I distinctly remember being mildly nauseated by riding in the passenger seat in afternoon traffic. I wasn't used to riding in the passenger seat at all, but now it was doubly vertigo-inducing: the speed, the oncoming cars and trucks, the traffic lights—

everything was light and sound and fury, an assault on nearly every sense. We never got out of the car but simply went through the credit union drive-through to deposit a check. Then we traced a large rectangle making our way back to the hospital, but not before stopping at Sonic.

A couple of days later, Kirstin absconded with me to a park ten minutes away, next to the grounds of a former art museum that had peacocks that had gone feral. Kirstin wrestled the wheelchair out of the back of her car as I listened helplessly to the struggle. As I transferred to the wheelchair and rolled up onto the sidewalk, Kirstin helped me up a small incline, and I briefly flashed on my parents—my mother, hale and hearty, pushing a wheelchair, my father white-headed and frail in the last days of his Parkinson's battle, resigned to this act of reverse chivalry only because the thought of sitting home and doing nothing was worse.

My inability to be chivalrous, to require logistical things be done for me instead of being able to do them for others, would be a major ongoing source of frustration for me the rest of my life. Whether I was born this way or learned it, chivalry was a deeply held virtue I did not really know I had until the ability to manifest it was gone. I would hold doors habitually. If the bus was standing-room-only, I would offer my seat to a lady, sometimes laying myself open to charges of sexism, especially in "progressive" Austin. No more. Pre-stroke, I had insisted on pulling my own weight and expected others to pull theirs. Now, it seemed I would never again pull my own weight.

As the light began to fail, it was time for the peacocks to roost, and we watched them make their way one by one across the grounds and up into an old spreading live oak, where they would be safe from cats and dogs and coyotes and other denizens of the night. Reluctantly, we drove back to the hospital, via Sonic, and Kirstin let me out at the drive-through circle, transferring back to the wheelchair. Just then Richard, my favorite nurse, was leaving work when a wide-eyed look came to his face, then a furrowed brow. He hemmed and hawed for a moment. "Um—what are you doing?"

"Oh, we just went to a park," I said, "and then to Sonic."

"Did you get a release?" he asked gently.

"What do you mean?" I asked.

"Well . . . you can't just leave."

"Oh—we signed out on the third floor and everything," I explained.

"That's for the *grounds* pass," he said. "If you want to leave the property, you have to fill out another form." This was never made clear to us, of course, but Kirstin and I sheepishly followed this rule from then on. It was explained to us that if there were too many trips outside of the hospital, the insurance company would begin to question if I really needed to be there. I couldn't spend the night at home, and I couldn't spend too long anywhere else without the red flag of questionable need going up. Big Brother was watching. Fair enough, as Big Brother was paying.

The one time I left the hospital after that was to see my youngest son, Ian, cross over from Cub Scouts to Boy Scouts at our annual Blue and Gold Banquet. I had set that as a goal, my first public appearance since the stroke. I could be away from the hospital a maximum of four hours, so I had to time things just right. In addition, I found it advantageous to only use the restroom at the hospital, so there were natural limitations put on my time away as well as corporate ones.

The banquet itself was wonderful. But there was an interesting mix of reactions in the room to my reemergence. Some of the other parents greeted me warmly, as one would expect. Others I had to seek out to say hello to. Still others seemed to avoid me, as if the stroke might be contagious. I was not angry with those people and understood in a strange way how they felt. Ian crossed over from Cub Scouts into Boy Scouts that night, which is what mattered most.

Ten days after my stroke, I turned fifty-one, which was loaded with all sorts of contradictory emotions. For everyone around me, it was "the happiest birthday ever," celebrating the mere survival of a loved one who had a real brush with death. For me, it was a combination of "Holy jeez! I'm the oldest fifty-one-year-old on earth," and "Hmm, I wonder if I'll live this way for twenty more years or thirty more years, and which of those would I actually prefer?"

Because my birthday fell on a Monday, we decided to have the family celebration on Sunday night instead. Kirstin, her mom, the boys, and a family friend brought in barbecue, cake, a flower arrangement and balloons, and decorated my room with a happy birthday sign.

The night of my birthday itself, Ed and Elaine ate supper with Kirstin and me in the little hospital dining room. A few nights later, they came back, along with other old friends Steve and Dina. We sat in the hospital lobby and ate Mexican food from a restaurant up the street and played a game called Yeti in the Spaghetti.

There were two security guards at the hospital's front desk—both entertaining in their own way. The first was entertaining purely for one reason—he had the highest voice of any man I had ever encountered. As a bass/baritone, I couldn't even imitate him in falsetto. When safely out of earshot, Steve, Ed, and I concocted tough-guy scenarios in a Mini Mouse voice—pulling a gun and chirping, "Reach for the sky, mother....er!" or "Drop the gun and you live!" shouted two octaves above middle C. I don't think I had laughed like that in twenty years. I probably came a hair's breadth from another stroke, but it would have been just about worth it.

The other security guard I got to know much better, as I often went down to the lobby to wait for visitors I knew were on their way. He was a character you could not even make up, a security guard at a neuro-rehab hospital who had suffered his own brain damage as a teenager while partying. Now in his thirties with close-cropped hair and wide, haunted eyes, he recounted to me the night when he was seventeen that he purposely combined alcohol and several different kinds of snake venom. The wild story included so-called friends who abandoned him to his fate, him lying unconscious on the kitchen floor for three days before coming to, and him seeing things "that only God was supposed to see." He told me this last bit with no sense of hyperbole nor as a figure of speech, but just as a matter of theological fact. Also, his hands were stained with engine grime, a sign that he worked on his car before coming into work. I found this to be strange for a hospital employee who was handing out sterile masks to visitors because it was flu season.

Time stood still at the rehab hospital, but life went on. Each day, I marked the progress on the upscale apartment building being constructed next to us. Rain or shine, cold or warm, the workers would be out there laying bricks, taking Sheetrock up the elevator, bringing in supplies and fixtures on flatbed trucks. Hopefully I would move out of the rehab hospital before they were finished with this building, but I had no idea.

The world went on in all sorts of other ways too. My brother Erren left the hospital for home in South Texas one morning while I was in therapy. I returned to my room and found a note on my bed, black Sharpie on a paper towel: "Be strong. Be brave. I love you. —E." A day later, he and Fernando were on their way to Morocco for a long-planned vacation. For two weeks, I watched his pictures roll into my Facebook feed—bazaars, camels, Marrakesh, Casablanca. It seemed impossible that he had just been with me, sleeping on the hospital cot, and now was on the other side of the world riding camels through the Sahara, but he was.

Nothing much ever changed at the rehab hospital. Even the weather seemed like a hologram. Raining or dry, freezing or mild, sunny or overcast, I was always in shorts and a T-shirt. I could only really tell what the weather was doing by the clothes my visitors were wearing.

Almost a week after insurance had denied our requested move to Dripping Springs, we received notice from the hospital's case manager that she had gotten a fax from Dripping Springs and that our stay there had been approved. There was no explanation or squaring of why it had been twice denied and then approved. It was simply, "Okay, go ahead and go." It now felt like they were simply jacking with us for sport. Months later, we discovered that the stay was actually approved during the peer-to-peer conference, but had been marked "denied" through a simple clerical error—a form put in one stack instead of another, the wrong key fat-fingered in some distant office, all the while Kirstin sick with worry over whether I would get any more intensive therapy or whether I would move home with one day's notice.

Now, I was leaving for Dripping Springs in less than two days. This triggered a flurry of action items. There was a wheelchair that needed to be exchanged, clothes that needed to be brought from home, two dozen cards that needed to be untaped from my wall.

I spent my final morning at Central Texas Rehabilitation Hospital in one of the gyms getting measured for a wheelchair. A few days earlier, I was groggily resting in my bed when one of my therapists came to my room to introduce me to a representative of a company with the over-workshopped name of Imperial Mobility. The wheelchair I was currently using was a loaner from the hospital, and when it came time to leave, I would certainly want a better one, said everyone. Now, with my discharge two hours away, the sales rep and two of his coworkers met me in the gym with two prototypes similar to ones I probably would want, they said. A nice woman interviewed me for twenty-five minutes, asking questions about the nature of my job and how far I would have to walk to my office from the bus stop each day. It was her job to build the case for me needing this chair, submit it to insurance, and get it authorized. And apparently, it required multiple pages of deft prose. It was never too soon to get this process started, we were told, because the insurance company could take up to six weeks to approve it.

I wasn't entirely convinced of the need for a custom chair, but Kirstin and I were focused on getting to the next step of the journey, and so I sat and answered these questions as the woman typed furiously on her laptop and the two gentlemen measured the distances between every two joints on my body as if tailoring a fine suit for me. They would have an estimate for me, including what our out-of-pocket would be, once the authorization went through in a couple of weeks. "Um, okay," I said.

Richard, my favorite nurse, was the last one out of my room. "Good luck with the next resident of Room 307," I told him. "Probably gonna be a max assist times three."

He chuckled. "You're probably right!"

Part Two

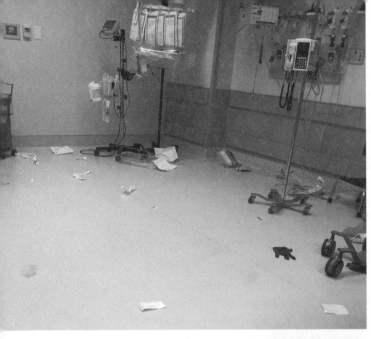

Surgery prep room, Dell Seton Medical Center.

Initial pre-surgery CT scans showing the bleed in my left hemisphere, face-on.

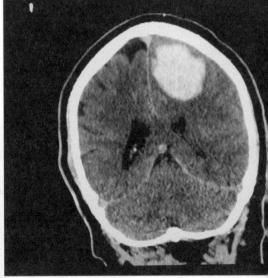

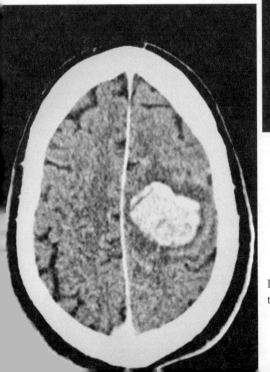

Initial CT scan, brain from the top with eyes at the bottom and a 4.7 centimeter bleed.

CHAPTER 9

Up on Cripple Creek

The tallest tree near the parking lot was a hackberry. The tiny leaves that were just coming in at the end of March were not much help in identifying it, but I knew it by its warty gray bark. From my wheelchair in the middle of the parking lot, I often would watch chickadees in that hackberry, trying to figure out their patterns and motives. The most interesting and striking birds were the cardinals. Were the church officials named after the bird or the other way around? I couldn't recall. I usually saw the males and the females hopping from tree to tree in pairs, the males being the classic red, the females having the same size and shape and orange beaks but being mostly brown.

The crepe myrtle in the flower bed was starting to bloom. The Easter lilies Jesse had spent most of a day planting about a week earlier were not faring well, but it wasn't for his lack of trying; if anything, he had overwatered them. The live oaks were pushing off their spent foliage, creating copious slicks of waxy brown leaves on the sidewalks. Yaupon holly volunteers were filling in the understory beneath the live oaks.

Near the parking lot where I sat in my wheelchair bird-watching after breakfast was a low limestone wall. I used the mortar between its stones to file the nails of my left hand, which seemed to grow even faster now that my right hand could not do a thing to help cut them. For five and ten minutes at a stretch, I would scratch the mortar backhand, one finger at a time, until I could feel it filing away my guitar callus, then I'd move on to the next finger. The calluses were starting to soften on their own from disuse after being rock-hard for thirty-six years. When I was finished, the nails were short, but they and my fingertips were green from algae growing on the stone.

It had been nearly a month since I moved to Dripping Springs. The day I moved had been a terrible one to be driving into the Hill Country, almost freezing but no ice on the road, and poor visibility. The heater was out in our car, and Kirstin had bought a space heater that plugged into the cigarette lighter.

From the small rehab hospital in central Austin, we drove south and west for an hour, through the town of Dripping Springs, until we finally came to a closed gate off the highway. We pulled close to it as instructed, and the gate opened.

I could not spot the new-looking limestone building featured in the slick video Kirstin and I had watched from my hospital bed, the drone footage underscored by inspiring keyboards, the trucking shots of high ceilings and spacious bedrooms glowing with morning light. Turns out that was a different campus, the new campus. This was the original campus, five limestone buildings set about one hundred fifty yards off the highway. It had been built in the early 1980s as a brain rehab facility and been added to over the decades. My building would be Oak Point. A lot of people who needed more care than I did started at Hilltop, the new campus, then graduated here to Oak Point.

Up the hill and farther away from the highway was the administration building and Cedar Point, a house for those who were never going to leave, lifers, as it were.

Oftentimes, as we would pull into the property after some outing, a gentleman stood next to the driveway, as if welcoming each and every visitor. But the welcome was disconcerting. There was nothing like a smile or a wave. There was just a hunched figure with a baseball cap over close-cropped hair, his mouth hanging open and a vacant stare on his face. This was Dusty. Dusty was the only person from Cedar we saw on a consistent basis, both because he stood out on the driveway so much and because he occasionally came to our door to try to gain entry. The staff knew him well, of course, and so were unalarmed, but many of the residents were unnerved by his presence. One night, my friend Tamika heard an animal moving through the underbrush on the property. It probably was an armadillo, or a whitetail doe, or a coyote. But that's not what she feared. She left the porch with the words, "That might be Dusty." He was the Boo Radley in a group of about thirty Boo Radleys, among whom I now counted myself.

Upon arriving in Dripping Springs, I was interviewed by no fewer than eight people. Some of them asked me what my birth date was. Others asked me how old I was. It seemed to me that the former could have been deduced from the latter. Several of them asked me if I was right-handed or left-handed. Again, I would have thought that the hospital might have conveyed this information. The admissions administrator asked what my highest level of education was. "Ma'am," I replied, "I don't much cotton to book-learnin'."

"Bachelor's degree," Kirstin said patiently.

They didn't all ask identical questions, but there was a good 20 percent overlap, and at the end of the eighth interview, I was so exhausted I could barely sit up. Three of the eight people questioned me extensively about the wheelchair—Was it a rental? Was it a loaner? Where did it come from?

During one of the early interviews, I was issued a plastic, battery-powered doorbell on a lanyard, which was, during waking hours, to be hung around my neck like the world's lamest hip-hop medallion. Mine was blue, as I was a boy. The women, of course, sported pink doorbells. The only exception to this rule was Merle from Houston, who had a stroke while working the gun counter at Academy Sports + Outdoors. I guess when you're seventy and work the gun counter, you're secure enough in your manhood to wear a girl's doorbell if that's all they have left.

Then I was asked, as I would be several more times, what my rehab goals were. *What kind of question is that*, I wondered—*what are my rehab goals?* My rehab goals were to do every single thing I did before the stroke, just as easily and quickly as I used to. Those were my goals. And while we're setting goals, let's throw in handstands, conversational Japanese, and complete financial independence.

Then they asked why those were my goals.

I wanted to do everything I had done before the stroke, of course, both because I wanted to enjoy my life and because I did not want to be a burden to my family. I would have thought that approximately 100 percent of new patients would have said the same thing if they could have, but I guess the point was to get me to articulate my own goals so that if my effort ever started to flag, they could hold these goals up in front of me and shout, "Mr. Seale, this is what *you* said you wanted to accomplish; we are just trying to help you do that!"

With me in my wheelchair, we went through a maze of hallways and dining rooms such that I halfway expected a minotaur to be patiently waiting in my room, tapping a hoof and stewing over his watch. The house, a feng shui nightmare of add-ons and retrofitting, finally terminated in my hallway, C Hall. My room was about fourteen feet square, with light blue walls, a ceiling fan, closet, a full-sized bed, night table, and a desk. In the corner of the room sat an armoire where a TV might go.

"Did you bring a TV?" the admissions staffer asked me.

Do people typically bring their own TVs to rehab centers? I wondered. For the price, which worked out to about a thousand dollars a night billed to insurance—it seemed like they might just throw that in, like music stores that will sometimes throw in a strap if you buy an expensive enough guitar. "No," I answered simply.

Now in my room, the intake interviews continued apace. The nurse supervisor, who was the seventh to interview me, asked which facility I had come from. I told her I thought it funny she didn't already have that information. "Oh no," she chuckled, "I haven't looked at a bit of the paperwork yet." She said this as if that were a great explanation, then proceeded to ask my age.

Finally, the clock struck five, and no more doctors or therapists or administrators came knocking at my door.

Darkness fell in the room, and a tremendous gray cloud formed over my spirit. I told Kirstin that I felt like a kid being dropped off at summer camp who didn't know any of these kids. We lay side by side on the full-sized bed in my darkening room, my feet hanging off the end, and I cried and cried, and she cried with me. She tried to get me to talk about my feelings. I struggled to get the words out, and the ones that finally came were "pathetic" and "helpless." That is how I felt. K said she understood but protested that I was anything but. Let me just say, nothing makes you feel more pathetic or more helpless than trying to blow your nose with one hand.

Six o'clock arrived, and a rap on the door signaled that dinner was ready. I tried to get into the first dining room, but there was no room for the wheelchair to maneuver, so I went to the second dining room, the one I had walked through with a quad cane and a physical therapist earlier doing my baseline eval. There, Jesse, a Latino in his fifties whom I had not yet met, shouted, *"Left, two, three, four. Left, two, three, four,"* and laughed crazily as I slowly made my way through the room. Another man slumped over his food and silently chewed, his face just inches off his plate. I sat tentatively at the corner of the table.

A young redheaded woman who was cross-eyed and had a tracheotomy scar sat beside me. Presently, she asked me, the newest arrival, where her room was. She wanted to go to her room but did not know where it was. I pressed my lanyard call button to get her help, and the staff, who knew her well, made her a peanut butter and jelly sandwich. She smiled sweetly at me and ate the sandwich with no more talk of her room.

Kirstin sat next to me as I used my left hand to stab at a plate of tough, pan-fried meat, macaroni and cheese, and boiled okra. It was she who first wondered aloud but in hushed, nonchalant tones if this was "the right fit." We both very much wanted it to work but were becoming more uneasy by the minute. Was there anyone here I could relate to? Was there anyone here who was even a potential friend? Was boiled okra, perhaps my least favorite dish in all the world, going to be on the menu every night?

At length, I decided the reasonable thing would be to test the facility by seeing whether or not they ever instructed me when and where to go to get my nightly medication. That seemed like a sufficiently weighty matter in which to fail. I would give them until 8 p.m. to tell me. If they didn't, I would cut our losses and have Kirstin drive back out here tomorrow and discharge me. We would go home, set up the wheelchair ramps she had bought, and figure it out from there.

Eight o'clock came and went. No signs of further orientation.

I was exhausted from the eight intake interviews that day and desperately wanted to go to bed. In light of the fact that one of my medications was an anti-seizure pill, I finally asked the nurse where to go. "Oh, there's the medication room right there," she said, pointing at a small storage room with a desk, chair, and a set of vertical file cabinets shoehorned into it.

Only one of my pills had transferred from the pharmacy, so I would go without my stool softener or the probiotic I had been taking and just hope I didn't have another stroke bearing down on the toilet the next morning. As is written in *Vitalogy*, "Constipation must be avoided as straining at stool is liable to precipitate an attack."

Over time, I figured out that the lanyard doorbells would tell the staff *who* was calling, but only if someone was sitting at the switchboard at the exact moment the button was pushed, which they rarely were. The doorbells could not tell them *where* they were, so every time a doorbell was pushed, a Keystone Cops-style search of the entire house ensued. "Did you push *your* button?" Knock knock knock. "Did you push *your* button?"

Still confused, I asked one nurse how they would know I needed help overnight without waking everyone up. Her answer was that there would be somebody staffed next door to me, and that I could just yell for them if I needed something. The yelling-for-help system, crude as it was described to me, at least would have been something, but this also turned out not to be true.

The resident next to me, Tommy, was not a staffer but a high-functioning stroke survivor with a penchant for moving furniture around in the middle of the night. That particular night, at 2:45 a.m., he decided to rearrange his room, banging the wall and scooting chairs around. It took me ninety minutes to fall back to sleep. "Yeah," one of my therapists sympathized, "a lot of stroke patients become impulsive like that." I suppose the key difference in Tommy's case was that not all stroke patients were strong enough to move every piece of furniture in their room.

The facility had failed the test it did not know it was taking—the medication test. And things had gotten worse with the bewildering call system and the middle-of-the-night home makeover.

In the next day's CaringBridge post, Kirstin characteristically put the most diplomatic face possible on our situation: "Our orientation felt incomplete," she wrote, adding, "we are still figuring this out." This hot mess notwithstanding, I was still reluctant to throw in the towel.

The next morning, in the nick of time, I made my first true friend.

Rachel had grown up in Lubbock but had a staccato Mexican accent that took me straight back to my Rio Grande Valley youth. I liked her immediately. We both worked in higher education—me at Texas, she at Sam Houston State. We both had some knowledge of the Sam Houston National Forest. I told her I had hiked a hundred miles through that forest the previous year. "There are some weird things in that forest," I said.

"Do you think there are bigfoots in there? Some of my coworkers said there were."

I smiled. "I think there probably are," I said. At breakfast the next day, I gave her a copy of *Monster Hike*. It felt good to have that small moment of connection to my old life, to talk about something, anything, that wasn't related to the stroke.

Lastly, we both enjoyed giving each other hell just for sport. It was when I met Rachel that I decided I could stick this out.

In the first week of January, probably two days after Wade and I had been in Sam Houston National Forest, Rachel was driving to work at Sam Houston State University in Huntsville. She started feeling funny but thought she could just shake it off, and proceeded to a car wash, where she detailed her car. When she put her hands back on the wheel, she noticed that the left one fell from the wheel, flaccid.

Still not knowing what was happening to her, she instinctively reached for the panacea, and proceeded to the nearest Starbucks for a cup of coffee. When that failed as well, she finally drove herself to the hospital in Bryan, where she had previously lived. Following that, she went to a rehab hospital in South Austin and thence to Dripping Springs, where she checked in on the same night I did.

We ate nearly every meal together and bonded over mild acts of rebellion against our newfound institutional restraints. In our first group therapy session, about nine of us in the house gathered in the front room to watch the documentary *Crash Reel*, the story of professional snowboarder Kevin Pearce who had sailed high over a half-pipe and, on his way down, bashed his head on the wall, then spent years trying to return to the sport after his fearsome brain injury. I suppose the intent of having us watch this film was to understand how brain injury in people with certain personality types can lead to impulsive and risky behavior. But with Pearce's poetic slo-mo backside 1080s in my mind's eye, and the Winter Olympics theme still ringing in my ears, I instead was inspired to innovate a new sport—the wheelchair half-pipe.

Just outside the front door of Oak Point, I noticed a concrete area designed to channel rain away from the building. Picture a canal four feet wide, sloping down to a center depth about three inches lower than the edge. Then picture that canal running about twenty feet and the whole thing losing about six inches. This was my half-pipe. The shallow concrete channel was subtle to the naked eye but had real effects on a wheelchair loaded with a 190-pound man.

It began tentatively.

I rolled down into the half-pipe perpendicular to the channel, and momentum carried me up the facing slope. As gravity took over, I stopped and rolled backward the way I had come in. I then used my good foot to stop myself from dropping back in. Forward and down, up . . . backward down, up and push out. Forward and down, up . . . backward down, up and push out. After a few more reps "dropping in" and pushing back out, I cast a cautious glance to make sure no staffers were watching. It was time to put down a run.

The top of the half-pipe was near the door, of course, and the bottom swerved, then ran directly into a limestone wall, the one I filed my nails on. I dropped in from the right side at a forty-five-degree angle, and as soon as my left front wheel hit the nadir and started up the facing slope, the chair creaked and groaned at the newfound torque it was experiencing. The chair, not having shocks or independent suspension, tried to square itself to the channel, but to keep the run going, I needed it to come out at forty-five degrees, so with a paddling motion with my left foot, I stayed diagonal to the channel. As soon as I came out of the valley, I violently stomped my foot to my left, made a right-angle turn, and dropped back into the half-pipe at -45 degrees. I was zig-zagging my way down the channel now, closer and closer to the limestone wall. Like Fred Flintstone slamming on his brakes, I stopped six inches shy of the wall.

Emboldened by my initial success, I began freestyling, whipping the chair this way and that, rolling the large drive wheel with my left hand and controlling my direction and braking with my left foot. Forward, backward, donut left, donut right. I discovered I could drop in at either end of the half-pipe and with a little extra digging with my foot, could tack my way against gravity and, using the valley, roll my way uphill.

The first morning it was just me. The next morning after breakfast, I asked Rachel to meet me outside. There, I demonstrated the technique, and before I knew it, it looked like we were both in a crazy carnival ride, randomly rolling down and up, side to side. "I haven't thrown down any back-to-back backside 1080s or a McTwist 720," I told her, "but I once thought I caught a little air, so it shouldn't be long. Soon, Rachel was smiling and laughing as we tried not to bash her kneecaps into the stone wall, and we agreed that every morning at eight thirty we would do the half-pipe. I think it was the first time that either of us had anything that resembled fun since our strokes.

With each passing morning we became a little more confident in our skills, and, perhaps as a result, a little less concerned about what the staff would think if they saw us. On about the third day, it became clear that the therapists had been watching us from afar. "What are you guys *doiiiing?*" asked one, with a mix of good-natured tsk-tsk and more than a hint of real concern. "Please be careful," she said with a nervous smile.

"No idea what you're talking about," I replied with a straight face, as Rachel joined in the fun, protesting, "We're just sitting here!"

I had found that chink in the regulatory armor, and Rachel and I were exploiting it fully. There was no rule against wheelchair half-pipe. If they wanted us to stop it, they would have to make up one, and what would that rule sound like? No wheelchairs outside? No wheelchairs going backward over one-half mile an hour for more than six inches? No riding in a wheelchair the wheels of which are forced to move in two separate planes? No laughing or smiling?

The half-pipe was well and good. It fed our souls, for a while. But soon the shine wore off, and new temptations beckoned. As my wandering eye surveyed the concrete landscape around the half-pipe, I was intrigued by the possibilities inherent in a much larger slope. On the other side of the half-pipe from the building, concrete stairs led up the hill toward Cedar Point, a flight that rose about six feet. But *beside* those stairs, a huge expanse of sloping concrete abutted a long concrete ramp. The long hillside ramp itself was quite the liability; more than once a staff member would come bolting out of the kitchen, which overlooked the area, because Gina, who was a hardy twenty-three-year-old but with very significant cognitive challenges, would be pushing another patient in a wheelchair up or down the hill. "Gina, honey, come on down!" the nervous staffer would shout. "You're not allowed to push other patients, sweetie!" Gina would furrow her brow over her crossed eyes, and reluctantly comply.

I found that with one good leg, I had all the power I needed to get up that hill, *if* I went backward. When Wade drove me back to Dripping Springs one night after a day trip home, I showed him the new trick, and he approved, dubbing the run "The Widowmaker." If the shallow little channel was the half-pipe, then I had found the double black diamond run of wheelchair sports at neuro-recovery facilities. A seam in the concrete marked the spot beyond which I knew I should not tempt fate, and aligning the chair precisely with the front door, I found that I could roll briskly down the concrete embankment, miss the landscaping stones on the left that lined the flowerbed, roll across the wide tile porch and all the way through the front door if it was standing open. Hushed side conversations among the therapists about Mr. Seale's behavior no doubt were increasing in frequency. "What is his target discharge date, again?"

As I was spending considerable time in the parking lot bird-watching and waiting to depart on group outings, I soon enough discovered a slight slope to the parking lot that, when compounded over fifty or sixty feet, really got a man my size moving at a respectable clip. The parking lot had no curb, and so I could simply roll into the weeds and dirt, which would slow me just as effectively as a runaway truck ramp in the Rockies.

As the days went by, the virus spread through the house, and soon, others were getting in on the act. One morning when we had assembled for a group outing but were still waiting for staff dealing with stragglers, Mark, a twenty-something who had broken his back and his neck in a car accident a year earlier, treated the assembled patients to a show of what his motorized chair could do when it was allowed to run flat-out in the parking lot. I think he said, with a mischievous grin, it could do fifteen miles per hour, even in the reclined position.

CHAPTER 10

The People in Your Neighborhood

I met a remarkable nurse named Idi. She was born in the Dominican Republic and immigrated to Massachusetts but moved here because Texas offered the cheapest nursing programs. She was studying for her nursing degree three hours away in Waco and working double shifts, sixteen-hour days, here in Dripping Springs to pay her way. I found a number of nurses pulling these back-to-back double shifts, so-called "double-doubles." I asked her where she stayed in Dripping Springs when she was not at work.

"My car."

"You sleep in your car," I repeated.

"Yes," she said matter-of-factly.

"What about in the winter, like now?" I asked. "Isn't that cold?"

"I have an electric blanket," she said. "It's fine."

My stay in Dripping Springs featured a rich parade of characters, and no class of them, whether patients, nurses, therapists, or cooks, were any less colorful than the others.

Of the roughly fifteen patients there at any given time, we were Anglo, Hispanic, and African American. We were two-thirds male and a third female. We were two-thirds strokees and a third traumatic brain injury survivors. We were introverts and extroverts, lefties and righties, walkers and rollers, Millennials and Xers and septagenarians, rednecks and intelligentsia, straight and gay.

The first person you would have noticed if you came to visit me in "Drippin'," as the locals call it, was Jesse because he always seemed to be in the common areas. He wore Houston Texans or Houston Astros gear at all times—baseball caps, jerseys, along with other swag like mugs and stickers. He was shorter than me but was made shorter still with extreme postural problems. His legs frequently gave out to one side, like one of those spring-loaded toys that collapses when the bottom of the base is pushed in. And he used a walker upon which he hung a heavy backpack full of water bottles and mugs. You also knew Jesse was near from the ever-present tinny strains of cumbia emanating from his cell phone.

There were two distinct Jesses. There was Exuberant Jesse, ever the life of the party. Exuberant Jesse was the self-appointed house host, who joshed and sparred with everyone. He was the Jesse who teased me with his drill sergeant routine as I walked through the dining room that first night before we'd even met.

Then, at turns, there was also the sullen, sleepy, Surly Jesse, the one whom the staff would have to coerce every day to go to his room for a nap instead of nodding off in the public areas. "Jesse, you can't sleep out here. You know that! Go to your room if you're sleepy."

Surly Jesse would sometimes lash out in anger, shouting at the staff if he thought he was being treated unfairly. He spoke in a way that was incomprehensible to all but the staff. English speakers assumed they couldn't understand him because he was speaking Spanish. But Spanish speakers could understand him no better because he slurred his words so badly. Once Rachel, who was over Jesse pretty much from the start, snapped at him: *Pronuncia tus palabras!* He also punctuated the end of nearly every sentence with an Anglo-Saxon vulgarity, which sounded like "shee." His asking the staff if the coffee was ready was a long, patience-testing series of repetitive phrases that I cannot even approximate, but in English would sound something like, "Hey, hey where is the where is the coff, where is the coffee? coffee? coffee? because the coffee where, where, where is the coffee at? Where is it at? Where's the coffee at— *shee . . .* "

Jesse was an extreme extrovert who, despite having lived in the United States most of his life, and even having served in the US military, spoke almost no English. The staff was scrupulous about not divulging details of other patients' lives to me, which I appreciated. On the other hand, this created an odd dynamic in a group setting, one for which living as a community was a central selling point. Many times, while making small talk with the staff, I would ask a seemingly innocent question about another patient and get gently and professionally shut down. "We really can't share those details," they would say, to which I'd reply, "Of course, that's not what I was asking, I just was wondering . . . ah—never mind."

But not being able to get at Jesse's backstory because of language and general speech quality made me want it even more. The first trickle came during our first session of Group together. We went around the circle and each said something about what we did, or used to do. Jesse proudly announced that he had been a sniper in the US Marine Corps, miming a rifle and making shooting noises with his mouth. "I killed people, *shee . . .* " he said without regret and with a dash of pride. He said he was a sniper in the Gulf War in Iraq, but insisted that it was in the 1980s, so I did not know how much credence to give this claim. I told him the United States military was not in Iraq until 1990, but he stuck to his guns, as it were.

He was born in Peru, emigrated to New York, then moved to Houston. One night in the 1980s, while he was on leave, he found himself at a fried chicken joint in Channelview, a sketchy part of greater Houston near the port. There, one of a small gang of men shot him in the head and left him for dead. Ever since the day Jesse left the hospital, he had resided in facilities like this one, perhaps even this very one, as it opened in the same timeframe. This fact distinguished Jesse from everyone else in the house. He was not a candidate for independent living, but for some reason I could never glean, he lived with us at Oak and not up the hill at Cedar with the other lifers.

After I had pieced this much of his story together, I often sat and wondered if, in their wildest dreams, the men who shot Jesse could have imagined that thirty-plus years later he'd be here, paying this terrible price for whatever mouthy, drunken, testosterone-fueled remark he might have made that night at the fried chicken joint.

The next person you would have seen was Merle, a seventy-year-old who would've stood over six feet were he not in a wheelchair. Merle's coworkers at the Academy gun counter in Houston called EMS when he began walking at a slant. The reason you would've noticed Merle next is because he was, as the old Visa commercial said, "everywhere you want to be." I was still 90 percent wheelchair bound at this point in time, and damn if Merle wasn't in my way everywhere I tried to go. Time for a bathroom? There was Merle parked in the doorway talking to some long-suffering nurse who is wearing a smile for him. Time to get my meds? Merle has set up a roadblock across the hallway. He was a sweet guy, and looking back I wish I had talked to him more, but he talked so much to everyone else, I didn't feel I had to.

Tommy was my next-door neighbor, the one who had taken to rearranging his furniture my first night. On my second day there, six of us slowly transferred into the Suburban and an assortment of PTs and OTs took us to

Anytime Fitness, with which the neuro-rehab center had a blanket contract. For the half hour we were there, the PT had me concentrate on leg presses and leg lifts and other exercises I could do while seated.

On the way home, Tommy and I shared the middle seat of the Suburban, and as I had yet to really say anything to him, I tried a little small talk. "So . . . I live in Austin. Where are you from?"

He stared at me straight-faced and simply shook his head, as if to say, "I don't know."

Oh wow! I thought. *Tommy doesn't know where he's from.* And at that, I began urgently recounting my lucky stars. But I didn't want to just awkwardly drop the conversation, if that's what this was, so I pressed on. "I didn't grow up in Austin—I grew up in South Texas."

Suddenly, Tommy's face came alive, and he began thrusting his index finger down, as if pointing to a map. "Yeah!" he said. "Yeah!" nodding vigorously. Aha! He knew exactly where he was from, South Texas, he just couldn't say the words. In the first two weeks I was there, I heard him say four words. On my way to breakfast, I said, "'Morning, Tommy." He said, "Yeah!"—and two exclamations of Anglo-Saxon origin that you can probably guess. In time, I also heard him using religious curses. It was a shame that he seemed to be gaining back linguistic capacity but only for words and phrases that were unusable in polite company. I was reminded of the old chestnut parents once used to stop their children making faces: What if the world froze right now and your face was stuck like that forever? This was the linguistic version of the ugly face frozen in time.

Finally, on a return visit to Anytime Fitness, we had congregated in the parking lot when I called, "Shotgun!" in order to claim the front seat. Good-natured Tommy said, "Awww." Then the therapists jumped at the chance for this "forced functional use." "You want shotgun, you can say it," they said. He demurred. "Go on, give it a try!"

"Shotgun," he said. It was a triumph, and I smiled, and we all cheered for him. But I had said it first, and I don't make the rules.

Brody stayed directly across the hall. I only saw him once without a black cowboy hat. His TV was on at all times of the day and night, playing "reality" shows with titles like *Gator Wars,* or *Mountain Man Wars, Trick Out My Truck . . . Wars,* bearded men with tattoos doing manly things like forging broadswords and modifying motorcycles and getting bleeped for cursing every few seconds. When my bladder would wake me in the middle of the night, I would transfer from the bed to the wheelchair and open the door to head down C Hall to the bathroom. There would be Brody through his open door, his TV at 130 percent volume, sound asleep but facing up into the bright overhead light.

Along with Rachel, Todd had arrived the same night as me and so was one-third of the three-headed monster that had overwhelmed the facility's intake process. He was about my age and was also a right-handed guitar player. We both had guitars and briefly entertained the notion of playing one together, him playing with his right hand and me playing with my left, but I think we were both too proud to try it and both thought it would represent some kind of surrender to our strokes.

Todd had a severe case of left neglect, which was a challenge in a group-living setting. Left neglect is just what the name implies. It occurs as a result of right-brain strokes and makes survivors oblivious to things happening on their left. It is not a visual problem—their whole field of vision might appear crystal clear; rather it is a problem processing that information. Kirstin's dad had left neglect. When a doctor presented him with a line drawing of a clock and asked him to fill in the numbers, he filled in 12, 1, 2, 3, 4, 5, and 6, then confidently set the pencil down, having finished the task in his own mind. Survivors with left neglect must take care not to run into the left side of doorways, etc. It's a curious affliction. There is such a thing as right neglect for left-brain strokees, but it is rare.

It was not Todd's only challenge, of course. He would roll into the front room for Group, and in the middle of the presentation, would be sound asleep, or else just impulsively roll to the door and start pushing on the door instead of pulling it—*rattle . . . rattle rattle rattle*—and the therapist would pause her remarks, help him open the door, and he would roll away for the balance of the session without explanation.

At mealtime we were asked to transfer from our wheelchairs to regular chairs, creating a sort of parking lot of wheelchairs in the foyer. But Todd could no more transfer out of his wheelchair than moonwalk to the dining room. So he'd roll into the dining room in his wheelchair with his left arm propped up on an arm rest and shimmed even higher with a pillow to keep his hand from swelling, and then occupy a space at the table meant for three diners. By the time he rolled away, the left half of his place was strewn with lettuce and cheese and croutons, and the left side of his mouth was smeared with ranch dressing. Todd also was the only one in the house whose status was "one-on-one." As I rose to visit the bathroom in the middle of the night, there a tech would sit outside his room in the dark hallway, his or her face lit only from below by the glow of a phone.

Gina, the sweet, cross-eyed redhead with the tracheotomy scar, was twenty-six and wouldn't eat anything, even scrambled eggs, without ranch dressing. She was from Arizona, and had one talking point: that she missed her family. Any sort of open-ended question like, "How you doing today, Gina?" resulted in the same answer: "I miss my family." If I tried to engage on this and get her to tell me about her family, it went nowhere. So, in order to avoid this predictable downer, I learned to ask, "How are those pancakes?" or, "How are the scrambled eggs this morning?" to which the reply inevitably would be a slowly enunciated, "They could use some ranch."

Jack was thirty-four, clean cut and lean with bulging forearms that suggested a previous life of extreme fitness. Last year at about this time, he had been out of the army for just a few months and was working as a bicycle repairman and as a doorman/bouncer at O'Tooles in Honolulu. St. Patrick's Day, of course, was a peak day at O'Tooles, even in a place almost as far away from Ireland as one can get. Jack had worked all night at the door, and the manager had determined that the place was such a mess that cleanup should wait for morning. Wanting to pick up another shift, Jack volunteered to come back at nine in the morning and help with cleanup. Being that he didn't get to bed until well after two, he got up late, and, wanting to make it to work on time, asked to borrow his friend's motorcycle that day because then he could weave through traffic and get there faster.

He worked all day long, then headed home on the motorcycle. The last thing he remembers is approaching a Y in the road. Everyone's best guess is that he fell asleep on the motorcycle and plowed right into the guardrail. He remembers nothing.

He was in a coma for eight days, and when he came to, claimed he had been in a helicopter crash—that he had taken a helicopter and tried to go to lunch at Burger King. His distraught father, fresh from Texas, tried to reason with him from the Honolulu hospital bedside that although he had repaired helicopters during his service in the army, he knew nothing about flying one.

"Ex-act-ly," Jack replied. "That's . . . why . . . I . . . crashed!"

Everyone in the house had a different cross to bear. Mine was mainly the loss of my dominant hand. The cross Jack had to bear, along with many others, was eating. For a full hour at every meal, he hunched over his plate and slowly chewed, with a speech therapist vigilantly by his side, ratcheting up the intensity of her gaze each of the many times Jack would start coughing. He had to have his water thickened. When I overheard this, I had no idea what that even meant. During one breakfast, I asked him what it was they put in the water to thicken it. Was it cornstarch, I asked, remembering a science experiment I had seen at UT in which students could walk on water that had been permeated with cornstarch. Jack said he didn't know, then returned to testing his water by holding the straw straight up, letting it go, then seeing how long it took to fall over. If the straw fell too fast, he would call for kitchen staff to thicken it more.

Every day, Jack used the stopwatch feature on his wristwatch to time himself from the chair in his room, up to the walker, down the hall, through the first dining room, around the corner, and then to the second dining room. When I arrived at the house, this task took him between four and five minutes. I remember the day he broke four minutes. Ten days later, he broke the three-minute mark, and we all applauded. One Saturday morning, I pulled out my phone, found a YouTube video of the old *Speed Racer* cartoon intro, and played it as he entered the room. A good sport, he smiled the knowing smile of a fan, and it led us all into a group discussion of the bizarre Japanese cartoon. Didn't the powerful Mock 5 have buzz saws with which Speed Racer could mow his way through forests? Didn't he have a monkey—Chim-Chim? What was that about?

Jack had resided in five facilities, working his way slowly back from Honolulu to his hometown of Fredericksburg in the Texas Hill Country, now only an hour away. As if all this weren't enough, Jack's brain injury left him with double vision. He wore a prismatic film over one lens of his glasses that largely corrected the problem. During Group one day, it was announced that Jack had lost that flimsy lens covering, and after the meeting, we fanned out over the house to search for it, but to no avail. Jack would have to live with double vision for nearly a week until his ophthalmologist got a replacement to him.

Jack's final contribution to house life was the forty-five-minute shower he took each night. I say these were contributions because he really made the most of his showers from a musical standpoint. Most of the time, the techs would get us onto the shower bench and then leave the bathroom but keep tabs on us with a baby monitor that hung in the shower. Jack took his waterproof radio into the shower and belted out hits from the eighties and nineties for the duration of the soaking while the rest of us listened from the dining room on the tech's monitor, cracking up. I think Jack knew all this and was fine with it. These karaoke showers probably did more for him than all his speech therapy.

As I've said, the cross Jesse had to bear was both linguistic and cognitive, but what he lacked in social skills he made up for with his outgoing nature. "Muchaaaaaaacho," he would sing out. Jack would answer him from down the hall. "Muchaaaaaaacho!" I picked up the habit, which was like a virus spreading through the house, and every time I saw Rachel, I started using Jesse's "Muchaaaaacha!" seeing how long I could hold the second syllable— sometimes fifteen or twenty seconds—before giving out. I know this practice annoyed the staff beyond measure, but we didn't care, because it was fun. Once, I was getting out of the shower in B Hall when I heard Jack rolling down behind me saying "Muchaaaaaaacho!" K. C., the burly, bearded nurse, long-blinked and mumbled, "Oh gawd. It's too early for this."

Jesse and I slowly got to know each other, after a fashion, and although we would never be able to communicate very well, we achieved a sort of friendship that was—not beyond an intellectual relationship—but perhaps, beside one. It was one based on call and response, like "Muchaaaacho" and hand signs. At one point I must have told him that I lived in far North Austin, and, as he had apparently lived in some northern part of Houston, he taught me a gang sign for "Northside." It resembled the sign language symbol for "I love you," only turned so the back of the hand showed, before beating two or three times in the center of the chest. "Muchaaaaaaacho!" he would call out if he saw me coming down the hall, to which I might reply, "Northside!" and beat the hand sign on my chest. It wasn't deep stuff, but it was nice to be able to connect with him on any level.

It seemed I had run out of answers about his history. He kept insisting he was a sniper in Iraq but was equally adamant it was the 1980s. Then a new theory occurred to me—1980s, Marines, Mideast. "Jesse, is it possible you were in Lebanon?"

"H-how'd you know that?" he stammered. I think he thought I was some sort of intelligence officer with secret knowledge of troop movements in the eighties. "How'd you know that?" he asked again.

"It's just history, Jesse. I watch the news and stuff. We were in Lebanon in the eighties, not Iraq. A lot of people know that."

There was one motorized wheelchair in the house; it belonged to Mark. My introduction to that chair was when it cut me off and beat me into the bathroom. When I would pass the open door of his bedroom, the chair would be reclined and Mark would look like an astronaut waiting for launch. Mark was also an auto accident victim. His back and his neck had been broken and his brain rattled good. He was bearded and thin and wore wire-frame glasses, but he said he used to be "swole" before the accident, swole being the preferred slang for muscular. I think catastrophic injuries must be especially hard on swole guys. The stroke did not change my physique much, but I did not have as far to fall as others.

The brand of Mark's motorized chair, which was stamped in a stylized logo on the side, was Permobil. I can only guess at the boardroom conversation in which this name was approved. "Hey, I know! Let's somehow incorporate the word 'permanent' into this wheelchair's name!" I say the logo was stylized— in fact it was stylized to the point I thought it said "Pornmobile." Mark, a mischievous sort, liked that, and so from that day on it was known between us as the Pornmobile.

Mark was among the chosen ones to go on my first "Community Mobility" outing. We loaded into the Ford Flex and twenty-five minutes later were at a pool hall named Boomers. There, in the dimly lit bar, the regulars, who were nursing beers at one o'clock on a weekday afternoon, lifted their eyes briefly to see who was joining them. We slowly filed in one by one, and we were a motley crew. I was by then walking short distances with a large quad cane. Mark had left the Pornmobile behind and was using a specialized walker that elevated one hand. Jack was in his wheelchair and opted for chess. Tommy had his trekking pole and opted for a huge Jenga game balancing on a table in the corner of the bar.

Mark and I circled the pool table with indescribable slowness as we each picked our shots and leaned precariously left and right, forward and back to achieve the correct angles. Each of us was accompanied by an OT whom we consulted about our shots and would hold the bridge in place while we took aim. "Little to the left," I'd say as they would scooch the bridge. "Too much. Back to the right a hair." It was my fifth turn when I finally sank the first ball of the game and called stripes. I proposed to Mark that he and I finish the game, and the outing, with a huge roadhouse fight, in which I would accuse him of cheating, and he would lay me out with a pool cue. It would have been the lamest fight in history, like a Sam Peckinpah western in which the slow-motion scenes were actually real time.

Back at the house, there had been some chatter among the staff that we would soon be joined by a violinist who played in the Austin Symphony. On March 5, we welcomed a man I recognized from the rehab hospital but had never met. Andrew was about thirty years old, had a black beard, Caesar's fringe, and an angry scar on his forehead above his right eye.

Andrew had been playing a gig with a small orchestra at a church on Christmas Eve when his stroke hit. He had the presence of mind to set his violin down before keeling over on the sanctuary's front pew. He also had gone to Dell Seton for brain surgery. And although I recognized him from Central Texas Rehabilitation Hospital, he left a few weeks before I did for another facility.

Not only was Andrew a violinist of a caliber to play in the Austin Symphony, but he was a string teacher in the school district where we lived. That was a lot of eggs in one basket. Then came the stroke, which took away his left hand, the hand used to finger notes. I had played violin as a child. Though I did not make my living performing music, it was indescribably precious to me, as it must have been to him. Part of me wanted to talk to him about all of that, but I didn't know what either of us would say beyond "Well, this sucks."

That day in Group, we heard the story of Phineas Gage. Mr. Gage was a construction foreman on a railroad in Vermont in 1848. One of his jobs with the crew was to supervise the use of gunpowder to blast out rocks when creating tunnels. First, someone would bore a hole in the rock about two feet deep. Another worker would pour gunpowder into the hole and run a fuse to it, then someone would pour sand on top of the powder, and finally, Mr. Gage would use a steel rod to tamp down the sand before they cleared out of the tunnel and lit the fuse.

But about four thirty on September 13, someone became distracted and failed to pour in the sand. Ol' Phineas, thinking the sand was in, dropped the tamping rod into the hole and the gunpowder exploded, sending the rod back out of the hole. It entered Mr. Gage's head below the cheekbone, went behind his eye, through his brain, and exited out the top of his skull. In a truly astounding turn, not only did Phineas not immediately die, he never even lost consciousness. His crew loaded him into a cart, and when they reached the nearest town, he simply sat on a porch while awaiting a doctor and even regaled a few astonished onlookers with the story of what had just happened.

After a several-week convalescence, he went back to work, but people around him began to notice changes in his personality. In fact, he turned into a real asshole and became totally unreliable. When he eventually lost his job as a foreman, he moved to South America and became a stagecoach driver, carrying the steel rod that had passed through his brain everywhere he went, because if that's not a good story, what is? Alas, he had seizures, as you do when a three-foot steel rod goes through your brain after an explosion. The seizures steadily grew in intensity, and, eleven years after his injury, Phineas Gage died.

I think what we were supposed to take away from this story was that this was the moment science really started to understand which parts of the brain controlled what—that the left frontal lobe controlled significant personality traits. *My* takeaway was that now that I had suffered a brain injury, I might become a totally unreliable asshole and lose my job.

The story of Phineas Gage wasn't the only one I learned that day involving explosive powder and a projectile through the brain. I had a new neighbor across the hall. Keith had taken his rifle out to his back porch because the cleaning chemicals were so strong and he didn't want the house smelling of fumes. For some reason, the rifle was pointed directly between his eyes when it fired the long-forgotten bullet that was still chambered. It was the kind of bullet that fractures into dozens of tiny pieces on impact, and so, even after the surgery in which a multitude of metal fragments were picked out of his brain, he would still carry around dozens more in his head for the rest of his life.

The first thing you noticed about Keith was the hole-shaped scar between his eyes. The second thing you noticed was a gigantic scar that ran along the length of his hairline from ear to ear, where apparently his entire scalp was peeled away for them to do the necessary surgery. The third thing you noticed was there wasn't a single thing that seemed to be wrong with him. In hushed side conversations, all of us wondered, "What is he doing here?" He walked completely normally. He spoke normally, looked you straight in the eye and answered in a voice you didn't imagine to be different from the way he had ever talked. When once we went as a group to Anytime Fitness, Keith benched two hundred pounds, more than his own weight. The best that we could surmise was that he had a few cognitive things to touch up before he returned to work driving a concrete mixer. Truly, his was a miraculous case.

Nevertheless, Keith completed a sort of sad cycle of guns. There was Merle, who sold guns, there was Keith who suffered brain injury from carelessly cleaning one, and then there was Jesse who had proudly killed people as a marine sniper before being shot himself and left for dead.

A frequent feature of my left hand was severe tremors called clonus. Whenever I exerted myself in any way, such as trying to stand from a chair, my hand would begin to spasm back and forth. It happened with my ankle as well, usually manifesting by my leg rapidly bouncing up and down whenever my toes would be touching the floor but not my heel.

Clonus is like the bump stock of a semi-automatic rifle; it is one motion setting off a chain reaction of reflexive motions back and forth. Each time I would clonus during therapy—which was often—all activity would halt while my therapist would make whatever sound they would make if I had hurt myself. She would try to soothe the tremors by having me stop whatever I was doing, then we'd try again.

One day shortly after arriving, I established a goal for myself of both setting my wheelchair brake and releasing the brake with my right hand. Releasing the brake by pulling was fairly easy because the biceps muscle is stronger than the triceps and because I could use Pancho as a hook.

Setting the brake, however, was much more difficult. At first, I activated my triceps by poking it with my left-hand fingers. This seemed to work. But then, to my great surprise, I started activating my triceps without touching it. I would simply hold my good hand outside of my right shoulder, and *bam*, the triceps would lock out the arm in an instant, as if the stroke had never happened. My therapists were confounded, and everyone I showed this to claimed never to have seen such a thing before. I speculated about what might have been happening. Was it just the suggestion of activation? Or was I somehow breaking the aura around my body with my left hand? Going forward, this was known as my magic touch, though, as I say, there was no touching involved.

Each morning and night, we were obligated to get our meds from the tiny medication room off one of the dining rooms, the Med Shack, we called it. Sometimes there was no wait, and I'd roll right in. The tech would take my blood pressure while she dug through the vertical files for my stash. But if I timed it wrong, the Med Shack would be bumper to bumper, like wheelchairs in five o'clock traffic. Jesse would be sleeping at the table right outside the doorway, the tinny cumbia ringing out from his cell phone speaker. Merle would have set up a roadblock across the hallway and be chewing Mark's ear about something in Korea or the Philippines. Gina would be scowling at her untouched plate of food, wondering where the ranch was. Jack would be in his fifty-first minute of eating. Andrew would be texting with a friend. When the Med Shack came available, the next person would roll in and don the blood pressure cuff.

These were the people in my new neighborhood. Their tenure ranged from a few days to life. I assumed my stay would be somewhere in the middle.

CHAPTER 11

Doctor, Doctor

Nature abhors the old, and old age seems the only disease; all others run into this one.

—*Ralph Waldo Emerson*

March 2 is typically the beginning of the Bahá'í fast, a period of nineteen days in which Bahá'ís are required to abstain from eating or drinking between sunrise and sunset. This is part of an ancient realization, observed across many religions, that abstaining from food and drink for certain periods is healthy for the body and helps develop self-discipline, among other virtues. Think Yom Kippur, Lent, and Ramadan, to name a few examples. But I would not be fasting this year, as I had the last fifteen. And that felt strange.

Instead, Kirstin picked me up, and we made the long drive to North Austin to meet my new, long-term neurologist. We decided to leave the wheelchair in the car, and I made the relatively long walk from the drop-off circle to the neurologist's office with my trekking pole. It would never have seemed like a long walk before, but now it seemed more like an airport than a hospital.

After check-in, the physician's assistant invited me to sit next to her desk and began asking me all of the same questions I had answered the previous week on intake at Dripping Springs, which were many of the same questions I had been asked at the rehab hospital, which were many of the same questions Kirstin had been asked in the ICU.

She asked me if I had had any history of surgeries, to which I replied that I had undergone three: a kidney-stone breakup, a hernia repair, and a vasectomy. There was a long silence, and then I added, "Oh—and I had brain surgery too. Forgot that one." She sat up straight, as if to say, "Ooh, that's a biggie!" I had just assumed that the neurologist would know that I had brain surgery six weeks earlier, but no.

The PA asked me if I had any memory issues.

"No," I replied.

She then asked if I had any mood swings.

Again, I replied no, then added, "and also, I haven't had any memory issues." Another long silence ensued, then Kirstin laughed, and I let the PA off the hook. "I'm kidding, just kidding," I said, and the PA allowed herself a relieved smile.

"Any allergies to medication?" she asked.

"Augmentin and Nystatin," I answered.

"What was your reaction to Augmentin?" she asked.

"Hiving," I said.

"And what was your reaction to Nystatin?"

"Well . . ." I searched for the right words, "it turned my penis four shades of purple and also into the shape of a mushroom."

The PA was quiet for a long moment while the wheels in her head turned, then said, "I think I'll just put 'discoloration' and 'swelling.'"

"Whatever you think," I said.

My questions for the neurologist were few. The first thing I wanted to know was whether my seizure preventative, Keppra, was making me inarticulate. He said no, and added that given where the bleed was, it was a wonder I had any speech at all. I was very lucky.

I said I knew.

He said some people, especially epileptics, take Keppra for their entire lives with no side effects. The fact that *some* people had no side effects was not that comforting. He ordered a cerebral angiogram, which was scheduled for about a month out. "Okay!" he chirped. "I want to see you back in about a month," and just like that, it was over.

Though I did not realize it at the time, I had just met one of the most important and consequential people in my life. Other than my wife, the most important person in my recovery and return to regular life would not be a therapist, and would not be a doctor—it would be my neurologist's assistant. Heed well this fact, my friends, and do not fail to grasp the gravity of this position should a similar fate befall you. An overwhelming fraction of your future happiness or despair rests in her—and it will likely be a her—hands. A prescription for more therapy or a piece of medical equipment? It starts with her. A letter stating that new flooring in your house is medically necessary and therefore tax-deductible? Her. Forms that allow you to return to work? She must fill them out and fax them to HR. A letter stating you are fit to have a driver's license? She must write it and, like all else, get the neurologist to sign it, sometimes the same day. Prescription refills for anti-seizure meds? A letter stating that you're disabled so the state will waive sales tax on a new car? A form stating you are disabled so you can get handicap parking permits? Her, her, and her. By the end of the year I was calling her so much people probably thought we were having an affair. But then I was faxing her just as much, and that's hardly romantic.

On March 14, I returned to Dell Seton for a follow-up visit with the surgeon who had boldly gone where no man had gone before, inside my brain.

I had never really known what they had done in there: how wide they opened up my scalp, how big a hole they cut in my skull, how they stopped the bleeding, and how they put me back together again. Finally, I would get the answers to these questions from the very person who had gone inside my head. K drove an hour to pick me up and another forty-five minutes to the hospital.

When we reached the check-in desk at the hospital, the receptionist told me nonchalantly, "Dr. Vasilev no longer sees patients at this hospital. You're going to be seen today by Mandy, the PA."

There was a long silence as I calmed myself. I kept my eyes down on the clipboard, filling out the paperwork jaggedly with my left hand. "That's extremely disappointing," I said in a low voice. "We were told it would be Dr. Vasilev."

At the end of five minutes, the receptionist looked up from her screen and said with no explanation, "It is going to be Dr. Vasilev."

"Good," I said softly. "That's good."

The first surprise of the visit was where the bleed was. I had been told, based on the original CT scan, that the hemorrhage was in the putamen (pyoot-AY-men), a part of the brain below the parietal and frontal lobes. For seven weeks I had been telling friends and family that my bleed was in the putamen. I had been bothering my therapists for information about the putamen and what the putamen controlled, smartly pointing out that the putamen was not featured on any of the line drawings of the brain handed out to us in Group.

"Oh no," the surgeon said. "The bleeding wasn't in the putamen at all." It was much higher up in the brain, a 4.7 cm area that spanned both the frontal lobe and the parietal lobe.

Through talking to Dr. Vasilev and from further research, I was able to piece together approximately how this went:

I assume I arrived at Dell Seton with an IV already in my arm from the other hospital. As the bleeding continued, I seized and fell unconscious. They began with emergency IV delivery of Keppra to stop the seizure, along with anesthesia so I wouldn't wake up. The anesthesiologist would have monitored my heart rate, blood pressure, breathing, and blood oxygen level throughout the surgery.

Then they cathed me. Multiple things were happening at once as eleven people tended to me. They positioned me on the operating table to access the top left side of my brain and placed my head in a device to hold it still. Perhaps because there was no time but perhaps because my hair was sparse and relatively short, they did not shave my hair over the surgical site but only cleaned it with an antiseptic.

They made a nine-inch incision in my scalp, pulled it open, and clamped the edges to control bleeding. They used a drill to saw an approximately three-inch hole in my skull to access the brain, then removed the bone flap and set it aside.

They cut open the dura mater, a thick outer covering between the skull and the brain. They then used a combination of foam coagulants applied with a syringe to stop the bleeding. I pictured the surgeon using a caulking gun to pump my head full of the expanding, hardening foam that you get at the Home Depot to seal gaps around windows. As we were talking, he said "anticoagulants," and I interrupted him— "*anti*coagulants?"

"Oh no—I meant coagulants," he said, and I momentarily savored the fact that I had just corrected a brain surgeon.

After they drained off the excess blood, they biopsied a piece of my brain in order to rule out a tumor. I didn't ask nearly enough questions about this part, such as, was it the size of a grain of sand? The size of a pea? A tangerine? Where exactly did you take it from? And what was that part of the brain responsible for? I wished I could have specified what cells they took: Could you please leave the multiplication tables and instead remove the cells that are storing the first names of the Kardashians?

I already had been blaming forgetfulness and every other shortcoming on the stroke, but now I had a splendid new excuse for every dropped ball, every under-planned birthday or forgotten anniversary. I had a new code word for forgetfulness: "Honey, *biopsy!*" This, almost eight weeks post, was the very first time I ever heard the word "tumor." As the sample came back clean, it thankfully was also the last.

He had reattached the skull-yarmulke using three small titanium plates to bring the manhole cover flush with the hole it came from. All of this was brand-new information to me, and it made more sense now that when I dragged my fingernails across my scalp, it changed pitch over the hole.

A drain tube was placed in my brain tissue to release pressure inside the skull created by cerebral spinal fluid and blood inside the closed skull, literally a brain drain. Forty staples closed the scalp, and that's when I rejoined the party.

The details were nice to have, but the main takeaway from the visit were the words "might" and "some." His take was that I "might" regain "some" use of my arm and hand. That confused me, as I had already gained back some, and he had not evaluated me. I tried to show him how much I could lift my arm. He was not rude, but I could tell he was not that interested. He was a surgeon, not a therapist, and he quickly steered the conversation back to the CT scans and MRIs on his computer screen.

I was availing myself of everything Western medicine could do for me, from Keppra and Prozac to multiple forms of therapy. But I was not content to stop at the edge of conventional medicine. It was somebody from work who first suggested I try acupuncture to speed my recovery. Kirstin and I had both long believed in the efficacy of this Chinese practice, and I had seen an acupuncturist the previous year for a frozen shoulder. He was a Taiwanese American whose son was friends with our youngest son, Ian. Also, it just so happened that on a Google search for "acupuncture in Austin" and "stroke," his was the only name that showed up. He agreed to meet us on a Saturday afternoon.

At length we found his office on the ground floor of a massive, tree-shaded office complex. A few moments in the waiting room, and he called us into his office. I leaned my trekking pole into the corner and took a seat next to his desk. He offered me some hot tea, a delightful touch that was definitely not a part of any regular doctor's visit I had ever had before. In another intake interview, we covered the basics of the stroke—when, where, why, what could I not do now? He wrote on a form in tiny Chinese characters. The cynic in me briefly wondered if they were merely doodles or irrelevant words and phrases, perhaps a grocery list of things he needed on the way home.

After fifteen minutes, it was time to get started. The treatment room was lit only by a lamp in the corner, and a CD of soothing Chinese music played on a jam box. If Western medicine borrowed nothing else from alternative medicine but its attention to *aesthetics*—lighting, music, hot tea—it would be improved tenfold.

I struggled onto the high table and, with K's help, removed my socks and shoes. As I reclined, he moved a heat lamp over my feet, disappeared to the kitchen where he microwaved a few towels, and returned, putting them under my neck and right shoulder.

Since right-side motor impairment was my chief complaint, I assumed he would concentrate the needles in my right arm and hand and in my right leg. But most of his attention was focused on my scalp, which made sense because Pancho was not the source of the problem; my brain was the source of the problem. As he continued to sink needles deeper and deeper around the scar in my head, I muttered, "Crown of thorns . . . to go with my Christ complex."

I pictured lightning striking my leg and my arm. Kirstin, who was resting on a couch five feet away, had already slipped into a deep sleep, and with the dim light in the warm quiet of the office, I soon joined her in unconsciousness. Twice during the nap, Keith knocked softly on the door and came back in to twist the needles in my scalp and stimulate more activity. I probably had only been out for eight minutes, but it felt like I had been asleep for eight hours.

We agreed that I would come back every weekend I could.

Acupuncture did not have the endorsement of Western science but was growing in popularity all the time. When I mentioned to my neurologist on a later visit that it was something I was trying, he was neither dismissive nor enthusiastic, but gave me a no-doubt well practiced few words along the lines of, "It won't hurt you." My experience with MDs is that they will take this laissez-faire tack with any alternative treatment unless and until it conflicts with theirs. For the price, I saw no reason to leave this stone unturned.

In reality, there were three lines of attack I was now pursuing. The first was Western science, which included medicine and therapy. The second was Eastern medicine. The third was prayer. Prayer, of course, did not have the endorsement of Western science but certainly was not in conflict with it, and the faith that I embraced wholeheartedly endorsed prayer along with medicine and skilled physicians as the best way of healing.

Many people told me they were praying every day for me, and I believed them. Many were Christian as you would expect in America. Many were from my own small but energetic faith community, the Bahá'í Faith. At one point, I received an email from a Bahá'í woman I had never met before. She said she had been visiting a synagogue with a Jewish friend on the previous Saturday and that the rabbi was asking for prayer requests from the congregation. Someone close to her softly said, "Avrel Seale." She recognized the name as one from the Bahá'í community. I knew that it must have been my friend and colleague Gary who had gone with me to the hospital on the afternoon of the stroke, called the med school dean to make sure I had the best surgeon, and now was offering up my name in prayer, and I forwarded her email to him with a note that simply said, "Thank you."

He replied, "Oh, you're welcome. Here's hoping that of all the prayers in all the languages to all the Gods, at least *one* of us is sending it to the right place!"

In the Bahá'í Faith, there is a prayer revealed by the prophet who founded the religion, Bahá'u'lláh, that goes:

Thy name is my healing, O my God, and remembrance of Thee is my remedy. Nearness to Thee is my hope, and love for Thee is my companion. Thy mercy to me is my healing and my succor in both this world and the world to come. Thou, verily, art the All-Bountiful, the All-Knowing, the All-Wise.

But there is a much lengthier prayer, the Long Healing Prayer. It is more than 1,300 words long and takes about fifteen minutes to say, which is not really that long in the grand scheme of things, and certainly not that long compared to stroke recovery, estimates of which ranged from eighteen months to eight years. And so I recited it, too.

Ten years earlier, I had gone on pilgrimage to the Bahá'í World Center in Haifa, Israel. I recalled a great number of people there in wheelchairs being pushed through the gardens and around the shrines, no doubt many of them stroke survivors, though I never had such thoughts back then. They were simply old people in wheelchairs being dutifully pushed by friends, or family members, or staff or volunteers at the World Center. Some of them surely did hope for healing of some kind. Others had probably never been on pilgrimage and wanted to go before their lives drew to a close.

I always wished I had been more vigilant about prayer. Bahá'ís are instructed to pray morning and night and on all sorts of occasions. I wished I had been more steadfast, more religious about it, if you will. I viewed prayer a little like acupuncture. I believed that it worked. I had seen some evidence it had. Of course, I had no proof, but what could it hurt?

Throughout my stroke recovery, I noticed that my body was forced into every traditional prayer posture: when I wanted to control my right arm or open my clenched right hand, I would interlace my left-hand fingers with my right-hand fingers, "praying hands" style. When seated in the shower, I would slump over and bow my head, letting the warm water wash over my scar like holy water. In physical therapy, I was taught "tall kneeling" posture, as if in a church pew, and then I was told to sit back on my heels, lower my head all the way to the ground, and force my arms all the way out in front of me, as if on a prayer rug. I see what you did there, God. Don't think I didn't notice that.

As long as I was trying three completely different approaches—Western medicine, Eastern medicine, and prayer—I would never be able to tell which one had been effective and by how much.

And even if I could separate these three approaches to healing, there was a fourth factor that muddied all the waters, and that was time. According to the saying, time healed all things. That is demonstrably untrue, but it did heal some things—a *lot* of things. Shortly after the stroke, a friend came to visit me in the rehab hospital. He told me the remarkable story of his grandfather who, in his mid-eighties, had a stroke. He was too old for the doctors to do surgery, so he was sent home with one of his adult children to convalesce in the woods of Maine. They made him as comfortable as possible, and after about three weeks, he got up and went back to his own home. He wasn't perfect, but the brain had healed itself well enough so that he lived another eight years, into his nineties, kicking around his house, even chopping wood for the fire. He might not have been any ordinary man, but he was proof that time could heal things and that the body could go a long way toward healing itself.

But my stroke was in no way a repeatable experiment. I did not have time for the scientific method—to control the variables, to stop therapy and see just how effective prayer alone was. All the research said that most of the gains were made in the first six months, with some still available to the patient at a year and some very few at eighteen months, but after that, improvement leveled off—the dreaded "plateau." This is why I elected for the both/and approach and not the either/or. Who cared what worked as long as something did?

What's more, my faith did not prescribe prayer alone, but specifically enjoined me to seek the counsel of doctors. In fact, one of the names for God in this relatively new tradition was "the Physician." One night as I was praying, I suddenly remembered that I had not used my electric stim machine yet that day. I respectfully but quickly wrapped up the prayer and broke out the e-stim kit for a thirty-minute session. Not only were prayer and therapy not mutually exclusive; to some extent, they were mutually reinforcing: the prayers prompting me to therapy; the therapy poses reminding me to pray.

My Austin acupuncturist had recommended a practitioner closer to Dripping Springs whom I could see midweek between visits with him, therefore getting my treatments up to twice a week. I found a hole in my therapy schedule, emailed her, and scheduled a visit. After multiple failed attempts to find a staffer who could drive me to this appointment, I decided to try a rideshare. I'm a late adopter of technology of almost every kind, including ridesharing, but I had downloaded the Lyft app when I was at a conference in Cleveland the previous fall. The staffers were dubious that Dripping Springs would be within a rideshare service area, but it was now my only hope. I hit the button, and within ten seconds someone was on their way from Johnson City, twenty-five minutes to the west.

Joanna, my driver, and I searched up and down the street for an acupuncturist sign. Finally, I spotted a tiny sign with Chinese characters on it. Joanna pulled as close as she could to the sidewalk, but there was a harrowing grassy downhill slope before getting to the sidewalk. The driver was kind and spotted me as I teetered my way down the hill. I tipped her the maximum amount.

As I reached the house, I came to a huge step, some eight inches tall, that I would need mount to complete the journey. Fortunately, just that morning, my physical therapist and I had worked on steps, and I had climbed an entire flight of them with only the use of a hiking stick. Talk about instant real-world applications—here we go!

She greeted me at the door, invited me to sit on a formal Oriental bench, and handed me a clipboard with six forms attached to it. "Paperwork," she said with an expression of apologetic inevitability.

Crestfallen, I took the clipboard, scrawled my first and last name, kindergarten style, and handed the clipboard back to her. "It would take the entire ninety minutes for me to fill this out with my left hand," I said. "What information do you really need?" She took my driver's license, copied my address and DL number onto the form, and invited me to a folding chair next to her desk.

"How old are you?" she shouted.

"Fifty-one—"

"So young!" she yelled. "You don't exercise?!"

There was a long silence. "Is that some sort of a joke?" I asked.

"Not a joke!" she barked. "You eat too much pork!"

Nope, not a fit. In the West, in America, for all our crassness, we've become accustomed to a certain level of diplomacy, especially when it comes to matters of health and blame. At this moment, I faced a mighty temptation to walk out of the house and see if Joanna, my Lyft driver, was still in range. I didn't know if I could accept help from someone with such an insensitive attitude. If I hadn't moved heaven and earth to get there, I surely would have left, but I didn't. Before long, she pointed me back to the treatment room. I shed my socks and shoes and precariously squirmed into a horizontal position on the narrow treatment table.

She asked if I wanted music. Sure, why not? She said it was monks, then corrected herself—actually nuns. "Sounds good," I said. She hit *play* on the little jam box, and soothing, *a capella* pentatonic chant started to play. The music was in octaves with some singers clearly nuns and other singers clearly monks. "I think there are some monks in this group," I said. "It's too low to all be women."

"You understand music!" she shouted. "I don't understand music!" Thus our discussion of Buddhist chant came to its conclusion.

She did not seem to focus on my head the way that my other acupuncturist had. Rather, she went heavy on the arm and the leg. She went deep, too. A couple of times I winced or lightly gasped in pain. Each time, she questioned me in disbelief that I was feeling pain, questioned me in a way that made me feel like a sissy. "What?!" she barked.

I wondered if she had ever actually received acupuncture before. "You realize, of course, that you're pushing needles into my body," I wanted to say, but instead, I just continued to gasp, "It's all right . . . it's okay."

At length, we reached the end of our session. She removed the needles and asked me to turn over, saying that we had a little more time and that two more "points" in my back would help immensely. She then raised my T-shirt and commenced slapping the living crap out of my kidneys with her cupped hand over and over again—eight, ten, twelve times. Finally, I reflexively reached behind me with my good hand and blocked her from hitting me further. There was never any mention of this on her website or in the treatment consultation. There was no warning of it before it happened, and no explanation of what it was meant to do following my desperate pleas for it to stop.

I then had one of those out-of-body experiences in which everything loses context and you see only what is happening in the moment: Why am I here? On a Tuesday afternoon? With a Chinese woman spanking my kidneys? It was like a scene out of one of the *Hangover* movies, and I was coming to after a roofie blackout. Am I in Thailand? Have I been sold into sexual slavery to a dowdy, shouting, middle-aged dominatrix?

As I got off the table, I found her to be a little too eager to praise me in my walking. I don't often eschew praise for anything, but this praise seemed a little too self-serving, a little too "It's a miracle!" Nevertheless, I appreciated her services, and what's more, she offered to drive me back to the rehab center.

As we got in her car, her stereo played a CD I did not comprehend. It was a man excitedly shouting in Mandarin. According to her it was essentially a Buddhist sermon. "What is he saying?" I asked.

She began listening more intently. "He says . . . you have to get rid of possessions that weigh you down and your worry about wealth. He says,"— she listened more—" . . . this is the way to a peaceful and happy life."

The significance of this outing was not solely the strange twists and turns it took; the significance was that it was the first thing I had done since the stroke on my own. It doesn't seem like much at this remove, but to contact someone cold, schedule an appointment at a time that did not conflict with other therapy, get myself there and back safely—it felt like I was rejoining the world of the living, the world of independent, busy adults.

I had made another acupuncture appointment with her and once again ordered up a Lyft driver to get me there. It was the last day of astronomical winter, and it was a beautiful day but with a biting wind. I was underdressed as Robert, my driver, picked me up. The nurses shouted after me that I still needed my meds, so I wheeled around, literally, snaking my way back to the Med Shack, and gulped them down. I used to take pills one at a time. Now, with the exception of the Keppra, which I affectionately called the horse tranquilizer, I thought nothing of swallowing three at once.

Everything about this acupuncture appointment went more smoothly than the last. I only had an hour to give her, so we got right to it. And at the end, there was no surprise assault on my kidneys.

As I struggled up to sitting and then to my feet, she said, "Say 'Buddha Buddha Buddha' and you walk faster!"

"I'm sorry?"

"You say 'Buddha Buddha Buddha,' and it makes you walk faster," she said earnestly.

What could it hurt, I thought, and I complied. I did walk faster for those few seconds, but I couldn't see this as a permanent fix. ("Have you seen that guy who hobbles around campus muttering 'Buddha Buddha Buddha' everywhere he goes?")

Again, she kindly drove me back, and still the Buddhist scripture played on her car stereo, the man yelling excitedly in Mandarin, and the doctor, still assuming I wanted to have every word translated, feeding me the scripture line by line as we passed the Dripping Springs Sonic.

As I braced myself to push up and out of her car, I turned my head toward her and said, "Have a peaceful and happy life."

"I do," she insisted. Her tone was one of indignance, as if I had implied by my wish that she didn't.

"Good," I said. "Me too."

As I walked across the parking lot toward my wheelchair still parked on the porch, I heard her door open and turned to see her chasing after me with a stack of business cards. "Tell everyone I give them one free treatment, but only on Wednesdays!"

CHAPTER 12

A Gift to be Simple

As an introvert, I have always been happy enough with my own company. I have a few very good friends, and that is all I have ever felt I needed. That said, I did know a lot of people. I had worked at the University of Texas for twenty-five years. There were many people I knew through my faith community. My closest friends tended to be from high school and elsewise from my hometown of McAllen.

The stroke brought with it a wave of social activity I was not used to. People show their concern by visiting the sick and afflicted. I now received way more texts than ever before. Everyone who had my cell number texted me to see how I was doing. But it was hard to give any sort of meaningful reply in a text, and so I resorted to whimsical sayings and pithy optimism like, "Slow and steady wins the race!" or, "Doing pretty good for the shape I'm in." My brother was coming through town from three to five. A high school friend wanted to come out from five to seven. My middle school choir director and his wife were in town. My childhood youth group leader. It was like a slow-motion episode of the old TV show *This Is Your Life!* Of course, I could have said no to any of them, and they would have understood, but I never did, because every gesture was precious to me. This sharp uptick in popularity and outreach was the best kind of problem anyone ever had.

On the second day after my arrival in Dripping Springs, there was a light knock on my bedroom door and a face appeared in the crack. It was one I knew from Facebook. "Avrel, you might not remember me, but I went to high school with you—Patrick Kufrovich. How are you, sir?"

"Hey, Pat—of course I remember you, bud! What's goin' on?"

Patrick sat in my wheelchair as I lay in bed, and we talked for about forty-five minutes, which was odd, because I don't think we said more than ten words to each other during all four years of high school. This was not out of any animosity—it was just a big high school, and you can't be best friends with everybody. But we were Facebook friends, he had seen news of my plight, and he happened to live in Dripping Springs. Whatever can be said about the perils of Facebook—its temptation to narcissism, its divisive political rants, its corporate Big Brother privacy failings—it does keep us connected to those we might otherwise lose track of, and that is a profound good.

Pat glanced at the armoire standing empty in the corner. "So where's your TV?"

"The rooms don't come with TVs. You've gotta—" I couldn't even finish the sentence before Pat had stood up. "We've got an extra," he said. "Can I bring it over to you?" Another ten seconds and Pat was on his phone with his college-aged son, asking if it was okay with him if they took the TV out of the bedroom he returned home to every few weeks. "All right, thanks," he said. "What else do you need?" Patrick asked.

I thought. "Well—I actually could use a lamp." The overhead light switch was of course at the door, so once that went off, the room was pitch black, a sketchy proposition for someone with a stroke trying to get from the door to the bed. "I think we've got one," said Patrick. "What else?"

"That's all I can think of," I said, "but only if it's not a big—" and Patrick was gone.

In fifteen minutes flat he was back in C Hall, maneuvering a forty-two-inch flat-screen through my door and around my wheelchair and searching for an outlet. "I'll be right back," he said after plugging it in and locating the cable box. Two minutes later he had returned with an old brass lamp for my nightstand.

Patrick texted me every two or three days, asking how I was. In one text, he asked if they allowed me to leave the campus, and if so, if I might want to come to his house to watch some basketball and eat something. Pat came to pick me up on a Sunday afternoon, and I was watching the parking lot for him from the wheelchair half-pipe. I was in an awkward phase of being able to walk but still using the chair as needed. So he hoisted the chair into the bed of his pickup as I made my way to the passenger's seat. His truck was a little taller than mine, but I hadn't gotten in my own truck since the stroke. I stood there awkwardly, wondering how to sit on something that high. I was no shorter than I had ever been, but I had never even thought before about how I got in my truck; I didn't sit then turn—I stepped in with one foot and my body slid fluidly onto the seat before the second foot left the ground. Now, I stood with my butt to the seat willing myself to be even one inch taller. Before I could get the words out, Pat had seized me under the arms and tossed me back onto the seat like a rag doll. At his house, I settled in with a Dr Pepper on ice, a true treat now, and nachos and, unfortunately, started slowly adding back the weight I had lost since the stroke.

On another occasion, Jay, an old friend I had made through the Bahá'í community, drove out and took me to dinner at a sandwich shop in Dripping. Jay is probably the most earnest person I know and also the most deferential. It does me good to hang out with him so that some of that earnestness and deference might rub off on me. When we were seated at the Dripping Springs Schlotzsky's and our order was out, he took a sip of his drink and said, "There's this thing I wanted to tell you about. You might have already heard of it—"

"TED Talk. Jill Bolte Taylor," I interrupted. Jay sheepishly acknowledged I was right and chuckled as he retracted his comment.

"I'm sorry," I said. "I shouldn't have done that. That was a jerk move. I blame the stroke." We both laughed.

Trips off campus like that one were the exception, and the vast majority of the time we were eating, sleeping, doing therapy, doing laundry, or queued up at the Med Shack door at Oak Point. There is something about dormitory life that is appealing in its simplicity. I got used to this. I had about ten changes of clothes, almost all T-shirts and shorts. I had one pair of shoes that worked for me, and I wore them everywhere—to the bathroom, to meals, out to eat, everywhere. I was a creature of routine anyway, and so eating promptly at eight, noon, and six was not an issue for me; I preferred it.

Life was boiled down to its simplest elements: eating, going to the bathroom, and enough physical and mental activity in between to utterly exhaust me. There were no commutes; I got out of bed ten minutes before breakfast in order to use the restroom, and from breakfast I could go straight to work thirty seconds away.

There were no bills to pay (not yet anyway). We even had a little allowance when we would go to a coffee shop or restaurant for a dessert and a Dr Pepper. It was like summer camp, not only in the way it was scary to be dropped off there with a bunch of kids I didn't know, but in the familiarity of the bonds that I developed. It was a comfortable existence, and at a remove of eight weeks, I could scarcely remember what my old life had been like. It was summer camp where everyone had brain damage.

Mealtime was a thrice-daily touchpoint with the rest of the residents, at least the ones who preferred the dining room I did. Those were Rachel, Gina,

Tamika, Jack, and Andrew. The other Tamika, Tamika the cook, did not suffer fools, or, really, requests of any kind, but had an infectious laugh. Techs and therapists would often dine with us, as a hedge against someone choking and to record in a binder what percentage of the food presented to us we finished. There were many patients who would take two bites and push their plate back. Thirty minutes later, they'd take a third bite, then call it done. Such was *not* the case with me. To the contrary, I was so hungry at every meal that I began eating foods that I had managed to avoid for fifty-one years, such as yogurt. After every meal, I would push my empty plate toward the middle of the table, turn to the nearest binder-toting therapist, and proclaim without fanfare, "a hundred percent." I would occasionally have to ask for seconds, Oliver Twist style, in which case I might report 150 percent or 180 percent.

The most memorable meals were the ones we had to prepare ourselves, and this back-to-the-real-world therapy included a trip to the grocery store to buy ingredients. My turn came about ten days into my stay. Rachel and I were accompanied by two OTs. The Ford Flex dropped us at the front door. When I made it to the shopping cart, I put the quad cane in the cart and, hooking Pancho to the handle, used the cart as a walker, as instructed.

We each had a list of about five items we needed to make lunch that day back at the house. Knowing that my OT was next to me to catch me if I stumbled or to stop the cart if it started to run away from me, I turned to the right inside the front door and entered the produce section. Proceeding toward the shelf where I thought the coleslaw dressing might be, I turned to ask her if she thought this was the right section, and she was nowhere to be found. Not only was she not in a position to catch me if I should fall, she wasn't even in Produce. This was real life. I was working without a net.

Every part of the store represented some impossible reality check. The very first item was blocked by a stocker, and I had to ask him to hand me a bottle. The next item was purple cabbage, for which I had to do a 180 in order to retrieve it with my left hand. Not having gotten the produce baggie yet, I then had to rip a baggie off the roll and get it open, something I could scarcely ever do with two hands. The next stop was ground beef, a five-pound tube of it. I retrieved it with Lefty and lobbed it into the cart with a crash.

I soon realized the error of my ways. I should have gone around the store clockwise so that I could grab all of the items with my left hand and not have to make a 180-degree turn every time I wanted to grasp anything. No matter, I was 60 percent through my list. Next, hamburger buns, sixteen of them. My OT made me pull these off the shelf with my right hand, requiring Herculean effort. Every time I flexed my right arm to bring it up to shelf level, my right foot would shoot off the ground, throwing off my balance. Lastly, I had been tasked with getting ground mustard, which was not in the mustard section, of course, but in spices. I told my OT that this task would have reduced me to tears in my best days before the stroke, and she graciously agreed to narrow the field for me by telling me it was a McCormick product, and that they were listed alphabetically. With much help, I grasped the spice bottle between the thumb and forefinger of Pancho and spastically thrust it toward the basket. It was done. I had completed my list of five items, and it had taken a mere forty minutes. It had been about seven weeks since the stroke, and this was far and away the longest I had been on my feet, and the farthest I had walked.

Part of the daily routine that particularly reminded me of preschool was "snack time." Snack time was between 10 and 10:30 a.m. and again between 8:30 and 9 p.m. Snacks could only be had during those times so that residents wouldn't ruin their appetites, and snacks were kept under lock and key in a pantry so that they wouldn't be sneaked into rooms with all of the attendant roaches and ants that might snack on them as well. At 8:30 p.m., residents would gather outside the med room. Each would spread out a napkin in front of them and get a baggie of trail mix. Sometimes we would talk and laugh, but other times we sat in silence and munched on the M&M's and peanuts and raisins, preschoolers in their forties and fifties.

At 11:15 one night, I awoke to a loud bang, and briefly thought a bomb had gone off in the courtyard outside my window. I then realized it was just a staffer taking out the trash who had let the lid on the trash can slam, then, I suppose just in case there was anyone still sleeping, slammed the door as he went back inside. I jumped, my arm spasmed wildly with clonus, and I made frantic transfer to my wheelchair to identify the culprit and tell them off. It was a hapless and apologetic young staffer, probably in his late twenties, who was taking out the trash at the end of his shift and had no awareness he had awoken neurologically fragile patients and scared the life out of them.

The next morning, I was sitting on the toilet in the C Hall bathroom when Jeanie from Imperial Mobility called with "great news." She had been the one who interviewed me at the rehab hospital and apparently written a masterwork of medical prose such that my insurance company had authorized the custom wheelchair I had been measured for several weeks earlier. She had run all the numbers, and the chair was going to be a little less than $8,000. Our responsibility would be only $1,450. Shall we go ahead and get started with building the chair?

I sat on the toilet, wishing I had something to write that number down with, and wondering if I had signed anything on the day Jeanie and I had met. I no doubt had signed something authorizing her to contact my insurance, but I think I would have remembered signing something with a dollar amount on it. "I'd like to pause this order," I said. "I just—I'm not sure I'm gonna need this much wheelchair. I'm walking more every day."

She said she was glad to hear that, and I tried to take that sentiment at face value. But the cynic in me could not help but hear the conflict in her voice. Here, I saw the medical industrial complex on full display. Getting authorization from insurance companies for high-dollar medical equipment was this woman's bread and butter and how her company stayed afloat, remained profitable and in business. To be sure, many people, including a lot of my housemates, would benefit from custom chairs. But from the get-go, this had been an elaborate mating dance between the wheelchair company and the insurance company; it felt as if Kirstin and I were hardly part of the conversation. How easy it would have been to authorize this purchase if I were any less together mentally, if I were confused, or simply did not have the energy or the willpower to press pause on the process. And just because $1,450 was a lot less than $8,000 did not mean this was a good use of $1,450.

The neuro-rehab center was filled with a cast of characters to be sure, but it was an ever-shifting cast of characters. First to leave was Brody, the twenty-one-year-old diesel mechanic who dressed like a cowboy and lived directly across the hall. I went down for a nap one day, and when I woke up, he was gone, and all the stuff off of his walls. He had been "disappeared" like a victim of the Pinochet regime. No use asking the staff for any information, living here at the odd intersection of communal living and medical privacy.

Merle, the Academy gun salesman who could relate absolutely anything you were saying to a long and detailed story from his own life, discharged a week later. Tanya, the high-functioning patient I thought was a staff member for the first three days, and who even pushed me in my wheelchair into Anytime Fitness on our first outing there, also disappeared.

Gina discharged, picked up by an uncle, and disappeared without goodbyes. In her place appeared Jordan, a quiet sort who had driven himself to the hospital experiencing chest pains and had a stroke during heart surgery. He did not share Gina's fondness for ranch dressing, and the supply in the house skyrocketed as a result.

About week eight, we got our first bill from Dell Seton. The first six days of medical care had cost $260,000. Emergency charges equaled exactly $50,000, a nice round number, don't you think? Emergency drugs, just those given me on the day of the stroke, cost $40,000. More than two years later, I received a collection letter for a $1,000 invoice from the first hospital because they had been sending invoices to the wrong address. Not having seen them, naturally I had not paid them. When I spoke to my insurance company to see if the charge was legitimate, the rep answered yes (plan years, deductibles, etc.). She then commiserated with me over the fact that I was facing two ER charges. In fact, she said that once she personally had an ER visit that lasted from 11 p.m. to 1 a.m., and was forced by the hospital to pay her portion of *two visits to the ER because her one visit technically spanned two days!* Does not a special place in hell await executives who design rules like this?

We also soon received two bills for the two ambulance rides I took on January 19. It turns out that in Austin, as in most communities, there is no such thing as "in-network" ambulance service. EMS is typically run by municipalities, like police and fire departments are, but unlike those other natural monopolies, EMS teams are not supported by tax dollars. Instead they are supported by insurance companies and patients. The aphorism "there's no fighting city hall" has never been so true. Since the EMS is a natural monopoly, they have zero incentive to negotiate a rate with insurance companies.

Therefore, the city or county says, "That 1.3-mile ride will be $5,000, please."

Insurance replies, "That's not reasonable. We will pay 80 percent of that."

And presto! You, the patient, who did not call the ambulance and had no say in the matter because you were having a heart attack or a lung collapse or a brain hemorrhage, just bought yourself $1,000 of transportation. This is a nationwide problem known as *balance billing.* And because I was taken to a hospital that was not the best one for a stroke, I took two rides and therefore got two bills. We appealed to my insurance and to my employer, and neither would give an inch, so Kirstin and I pay $10 a month times two to this day. Patient-centered care.

CHAPTER 13

Head Games

After our visit to the brain surgeon, Kirstin drove me back to Dripping Springs. On our way, we stopped at Donn's BBQ, barbecue being one essential food group in Central Texas, the other being Tex Mex. As we pulled into the parking lot, I noted with dismay that the one handicap space had already been taken. What's more, I saw a handicap hanger on another car that was not in the space. "How many of us *are* there?" I wondered aloud. Looking covetously upon those sweet, close-in parking spaces for half a century and now finally being licensed to use one but not able was a little maddening. "Whoever is in there," I said, "had *better* be in a wheelchair."

We arrived back in Dripping just in time to join my group on an outing to Thyme and Dough, where I enjoyed a tiny Dr Pepper, a piece of carrot cake, and a game of Battleship against my housemate Mark, driver of the Pornmobile whose neck was broken in a car accident, and Keith, who shot himself between the eyes while cleaning his .22. I proposed to Mark that we execute our fight that was never realized at the pool hall. He could overturn the Battleship game, red and white pegs flying all over, and I could break my Dr Pepper bottle on the table and threaten him with its jagged remnant. He said that would be good, but once again, we never followed through.

The Ides of March was true to form. The wind came out of the Gulf bringing warmer and moister air to the Texas Hill Country, but I suppose that there were otherwise no bad omens. My family meeting was that day, with my physical therapist, occupational therapist, speech therapist, the medical doctor, and administrative coordinator. They went around the table, and each one reported on my progress as Kirstin listened in on the speaker phone. Could we stop the Flomax now? Was it time to consider Botox to relax Pancho? What outpatient rehab facility would we like to use? Rehab Without Walls, we thought. Was the doctor's form ready that would tell the IRS that the new floor in our house was a medical expense? Also during the meeting, we set a discharge goal date of March 30. If we met it, I would have spent five weeks in Dripping Springs.

I have not spoken much of the therapy I received in Dripping, mainly owing to how rich the cast of characters was there with me. But of course, therapy was the main event and the reason we all were there.

Each day was different, but a typical afternoon was a solid block, four hours of back-to-back therapy sessions. After lunch, we piled into the Flex and motored the five minutes to the Hilltop Campus, where we went twice a week for "gait clinic." There, I was strapped into a LiteGait, as I had been in rehab hospital, but this time, instead of rolling down a hallway, the LiteGait was stationary and the "Diaper of Power," as we called it, suspended me over a treadmill. There I walked for twenty minutes—0.43 miles—as PT Samantha sat on the edge of the treadmill tugging my right shoe forward by its shoestrings with every step.

When forty minutes was up, we piled back in the Flex and sped back to our campus. Now OT Roni took over. She worked a while to try to claw Pancho open, for he did not want to open, and he very much had a mind of his own. Then she asked me to lean on my right forearm to "put information" into my wrist. This weight bearing helped my fingers relax and would become a necessary exercise/stretch many times a day to the present.

Next, Tim took over for an hour. He wanted to move me from the quad cane, which had four feet, to the single-point cane. I was game. We went back outside, and I demonstrated my expertise at climbing the Widowmaker, which was actually easier with the single-point cane than it was with the quad because I could stab it vertically plumb into the ground, whereas the quad cane remained perpendicular to the ground no matter what the angle of the ground was.

Tim I had come to regard as a friend as well as a therapist. As we slowly strode up the hill on the winding asphalt path, he picked my brain, such as it was, about the causes of the Vietnam War, and for some reason, we veered into the Iranian hostage crisis of 1979, which he had never heard of, hastening to remind me that 1979 was the year of his birth.

At the far end of the quarter-mile loop, we sat in the shade of a gazebo, where he told me about his plans to have clients build picnic tables that could be set in the shade of a spreading live oak, a sort of benevolent forced labor like the kitchen work, I suppose. We also talked again about the field of for-profit rehabilitation, the vagaries of insurance, and of the interplay between the two industries. Tim made the point that the really good administrators in the rehab business knew the buttons to push and the people to ping on the insurance side. To make the levers move and get the authorizations needed that fueled the whole system, the rehab admissions professionals needed to know the insurance companies better than they knew themselves. I reminded him of my backstory, of the insurance company that screwed up our case in every way it was possible to screw it up, denying me twice, then, with no explanation, approving me but never telling me I was approved. And this was from the leader in the field, the company that providers *liked* working with.

Each day, I had an hour scheduled for something called Walking Program, in which those of us who were able would slowly walk around the house or smooth parts of the grounds while a tech or therapist walked behind us spotting us on each step. But since I had been cleared to walk by myself inside the house, this became something of an independent study. I asked Samantha, one of my three PTs, if the porch counted as the house, ever angling for independence farther afield. She said yes, and then added that I could even go on any of the concrete surfaces outside the house. This included what I called the half-pipe, and the Widowmaker. As soon as she said this, I made a beeline up the steepest part of the concrete. I walked all the way up the hill to the pool, which was still covered in plastic for the winter, and slowly, ever so slowly, made my way back down. I may have been a daredevil in the wheelchair, but with only a cane, I was an ultra-cautious old man.

Many therapists were too artful by half when it came to terminology. One day, when Samantha invited questions, I asked what the best strategy would be for getting up after a fall. "Yes, good question! That's very important. If you have transferred to the floor, you'll want to find a sturdy piece of furniture ..." Wait—what? I suppose "floor transfer" was the clinical term for a "face-plant" or a "yard sale." Other therapists opted for "upper extremity" and "lower extremity" instead of "arm" and "leg."

I also noticed that none of the therapists would use the word "help"; it was always "assist," "offering assistance." As a writer from the Orwell school and a defender of the virtue of plain English, I was against this sort of thing. Help is "help." "Arm" is a perfectly sufficient word. A fall is a "fall"—not a "floor transfer." Again, these things were said with the best of intentions, but were nonsense and only moved the finish line, only delayed understanding. Clearly, this was part of their training, but it was folly.

Even though I had been discharged from speech—i.e. cognitive—therapy in the rehab hospital, here I was right back into it. This was mostly a function of the fact that everyone got it, I guess because if they didn't it would mess up rotations. And I will hasten to add that there was a need, my early graduation from speech at the hospital notwithstanding.

My hour-long sessions with Sherri, my speech/cognitive therapist, were always in a quiet corner of the house, the back living room, with large windows shaded by oaks that looked out on pastures to the southeast and a chalkboard with a hand-lettered sign reading "Think Like a Proton—Stay Positive!"

I have mostly fond memories of those hours, but they were taxing. It was Sherri's job to toughen me up mentally so I could return to work one day. There were many exercises and games that were no doubt given to everyone. We played the board game Pente, a glorified version of tic-tac-toe in which players in alternating turns try to place five stones in a line without getting blocked. I desperately hated the timed spatial reasoning challenges she would give me on an iPad. I was rarely successful at these and doing them put me into a spiral of frustration and anger she would then have to dig me out of.

But knowing I was a writer, she doubled down on word games. This meant lots of Scrabble, at which she was awesome and at which I had never been any good despite being a "word person." Also, we played lots and lots of Bananagrams, a cousin to Scrabble that was played with letter pieces on a table. She beat me like a redheaded stepchild every time, but there were worse ways to spend an hour.

It also fell to speech, and therefore to Sherri, to teach me how to "pack out my meds," putting all my morning meds in one compartmentalized plastic box and all my evening meds in another. Again, I flashed to my father, who had an enormous multi-compartment box of meds each day. I've seen smaller tackle boxes.

One afternoon, Sherri gave me a memory test with a story that went like this:

"Mike and Kathy miss their children, Pam, Rachel, and Mindy. So they planned a trip on Saturday to their college. They would drive through the country and reach the campus at 11 a.m. There they would eat at the Hungry Hut campus diner, where the girls would likely order hamburgers, french fries, and a strawberry malt. If time permits, they would then have a shopping trip and could buy Mindy a pair of badly needed shoes. Mike wanted to leave by four so that he and Kathy could get home in time to watch the big game on TV at six."

Sherri told me she would ask me to repeat this story every fifteen minutes for the rest of the hour, including as much detail as I could. In between tellings, we would play Scrabble, during which she always complained about the hand she had drawn before soundly beating me as I slumped in my chair.

The first time, I repeated the details of the story pretty well, probably regurgitating ninety percent. She then read the passage to me again, and I picked up on a few details I had missed. For instance, it was a strawberry *malt* that the girls normally ordered, not, as I previously said, a milkshake. Also, the three girls' names I guessed were Mindy, Rachel, and, not knowing what the third one was, I decided to play the numbers game and simply threw out Jennifer, as good a guess as any.

By the third time I told the story, I was no longer content with mere accuracy, and some embellishment began creeping in. I started it before I was even asked to, while I continued to study the Scrabble board. "You know, Mike and Kathy really need to learn to let go. I mean, how are the girls ever going to learn the value of a dollar if every Saturday Mike and Kathy drive through the country and buy the girls lunch at the Hungry Hut?"

The next time, the story got even more subtext. "It's clear that Kathy and Mike need to address their own problems," I said. "I mean, honestly, Kathy's sort of been a tramp ever since college. She's trying to fill an empty spot, because her father was so emotionally distant, but that's not Mike's fault! Deep down, Mike knows she's cheating on him, and that's why he drinks. The big game at six? Maybe six is when he starts getting the shakes if he's not nursing a Seagram's."

Then Sherri began getting into the spirit of it. "Yeah, and Kathy only wants to get home because she's having an affair online and needs to drown herself in white wine because she's so desperately unhappy." We started feeding off each other with a crazy plot line.

"I mean, sure," I said, "Mike had the thing with the babysitter, but that was *eight years* ago. Does she have to keep bringing it up? And okay, yes, the babysitter was in high school and he was thirty-five, but it was purely physical, and it was only the once! If she can't forgive him, she ought to just move on—not keep having these serial revenge affairs. Mike has suffered enough for his crime."

To get to supper that night, I decided to take the single-point cane, but not to use it unless I had to. I held it six inches above the ground, and labored waddling down the hall, around two corners, and to my seat. This was a major victory, although like all things in this journey, it was not pretty compared to a healthy body. All the same, I was proud as I strode into the dining room, my cane floating gingerly above the ground. I tried to not make a big deal of these things, as they could become points of jealousy or sadness for my housemates, but I was not going to use a wheelchair or a quad cane one moment longer than I needed to. I was here to build strength.

Friends, who were not therapists or staff and not used to being around those with a stroke, offered the most help. "Let me know if I can do anything," they would naturally say. They positioned their hands in front of me and behind me and beside me and everywhere they thought I might fall, all with the best of intentions. But this communicated worry and reinforced my frailty.

Saturday was St. Patrick's Day, and I gave a thought to Jack and his motorcycle accident a year earlier, but I remembered it too late to dig for a green shirt. Kirstin picked me up at nine thirty to take me to Austin, first for my acupuncture appointment, then a haircut, then a Bush's Chicken lunch at home. I donned my Scout uniform, and K drove me unannounced to an Eagle Scout ceremony, where the other Scout parents were surprised and happy to see me.

Kirstin and I had decided to bite the bullet and refloor a large portion of our house to make it easier for me to get around. The previous Saturday had been occupied by packing up books so that the large free-standing shelving units in our dining room could be moved to the garage and the floors laid. Now the floors were in, and this afternoon was taken up with putting all the books back. We ordered Chinese with some of the Grubhub money we had received from friends. Each week we prevailed on a different friend to make the two-hour round trip to Dripping to get me back to the neuro-rehab center—Wade, Dave Harmon, Elaine. Tonight, it was David who loaded my wheelchair into the back of his car and made the long trip with me.

I seemed to have turned the corner with regard to sleep. I no longer needed the ten hours I once did. Don't get me wrong, I was still good and tired at the end of the day, but I was no longer a slave to naps, and I regularly woke up in the five or six o'clock hour if I went to sleep in a timely way.

We had established a long tradition of taking a spring break vacation with Elaine and Ed and their kids, renting a house for a few days in various places around the Hill Country. Clearly our family was in no condition to observe this tradition this spring break. But there was one element of these joint family vacations that we could observe—the talent show. The Cavazoses had arranged to meet us at a park in Dripping Springs. Kirstin and the boys picked me up and soon the show was underway. For my act, I performed an interpretive lip-sync of "Puttin' on the Ritz," twirling my aluminum cane while seated on a picnic bench and mouthing words about Park Avenue and spats and lots of dollars. Cameron tapped a sixteen-penny nail all the way into his nose with a hammer as his mother and I looked on with a mixture of horror and pride.

On Monday, March 19, I crossed the two-month mark since my stroke, and my therapists worked me like a rented mule. I started with OT, then went to Anytime Fitness with the exercise group. After lunch it was back in the Ford Flex and over to the Hilltop Campus for gait clinic. At four, it was PT with Tim, who set up tiny parking cones in the hallway and made me weave back and forth through them.

The next day, I had psych with Dr. McKetta. These were low-intensity affairs that happened about once a week. I told her that life was now bifurcated into pre-stroke and post-stroke. There were many ways life could be bifurcated, pre-marriage and post-marriage, pre-kids and post-kids, the years when your parents were alive period and the years after they died. But it seemed all but inevitable that this was the new Year Zero. Maybe I would look back on these days as nothing but a hiccup, but it certainly seemed more profound than that, more fundamental.

On the evening of March 21, I normally would have been breaking my fast on the final day of the Bahá'í fast and celebrating the new year, keyed to the first day of spring. But instead, a small group of us loaded into the Flex and made the one-hour trip to North Austin. We were the ones who were good candidates for returning to driving, and there was a stroke support group meeting there with an occupational therapist who was an expert in the subspecialty of returning to driving.

In a rich irony that was at once hilarious and terrifying, the staffer tapped to get us there and back was a terrible driver, maybe the worst I've ever seen. There was needless hard braking, tailgating, sudden lane changes, swerving. Another staffer who was tasked with going along shared the middle seat with me and was equally alarmed by the quality of driving, quickly palming the seat in front of her when the brakes were stomped, inhaling through her teeth when we swerved out of our lane. Finally, we both simply chuckled, a mixture of disbelief and a resignation that if these were our last moments of life on Earth, it was better to go out with smiles than with faces twisted in horror and pain.

The OT we met was known far and wide as "One-Armed Bob." Bob was an inspirational figure in his own right. Having fallen off a tractor at the age of four and losing his right arm, he had spent practically his entire life "shorthanded," as he loved to say. Seeing all that he could do with one hand abruptly took away all license we had to pity ourselves and replaced it with a breathtaking example of manual competence and fierce self-reliance. Bob Whitford had a tone that was reassuring but free of all bullshit: this driving thing would be work, but we could absolutely do it.

Of my three PTs in Dripping Springs, I spent the most time with Susan, who was from Kentucky and had rich Southern accent to match. "Tall and handsome!" she would cry out whenever I would walk crouched. In physical therapy, Susan led us in a group workout in which we crawled on the floor, neither tall nor handsome. She was a big believer in crawling, and even went to her own weekly workout group of crawlers. It might sound easy but was some of the hardest work I had done to date. There's no doubt that it is a good core workout, and it follows a school of thought in neuro-rehab that brain recovery can recapitulate brain development. We all crawled before we walked the first time around as babies, so perhaps strokes were like reinstalling software and we ought to master these tasks in the same order.

Once during a therapy session, I played Susan the most recent mix-downs from David's and my album. The following day, as I rested at a picnic table during a walk along the loop, she took out her phone and played me two tracks off a folk demo she had recorded when she first moved to Austin a dozen years earlier. It was legitimately good, and I told her so. There's a trope about everyone in Austin being in a band, but there aren't remotely enough clubs to keep that many musicians employed. So I wrote for a university communications office, and Susan was a physical therapist, getting stroke and auto accident and gun accident survivors back on their feet. Ninety-nine out of every hundred of us had been cast out east of Eden, and now had to work the land and toil for our bread. As I rose from the bench and continued down the trail, she barked, "Tall and handsome!" and away we went.

That Saturday morning, K picked me up for my weekly trip home. I rolled myself out to the parking lot and found the vantage point at which I could see the easternmost stretch of US 290 to see how soon I could spot Kirstin. I saw the silver Honda Pilot within half a second of when it first cleared the cedars and live oaks. She was alone, as the boys were away camping with the Scouts.

After my acupuncture appointment, and a cheeseburger from a drive-thru, I felt like going to Lowe's, the megalithic home-improvement store at which I had shopped hundreds of times over the nearly twenty years we had lived in our neighborhood. The new floors at home were fantastic, but the rooms were echoey and needed an area rug to absorb some sound and warm them up visually. It was the first time I had been back to Lowe's since the stroke. We took the handicap spot nearest the entrance, and I shuffled through the front door.

"I'm baa-aaaaack!" I shouted as I entered the door. The lady at Customer Service did not look up but busily continued processing a return. It took me nearly ten minutes to reach the carpet section at the back of the store, at which point I was nearly out of steam and was without anywhere to sit down. For the first time, it occurred to me that there were places in the world without benches or chairs, lots of them. As we were now near the restrooms, which were at the back of the store, I thought it best to press on to the restroom simply because it afforded me a chance to sit down.

There were two handicap stalls. One was occupied by someone already. The other had poop all over the seat, and none of the rest of the stalls, of which there were many, had grab bars. I would have to make do. I made the long journey down to the toilet, my knees bent now at an acute angle. When it was time to get back up, I relied on the plastic toilet paper dispenser bolted to the wall and prayed it would support me when I pushed down. We did not buy a rug.

Kirstin and I had decided to say no thanks to a custom wheelchair. But we felt we needed some kind of basic chair at home. What if I had some sort of a setback? What if I sprained an ankle? Crutches would not work. OT Roxanne sat with me and looked at wheelchairs on Amazon. I sent Kirstin the link, she hit the purchase button, and the wheelchair arrived on our porch, fully assembled, ten hours later. It was $195, free shipping.

Back home, Kirstin cleaned off the shower bench and moved it into the bathroom for me, where I turned on the water and proceeded to shave with a razor for the first time in nine weeks. That night, Dave Harmon brought over a spaghetti dinner and we shared it with him. After dinner, I made my final trip back to Dripping, my e-stim unit trying to shock the life back into Pancho.

CHAPTER 14

I'm My Own Grandpa

My time in Dripping Springs was drawing to a close. It was the last of everything—the last Monday, the last Tuesday. The cast of characters had changed markedly even in the four and a half weeks I'd been there. Some had come and gone since I'd been there. Others were there long before me and would be there long after.

My OT marveled at the new wheelchair that had cost less than $200 and made a few fine adjustments. I walked with Samantha. We made my last trip to Anytime Fitness, to gait clinic at the Hilltop Campus where I recorded a personal best of 0.37 miles on the treadmill, no Diaper of Power needed.

The next day, another OT tested me on all sorts of metrics including some of the things I failed when I first got here, like how many circles could I count in a tangle of circles and ovals and squares and triangles? She then produced a machine that would measure my grip. She took my right hand and fed my fingers through the handle, then ask me to squeeze as hard as I could. This produced fourteen pounds of force. As she started to put the machine away and record the number, I asked her if I could do it with my left hand too, just so I could know what was normal. I squeezed the handle, and her eyes grew wide. "Wow! I've never actually measured a number that high," she said. "Fifty-four pounds is considered very strong; you just did eighty-four." Naturally, I took pride in this fact, but another part of me simply lamented how far Pancho had to go to catch up to Lefty.

In PT, Tim and I decided to walk outside. It was misting but not quite raining, so we pressed on up the trail. As we moved slowly away from the building, I set up the performance evaluation scenario for him: "So let me get this straight, Tim. You took a patient out in the rain, the ground was slippery, lightning was threatening, he could have gotten hypothermia."

In Group, which this day was branded "Life 101," Dr. McKetta said she wanted Rachel to share a question that had been on her mind with the group:

"Why? Why has this happened to me?" she asked. "Why did I get cervical cancer? And then why did I get colon cancer? And now why did I have a stroke?"

I offered that I long ago had given up on the notion that bad things could not happen to good people. My own dad had died of Parkinson's four years earlier; he didn't deserve that. Nor my mom to lose her colon. Nor Erren to have scoliosis. There was absolutely no evidence to suggest that suffering comes only—or even mostly—to the wicked. Life would be a lot simpler if it did.

Jack, on the other hand, said he couldn't understand why he was saved. At first, he was angry that he would have been saved when so damaged. Then he remembered that he had children, and they would have been fatherless. He struggled to get the words out, like he struggled with all words: "They . . . are . . . my . . . life."

Another said that the question of why never crossed his mind, he just kept doing the next thing, he just kept doing whatever made a difference.

Andrew said he asked why a lot in the beginning, but because it didn't do any good, he stopped. It was just a rabbit hole that led nowhere.

Dr. McKetta invited Tommy's thoughts, and he said, "Yeah. Well . . . yeah."

I also added that we have to cling to silver linings. We don't know what the future holds and what these events portend for our lives. "If I had never had a stroke, I would have never met you," I told Rachel. "I would have never had all sorts of experiences—reconnections with out-of-touch friends—that I've had. I would never have had this deeper appreciation of the little things we always took for granted, a stroll at sunset, strumming the guitar, all of that. Life is a package deal, and we have to try our best to see the whole package at once."

Shortly before dinner, I rose from my wheelchair and walked from my room to the dining room. No one was there yet, and with no sign of imminent food, I returned to my room for a few minutes. Wanting to check my email, I decided to sit back down in my wheelchair. Either one of the brakes had never been properly set or I just approached it wrong, but this would be my first unintentional "floor transfer." The wheelchair slid out from underneath me with lightning quickness. I let out an oath and tumbled to the ground, landing halfway in my closet and turning over the plastic hamper. There, I just lay on the floor assessing the damage. Head—no damage. Arms, wrists, fingers, no damage. Knees, hips, nothing hurt.

I did not want to resort to pressing the call button. I could not do that next week at home, and moreover, they might have downgraded me to "supervision" or "contact guard" or even "assisted transfers" until I left. For all I knew they might even extend my stay. No, no staff could know about this.

After a minute or so, my heart rate had returned to normal, and I set about the grueling work of getting back to my feet. Of course, we had practiced getting off the floor in physical therapy and occupational therapy, but it was different furniture, and a different floor. I squirmed until I got to kneeling and stared at my bed. Having my bare knees on the linoleum was more painful by far than the fall itself. I could not get enough purchase with my feet to get close enough to the edge of the bed to make my move. At length, I went down on one shoulder and rolled over. Then I pushed myself up off my back with a good arm and scooched the good foot toward the bed. This felt like the most athletic thing I had ever done. I looked at the desk three feet away and thought that was a more reliable piece of furniture on which to push, but when I got there it was too high.

Finally, I turned to my second wheelchair, the loaner, which was still in my room. I brought my right knee up and got enough of my right foot under me to stabilize myself. Then I put my strong left arm on the seat of the old wheelchair and pushed with all I had, quickly scooting my left foot forward and rising to standing, panting. I was up.

Stephen and I had been friends since first grade, and he was another transplanted McAllenite. He and his wife, Dina, picked me up and took me to a Mexican restaurant one night when I was still using the quad cane. As we rose to leave, and I glacially made my way toward the door, a man at the neighboring table asked Steve if I was his father. Not only was I not Steve's father, Steve was all of fifteen days older than me. A few days later, a distant cousin of mine who lived in Dripping Springs came to bust me out for a bit and drive me around his ranch. Another patient asked if he was my son. I was fifty-one, and Hank was fifty-four. I seemed to be aging so rapidly that soon, people would be asking me if my seventy-eight-year-old mother was my daughter. As the song goes, I, indeed, had become my own grandpa.

We, the diners of the west dining room, had become supremely comfortable with each other, as you do after a month of three meals a day. I think it was Jack who started it—flicking a cross section of carrot, like a hockey puck, from his salad across the table to Rachel. A minute later, she flicked it back with a deadpan look. Andrew looked up from his phone—what was going on? "Ay!

You're like a monkey . . . throwing poop!" Rachel laughed. I flashed on our Speed Racer discussion a few days earlier as Jack had timed his bedroom-to-dining room splits, and added, "caca de Chim-Chim." Rachel squealed with laughter and rebuked me. "Don't *say* that! You're so nasty!" Staffers glanced at each other warily. Then the carrot went from Jack to Andrew. This was slowly becoming more interesting than his Facebook feed. He set his phone down, positioned his arm just so, and flicked it to Rachel. I assumed the role of color commentator, "You've got to appreciate the focus and determination these players have shown to get to this this level."

Thursday, March 29, was my last full day in Dripping Springs. My morning schedule was light, just my ITM, my "intra-team meeting." Kirstin was calling in for this one, as she had just been here the night before and would be here again tomorrow afternoon. The meeting was scheduled for 10:15, but I got a thirty-minute head start because I had never done this walk by myself before, and it was a little like Everest to my eyes. Plus, I had nothing else to do. One by one the doctors and therapists came in and closed the door behind them as I sat out in the foyer waiting to be called in.

At about fifteen after the hour, they opened the door and invited me in. I rose to my feet and hit play on the YouTube video I had cued up on my phone. Timpani pounded. The theme to *2001: A Space Odyssey* blared its triads and major to minor chord shifts as I made my dramatic entrance with no cane and no trekking pole. At the final chord change, I stood at the head of the conference table with my left arm outstretched and my head thrust back. The entire group broke into applause and laughter.

We went around the table and each person gave their report. Then they asked if I had anything to say. "I want to thank all of you for everything you've done for me," I said. "I know this must sometimes seem like a thankless job, but I'm glad you do it. I'm glad this place exists. I'm glad my insurance company saw its way clear to let me come—whether or not they would have ever told me."

That afternoon, I had my last OT session with Roxanne. My last gait clinic with Samantha. My last PT with Tim.

In late afternoon, I started making the rounds with my white plastic ankle brace, getting all my housemates and therapists to sign it like a cast in grade school. I saw Jesse in the dining room and asked him to sign it. He wrote, "Good Luck, Jesse M." It must have hit him just then that I was leaving, because a few minutes later, I was outside when Jesse came rolling out. "Gonna miss you," he said, in English. He was angled away from me, and

I couldn't see him that well. Rachel whispered, "Look at his face." When I did, I saw Jesse's face twisted with grief. "Gonna miss you—miss you, *shee . . . !*" he repeated.

I signaled for him to come to me. "Love you, bro," I said. "I'm gonna miss you too. It's gonna be all right. I'll come back and see you." He nodded but continued to sob like I had not seen another grown man weep in many years, except the man in the mirror.

An hour and change later, our eyes met as he came out of the bathroom, and he started up all over again. He gave me the hand sign for Northside, weeping violently, cursing *"Shee . . .!"* and proclaiming how much he would miss me.

Patrick came for his TV and lamp.

March 30 had arrived, Good Friday. It had been ten weeks to the day since my stroke. I had been here five of those weeks—so long I could scarcely remember a time before gait clinic, and Group, and Bananagrams, and snack time, and wheelchair half-pipe. And yet, as my friend Dave Harmon put it on a trip out here a few weeks earlier, "All this—all this therapy for these five weeks—is going to be edited down to a thirty-second eighties music montage in the movie."

Kirstin would be here around twelve thirty, and my morning was lightly scheduled—only one therapy, a Group session billed as "Coping and Adjustment." As was my habit, I got breakfast, hit up the Med Shack for my morning doses, and reported five minutes early.

Nine o'clock came and went.

At 9:05, Mark motored into the room in the Pornmobile. "Is this Coping and Adjustment?"

"That's what I've got," I replied. "I'm assuming it's in here, but that's only an assumption because it's a scavenger hunt every time there's a meeting." That part had gotten a little bit better in the five weeks since I had been there, as we no longer met for Group in the front room except for group exercise.

At 9:10, Andrew wheeled into the room. "Is this Coping and Adjustment?"

"That's what I've got," I replied again. "I'm assuming it's in here. At nine fifteen, I leave," I said. I figured the best way I could "cope" with and "adjust" to staff members being late was to help them by creating a consequence. The stroke had done nothing to blunt my long-standing indignance over tardiness. Nine fifteen arrived, and I made good on my promise.

I went back to my room and gathered a few more things, trying to straighten out piles of shifting paper, unplugging things that I could reach, peeling back and trying to fold the wool comforter that had covered up my bed but winding up with it in a loose wad despite my best efforts.

The morning dragged on and on, with no TV and little to do but run down my phone's battery looking at Facebook and wait for Kirstin and the boys. At eleven, I wheeled into the dining room and found Rachel eating pancakes leftover from breakfast. She had been gone all morning at a doctor's appointment in South Austin, getting her gallbladder and liver checked. "You made my stay a lot more bearable," she said.

"It was after I met you," I replied, "that I decided to stick it out after that shaky start. Thanks for everything."

Lunch was three pieces of shrimp on fettuccine and a leafy green salad. I had finished up and walked out to the parking lot to await Kirstin and the boys' arrival. I leaned casually against the split-rail fence, and presently saw a silver Honda Pilot coming from the east down 290 and slowing into the left-turn lane.

When they arrived, Kirstin and I did a quick exit interview with my case manager, then we walked through the house and I systematically told everyone I could find goodbye. I didn't want to be just another disappeared patient.

Mark was sitting in the doorway of his room. "I want to see pictures of you in a few months, swole like you used to be," I said, and reached for a knuckle punch. He softly obliged.

"I'll always be your nemesis," he said through a smile.

Making sure my sons were out of earshot, I pointed to his chair and mumbled, "Take care of the Pornmobile."

Rachel and Tamika were in the back living room. Tamika reached for a hug, and I eagerly obliged. I then hugged Rachel, looked her in the eyes, and said softly and earnestly, "Caca de Chim-Chim." I turned and left before the tears could come.

Jesse was the last person I saw at the neuro-rehab center in Dripping Springs, an appropriate bookend to that first night when he was shouting "Left, two, three, four!" and laughing crazily at a person he had never met before. He mumbled and stuttered something I could not understand, and then he handed me his Houston Astros baseball cap. "I washed it," he said.

It was perhaps the most meaningful gift anyone has ever given me because it was the only thing he could give. I tried it on, and it was much too small, so I turned and handed it to my son. Jesse handed Kirstin his phone, to which he had opened a new contacts page and asked her through gestures and stuttered Spanglish if she could put my number in his phone. She did.

I gave Jesse the Northside gang sign, resembling the American Sign Language symbol for "I love you." "Northside," I said and thumped my chest. Then I said it. "I love you."

He broke down again crying hot tears, face wrenched in pain. I wondered how long it had been since someone had told him that. "It'll be okay," I said. "I'll come back and see you." I meant it, but he knew better.

I walked slowly with my family down the long porch as Jesse struggled to get back inside the house with his wheelchair. I looked back at him before I turned the corner into the parking lot. "Love you!" he cried.

"You too," I reassured him, and then we were gone.

Ten minutes later we were pulling into Sonic to get me some celebratory tater tots and an orange cream slush. Once we had all given Kirstin our complicated orders, she pushed the order button and a voice exploded through the speaker, "WELCOME TO SONIC. ARE YOU READY TO PLACE YOUR ORDER?" It was so loud I almost had another seizure, and once I recovered from the shock, I doubled over in my seat, wheezing and laughing uncontrollably. "So loud!" I coughed, gasping for air and still laughing. "So loud!" That started all the boys laughing, leaving Kirstin alone to place the order. It was the laugh we all needed.

That night, being Good Friday, the last Friday of Lent, was the biggest night of the year for Catfish Parlour, the restaurant for which Kirstin worked as a part-time bookkeeper. Although I had never known this before, growing up Protestant and all, Good Friday is to fish restaurants what April 14 is to CPAs and Black Friday is to retailers. Kirstin had parlayed her job there into occasional work opportunities for our two oldest sons, and seeing sons work makes moms and dads happy and proud.

That night, I settled into my own bed next to Kirstin for the first time in ten weeks. "I love you so much," she said. "I missed you so much."

"I love you too," I whispered. "It's so great to be home." Then I tried to turn toward her, but instead backhanded her in the face with Pancho. There were many more things to relearn.

Part Three

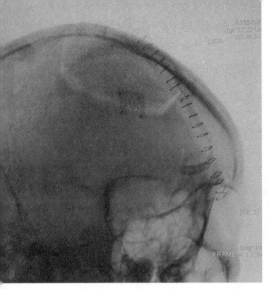

Post-surgical CT scan showing cuts in the skull and, at top, one of three titanium plates refastening the bone.

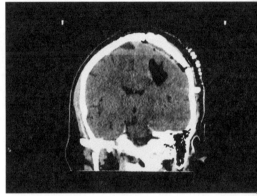

Follow-up CT scan one week post-stroke. The dark spot indicates dead brain tissue, but no blood. Note the staples in the top right of image.

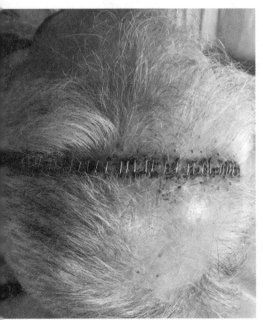

Week two, bird's-eye view. Photo: Ansen Seale.

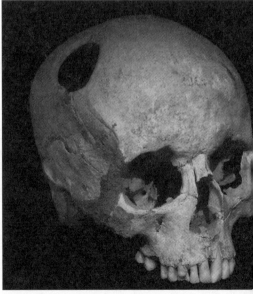

Trepanation of a fifty-year-old woman's skull, circa 3500 BCE, France. The rounded edges of the hole indicate she survived the surgery. More than 1,500 "trephined" skulls from the Neolithic Age have been discovered throughout the world.

CHAPTER 15

Home at Last

Saturday, my first full day at home, Kirstin made me breakfast. At ten we assumed our familiar Saturday routine with a trip to the acupuncturist, me getting needles twisted into my scalp, her napping peacefully on the short couch next to me. On the way home, we saw a man in his sixties power walking along the road almost at a jog. "That's a stroke," Kirstin said. "Look at his arm." His long, even strides were eating up the sidewalk, one step per section of concrete.

"Maybe that'll be me in a year or two," I said.

When we got home, with some help from Ian, I hung my olive hammock in its usual spot between two live oaks in the front yard.

Sunday was both Easter and April Fool's Day. I decided to try to walk down to where our street T's into a cross street called Hillside Oak. I didn't know if this rising on the third day home was more symbolic of Easter or of April Fool's, because it was probably foolhardy to make this first outing alone, but I needed to do it. Maybe the man we saw on the way home the previous day had inspired me.

The route I chose was one I had often used to walk Gracie and was six blocks total. Setting out with my black trekking pole, I immediately encountered my first challenge, getting around a neighbor's car, which was parked across the sidewalk. The trip around the car—down into the street and back up to the sidewalk—took about forty-five seconds.

As I came to the end of my block, I had to cross the main artery that ran through our neighborhood. Split Rail Parkway was a winding thoroughfare, and this section was right at a blind curve. I stopped and listened for about fifteen seconds for cars, and, hearing none but those on highways in the distance, I made my move, like a spindly, incredibly tall sloth might "make a move." At the midway point of the street, I remembered the exercise I had done at Dripping Springs, walking down a hallway as my PT would ask me to look to my left while continuing to walk, then look straight, then right, then straight. This was a real-world application with life or death consequences.

When I reached the other side, I stepped up to the next section of sidewalk, unleveled by large roots and immediately twisting and turning as it had been poured to circumvent a tree. I gravitated to the left edge of the sidewalk, I think subconsciously wanting to be near the grass in case I fell. This made little sense, because if I did fall, it probably would have been to my weak side, my right. It probably was a habit I had developed in the rehab centers as I always walked on the left to hold the handrail with Lefty or to hold the wall or just be near the left wall if I lost my balance.

By this point, I had to stop at every driveway to rest. I passed a house with an insane barking indoor dog, familiar from my many walks with Gracie. Shortly thereafter came the house where the red-tipped photinia came crowding in on me and branches of crepe myrtles arched over the sidewalk, forcing me to duck. Seeing these obstacles was tricky, because my eyes defaulted to the ground, and I heard in my head Kentucky Susan rebuke me. "You didn't use ta look at the ground when you walked, didya?" she would ask. "But ya didn't fall, 'least not very often."

As I walked, I would coax myself to look up, even if it was at the sidewalk fifteen feet ahead. "I lift mine eyes," I whispered. I knew it was a Bible verse but couldn't recall who said it or why they were lifting their eyes, but every time I found myself staring at my feet, I would say, "I lift mine eyes . . ." Turns out it was King David, and he was lifting his eyes to the hills, whence his help came. No hills around here, despite my goal being Hillside Oak, and no help today.

At last I reached the turnaround at Hillside Oak. I knew this would be my regular walking route, and I planned on timing myself as Jack had in Dripping Springs. So that I wouldn't cheat on future walks just to improve my time, I decided I would force myself clear to the curb cut before slowly scooching 180 degrees and starting back: low-hanging crepe myrtles, house of the barking indoor dog, around the tree, stop at the cross street, listen hard for cars, make the dash, back home to the cul-de-sac, up to the porch, through the storm door, and hitting *stop* on my phone's stopwatch. It had taken me fifty-one minutes to go six blocks. It was impressive only as a feat of endurance.

Funny—I used to walk every day chiefly as a means of brainstorming. From my earliest days as a newspaper reporter and columnist, I would leave my desk midmorning and circle a city park one block from my office. These walks would always produce the best ideas for my column or provide the breakthrough angle or the clever headline I needed for my next story. It was as if my legs were pumping the ideas up to my brain. I could solve all the problems of the world on a twenty-minute stroll. On my one-hundred-mile hike a year earlier, I basically wrote a whole book in my head as I wound along the forest trail. Now when I walked, I could think about absolutely nothing but the mechanics of walking itself—foot placement, arm swing, balance, momentum, not falling, not falling, not falling.

That afternoon, we went to the movies to see *Black Panther*. I hung tough for most of the show, but at length my bladder began to signal to my brain that whatever was happening to the vibranium in Wakanda was of secondary importance to what was about to happen in my pants. The trip to the bathroom was slow, steady, and uneventful, but just as I came out of the restroom and headed back toward the theater, another movie let out, and I froze as dozens of people streamed past me as if I were a salmon going the wrong way in a river.

After our weekly Sunday night dinner at my mother-in-law's—a ritual I had not participated in since the middle of January—Ian helped me build a foot-powered nail clipper to cut the nails of my left hand. A scrap of heavy HardiePlank formed the base. We used rubber bands to hold the clippers in place. Setting the apparatus on the kitchen table, we then ran a string from the top lever of the clippers through a hole in the bottom lever and down to the floor, where it was tied to a board that functioned as a pedal. Though bulky, it worked well, and I posted a video of it in use. K's dad, a fellow strokee, commented it was a "million-dollar idea."

Then came a comment from a friend that I'll never forget, one that caused me to rethink my social media activity entirely: "Cool! The fun never stops!" Wow, I thought. I have done the impossible. I have sold a crippling 4.7-centimeter hemorrhagic stroke as "fun." I had not wanted to depress people by posting about all the struggles and garbage I had to put up with every day, but maybe I had gone too far in the other direction. Another friend commented on a video of me slowly walking out of a store with my cane: "Seeing how well you're doing makes me not so afraid of a stroke." No! I thought. A stroke is a catastrophe! Be as afraid of it as hell!

Monday morning was eerily like the morning of my stroke. The kids were getting ready for school. Kirstin was getting ready for work. The chief difference, of course, was that I was not getting ready for work. Soon, all the boys had finished their cereal and one by one left.

I stared at Gracie and she at me.

The house was quiet—so quiet. After the binging of the ICU and the binging of the rehab hospital's unstaffed nurse station and the closing doors and flushing toilets of the Dripping Springs house and the weekend milling about of my family, now, all was silence, hear-the-house-settle silence.

As I began to move around, Gracie was underfoot. Everywhere I wanted to go, there she was, usually sideways, like a roadblock, but sometimes head-on, just watching me with a quizzical look. My movements were so spastic and slow that she did not even recognize them as walking, but just stared at me, puzzled, until I said, "Bump!" our family's cue for her to kindly move out of our path.

It had been more than two days since I had hung my hammock. I had put on the tarp the previous day in case it rained, but I had not secured the guylines, and, like an object lesson in chaos theory, two of the guylines had become impossibly tangled with an elastic cord that hung loose from the hammock itself. The tarp was in such a state that it was no longer over the hammock and never would be until I untangled this bird's nest.

I got a canvas camp chair out of the garage and sat in it next to the hammock. There, I commenced slowly reasoning out the tangle, pulling on the loops, as I had learned to do from long experience, and *not* on the ends. The strands came free of each other in ten minutes, and I thought about what to do to keep the lines from getting tangled again. Normally, I would have just tied two taut-line hitches around other trees to secure the outer corners of the diamond-shaped tarp. The taut line was a "friction hitch" that allowed the line to be looped around some object, like a branch or a stake, and then fastened back to itself. The point of it was that, once tied back to itself, one could slide the knot up or down the guyline and it would hold in place, and therefore make the line taut. The knot required three wraps of the working end around the standing end of the line, the last of the three passing through a smaller loop above the first two.

Well, I thought, I'll never know until I try.

Ten minutes later, I was looking with pride upon the smooth, tight tarp, which I had secured with two taut-line hitches tied with my left hand and my teeth.

Moving home was accompanied not only by the familiar environs of the house and the rhythm of family life but with an unprecedented tsunami of doctor's appointments. A new long-term neurologist, a follow-up angiogram CT scan, an EEG to inform my anti-seizure medicine dosage, a neuropsychological evaluation to clear me to return to work and a follow-up appointment to get those results, and my acupuncturist, whom I now began seeing twice a week.

In addition, there were all the run-of-the-mill appointments I was now overdue for, such as my eye doctor and dentist and dermatologist. When I came down with flu-like symptoms, I went to see my family doctor—my GP, whom before the stroke I would have simply called "my doctor." Of course, he did not have any inkling about my stroke until he asked me to "hop up on the table" so he could take a look at my throat. As I struggled out of my chair and shakily climbed onto the examination table, I broke the news to him. "Yeah, so I had a stroke and emergency brain surgery earlier this year." Odd that I would need to tell my doctor something like that.

Anyway, it was almost immaterial whether I was capable of going back to work, because with all of these doctor visits, there would have been little time left to do any work. "A doctor a day keeps the apples away." That is the saying, isn't it?

My new neurologist ordered a CT angiogram, in which dye is pumped into one's veins. After warning me that I would feel a warm sensation, the techs evacuated the room to avoid radiation, and the grubby white CT scanner whirred into motion. The machine running the IV clicked on via remote control, and within five seconds I felt that warm sensation, first in my throat, then the back of my neck, then in my genitalia, and finally through my torso.

All looked as it should have. But the angiogram was only one of two reasons that hospital visit was memorable. Before we left, I succeeded in using a urinal for the first time since the stroke. It might sound silly, but it was a significant step back toward normality. No longer would every trip to the bathroom involve the time- and energy-consuming ordeal of getting my pants down with one hand, lowering myself to the seat, then shakily rising from a toilet that was nearly always too low, getting my underwear and pants back up and centered with one hand while somehow also tucking my shirt with the same hand. And if it was a step toward normality, it was also one back toward manhood.

Though I was no longer institutionalized, I was not by a long shot done with rehab. I began outpatient therapy with a company known as Rehab Without Walls. They had sent a case manager to interview me in Dripping Springs, and with about a ten-day break from therapy, I was now ready to start anew. Rehab Without Walls was a service in which one PT and one OT made home visits multiple times a week.

My new physical therapist, Anna, was an introvert who was all business on our first meeting and had little interest in my irreverent asides or attempts at humor. I think it was just extreme concentration. We began, as all rehab begins, with assessments, baselines against which progress would be measured in coming weeks. The Berg assessment was a favorite that by now I had almost memorized. I had done the Berg just ten days earlier with my last PT, to show the improvement I had made with her over her baseline measurements taken five weeks earlier. How long did it take me to turn in a circle? Could I hold my hand out in front of my face and then reach a foot farther? Could I pick up a pencil off the floor? (I could.) Could I stand with one foot in front of the other as if on a tightrope, then reverse it and put the opposite foot forward? (Not too well.) Could I tap the top of a footstool with my feet alternately eight times, and how many seconds did that take?

The next day was my initial meeting with my new occupational therapist, Debbie. She was blond, blue-eyed, two years younger than me, and about 4'11" in heels. I towered over her. Debbie was the very embodiment of positive extraversion. I would bet everything I own that she was a high school cheerleader, perhaps even college. She was also notably "swole," as my sons might have said, with a stomach flatter than Kansas and veins that showed in her bulging biceps and quads even at rest. Debbie and I began our time together by touring the house for potential challenges, benchmarking my range of motion, and me getting the first of many long talks about weight bearing and repetitions being the keys to success. "Weight bear, weight bear, weight bear!" she would cheer. When she spoke of exercise, she would speak not of reps of ten or twenty, but of reps that totaled in the thousands and tens of thousands.

The following day, I was to be fitted with a custom ankle-foot orthosis. I had worn an off-the-shelf AFO since early Dripping Springs days, but all agreed, even insurance, that a custom brace was the right call. We had been referred to an interesting man who I vaguely suspected created AFOs by day and fought crime as a superhero by night. Perhaps this was because he was a fit, bald, black man and I had just seen *Black Panther*, or perhaps it was because he had the coolest name of all time and one perfectly suited to a superhero: Malcolm Slade. In any case, if this was his cover job, then he had been fighting crime for thirty-two years. Malcolm told me he had felt called by "the man upstairs" to work in the field of orthotics.

"Oh wow," I said. "I thought this was a single-level building." Kirstin sighed, and Malcolm picked up long rolls of gauze impregnated with dry plaster of Paris. He dunked them in a bucket of water and began unrolling them around my foot and leg. Perhaps it was his earlier references to being "called," but there was something distinctly Christ-like about the scene, a faint echo of Jesus washing His disciples' feet.

As the cast hardened and dried over the next five minutes, it grew warm inside. Then he sawed it down the front with a jagged vibrating disc and took it off. He explained that he would use it to make a positive mold, and then use that to create the AFO, pouring plastic over it. I ordered a black one because I had seen one such orthosis at Dripping Springs and thought it would be funny to put a Batman logo on it. It would be ready in about a week.

On Thursday, the end of my first week home, I awoke, for some damned reason, at five in the morning, refreshed and ready for the day. I showered, then went back to bed until eight. When it was time to get up for real, I readied myself for my daily walk, wearing sweats and donning the air-cast to keep my elbow straight, my arm out of its "chicken wing" flexion pattern. It was 9:03 when I left, 9:24 when I reached Hillside Oak and took my split, and 9:43 when I struggled through the storm door and marked my finish time. I had beaten my goal, dropping eleven minutes in four days.

On Friday, the boys went on a Scout campout, leaving K and me alone in our own house for the first time in modern memory. Saturday, we headed to acupuncture. In keeping with Christian symbolism of the week, I acquired a stigmata from the needles in my palms to go with my crown of thorns. I think the doctor was becoming impatient for improvement and was getting aggressive. He put four needles in my scalp instead of the customary two. After the needles came out, we went to the dollar movie to see the Churchill biopic *Darkest Hour*. At home we dined on tamales, a gift from the guys at my office.

During my next OT, Debbie brought out Jenga blocks for me to start picking up with Pancho. After the workout I fed myself with my right hand for the first time—a fried, bready, cheesy concoction from a local pizza joint called a pepperoni roll. Anything is possible with the right motivation.

Thursday, we returned to pick up my AFO from Malcolm. He tested the black plastic brace on me, made a few marks with a white grease pencil, and retreated to his workshop, where he spent thirty minutes attaching hardware and Velcro straps.

Next morning was my second neurologist visit. When the doctor came in, he asked me a series of rapid-fire questions. At the time, I was down to two prescription medications: Keppra for seizures and Prozac for depression and possible motor return benefit. "I want to keep you on the happy pill till you're back at work. For the Keppra, I want to see an EEG. They'll set that up at the front desk. If there's weirdness, we'll talk; if there's no weirdness, we'll talk. I wanna see you in three months, 'kay? Tremendous." And in a flash, he was gone.

I scheduled said electroencephalogram, better known as an EEG, to see if I had any "weirdness," as he put it, also known as seizure risk. The test would be at a sleep center housed, oddly, inside a credit union. When Kirstin and I arrived, we were led down a long hallway lined with windowless bedrooms. I was instructed to lie diagonally on the bed so that my feet would not hang off, and I settled in for twenty minutes of uncomfortable scrubbing of my scalp. The technician pasted twenty-five electrical leads to the spots she had scrubbed on my scalp. I was an electric Medusa.

She got some baseline readings by having me open my eyes and stare at the ceiling, then close my eyes, then open my eyes, then close my eyes. At last we were ready for the test. She told me to close my eyes and keep them closed, then turned off the lights. She positioned a powerful strobe light directly over my face and told me that I would see a series of flashing lights, each one separated by ten seconds of darkness. The first bursts of light came at about half-second intervals. Each series of bursts of the strobe was faster than the last. As the bursts came faster and faster, my field of vision became a swirling kaleidoscope of colors and shapes, a psychedelic acid trip without the Jefferson Airplane. In doing this, they clearly were trying to induce a seizure, so it was strange that I don't recall emergency quantities of Keppra standing by.

After that, she said, "Okay, now I want you to try to take a nap." For about ten minutes, all was dark and silent, with the exception of her loudly rustling paperwork. When the lights came back up, I asked if she could tell when I was asleep.

"Oh, yeah," she said.

"I would guess about four times. Is that right?" I asked.

"I can't say," she answered. "I can't give you any of the results. Your neurologist will have to do that." One would think one had the right to know the activity of one's own brain, but one would be wrong. This was followed by the detachment of wires and fifteen minutes of scrubbing my scalp clean with warm water to get the paste out of my hair. She walked us to the front of the building, told us she would write up her findings, and wished us a good day, whereupon we left the credit union.

That Sunday, I returned to the Bahá'í Center for the first time since my stroke. I attended the adult class, the title of which was "Beyond Left and Right." The speaker made the case for the Bahá'í practice on noninvolvement in partisan politics and for breaking out of our comfort zones and looking beyond our own biases and media bubbles when it comes to hearing other points of view. It seemed to me that the health-care debate could use a heaping dose of such open-mindedness. Like so much else, we had become locked into partisan viewpoints on it: one representing free-market capitalism, the other, essentially socialism, with single-payer models. I confess that living with the chaos of the "free-market" model had made me more apt to choose the latter than the former, but I'd lived long enough to realize that the ideal probably lived somewhere between the two extremes.

How do we incentivize people to work? How do we make health care profitable without making it obscenely so? How do we create an actual system where information flows more seamlessly and where it does not fall to the patient to recreate the wheel at every step of the process?

On Monday, I wore my new AFO on my walk and as a result dropped my time to thirty-three minutes.

That afternoon, I received an urgent letter, which apparently was the "3RD AND FINAL NOTICE" to call a company that was a "partner" (subcontractor) of my insurance company. They wanted to speak with me immediately regarding the "injury or illness that required treatment on the date shown above." The contractor provided "subrogation services" to the insurance company, which meant the insurance company hired them to try to find anyone else who might be liable for the accident or injury or some other insurance that might be primary. "Please indicate whether the injury on January 19 was the result of a:

- Work accident or condition?
- Auto or motorcycle accident?

- Injury at home?
- Injury on property owned by another party?
- Assault?
- Illness or condition unrelated to an accident or injury?
- Product liability?
- Medical malpractice?
- Other"

All of this, of course, was automated; they had no idea whatsoever what my injury was. Once again, a subcontractor of my insurance company hadn't the slightest idea I had had a stroke nearly three months earlier or anything else about me. The burden of supplying information fell on the patient. Guilty until proven innocent.

In this one respect, it was very much "patient-centered care," because the patient was the only one through which all agencies communicated. Again and again, I was forced to observe to some unperturbed soul on the other end of the phone line, "It seems odd—even alarming—to me that you would not know this."

The reason for this phenomenon of unintentional "patient-centered care" throughout the health care sector (I no longer call it a "system") was a sort of fetishizing of privacy. In most instances this was well-intentioned, but it also served as cover for abject incompetence and putting the onus of coordination solely on the shoulders of the patient. Perhaps I'm just more resigned to the loss of privacy than others, but my attitude came to be, please don't worry about my privacy. Share away! Just don't make me go through this form one more time. What good is privacy if it means a lifetime spent filling out forms? To what end? You guys just sort it out yourselves. Plug into that big computer in the sky that's bound to have all this stuff anyway.

If Google and Facebook can do it without anyone even knowing, why can't massive health care agencies? If Facebook knows that I'm a male over fifty living in the Austin area who loves Jerry Reed and Planet of the Apes and that I'm having a birthday and that I have browsed online for AFOs and wheelchairs, why, in the name of Taco Charlton, can't my insurance company tell its own subcontractor I have had a stroke, when I have been telling them that repeatedly, and they have been paying through the nose for it, for three months?

Not only was I the only point at which these massive systems intersected, many were the times that I had to inform one department of a company what another department *of the same company* was doing. The departments themselves were communicating through me instead of with each other.

Being mad about such things did nothing to lessen a general sadness. I had been put on Prozac early on, ostensibly because studies had shown it was associated with increased return of motor function. At a minimum, it lifted my mood enough that I was able to imagine a positive future and so work a little harder to realize that future.

But even with Prozac, I was prone to sadness, especially in the morning. Maybe it was the disappointment, upon waking, that it was not all a bad dream, that it was still true. March had come, and every morning I woke up and it was still true. Now April had come, and it was still true. Maybe mornings were worse psychologically because it was such a struggle to ready myself for anything, such a hard shift from peaceful slumber to this drag of a life. The third Tuesday of April was one such morning. Anna showed up at the house for PT and knew it instantly from my red eyes, my mouth-breathing, my defeated posture. She suggested we go for a walk, and she didn't correct me once. She just walked with me. That was nice.

Late in the walk, my mood eased, and we did talk a little therapy. Anna was the mother of a toddler, and she said Virginia had many of the same motions and reactions I had. She did the stiff-legged "zombie walk," as I called it, and sometimes went into "chicken wing" with both arms as I did with Pancho, because I couldn't flex my leg without flexing my arm too. Her startle reflex was also dramatic like mine and sent her arms flailing.

Of course, she was a perfectly healthy two-year-old. The reason little Virginia and I were in the same boat was that we both lacked cortical control. Anna explained that when we are born, our actions are governed by our brainstem, the deepest, most primitive part of the brain. As we grow and the wiring in our brains begins rather miraculously to hook itself up, our neocortex begins to exert more and more control over the brain stem. Soon, loud noises don't send our arms flying up, arms and legs glide smoothly instead being jerky and spastic, and we find our balance. If we have a lot of cortical control, we can even disguise our true feelings.

This comparison between little Virginia and me cast the whole stroke in a different light. Instead of a degenerative catastrophe, this was generative event—a do-over. How long did it take a newborn to learn to walk? About a year. And to walk smoothly? Two or three. How long did it take before their startle response wasn't flailing? About the same. Instead of being permanently out of commission, maybe my arm and leg merely had been born again. No analogy was perfect, and I never harbored any fantasies of total "you'd-never-guess-he-had-a-stroke" recovery, but this did help frame the situation differently.

In about a week's time, I planned to make my first visit to work—a return to the scene of the crime. I scheduled the visit with Debbie, my occupational therapist, who would accompany me at last to my occupation. Then I realized that if it was my very first visit back, I would be able to accomplish almost nothing with Debbie because I would want to visit, and so would everyone else.

So I hastily scheduled another, preemptive visit. It was April 19, three months to the day since the stroke. Q1 of my new life was behind me. Kirstin parked the car near my building, and I walked over the uneven bricks warily, as college students, almost all of them looking at their phones, whizzed around me on the way from their sorority houses and condos to class. Down the familiar sidewalk and through the front door I went, then up three steps that the person who designed this building in 1961 never thought twice about. Up a floor in the elevator, a quick sip from the water fountain, and we proceeded down the long, snaking hallway toward my office. I heard the front door of the office open and close. It was a friend and coworker who had been there the day of the stroke. Surprised, she hugged me and her eyes filled with tears—gratefulness to see me but also, I imagined, a mixture of shock at the change in me and traumatic memories from that day.

When the office door closed behind me, I said loudly, "Now . . . where was I?"

Teresa had moved on to a new job, and I met her successor, Andrea. She could not have been more supportive, even offering to share her office with me if I thought my dictation might disturb others in the big room. This meeting marked a strange transition in my life: it was the first of many introductions to people who had never known me before the stroke. All they knew was the man before them now, a shaky, unsteady man made old before his time, a perpetually tired man, a struggling man, a man unsure of his place. To Andrea and to a long line of new colleagues who came after her, there was no past-Avrel, only stroke-Avrel.

I gave awkward one-armed hugs and made awkward conversation with most of my coworkers, a lot of nodding and smiling and just saying "Yeah," over and over again. Although I was willing—perhaps even eager—to recall the details of that day, understandably no one else was comfortable doing the same, opting for a lot of pleasantries about how great I looked, how good it was to see me, and me reciprocating about how great it was to be there and to see all of them. The visit served its purpose. It remained to be seen whether I could actually do the job.

CHAPTER 16

Turn the Page

When I arrived home from Dripping Springs a month earlier, it had taken me fifty-one minutes to walk a six-block loop. May 2, I did the same loop in twenty-six. Praise God—the wheelchair was in the garage collecting dust. In a recovery with a thousand shades of gray, this was a clear win, an unambiguous achievement I could cite and celebrate.

So it was very odd to have to get back into the chair for one night. *Wait Wait . . . Don't Tell Me*, the NPR news quiz, had traveled to Austin. It was a sold-out show on the UT campus, with more than 3,000 attending. The only catch was that Kirstin had bought our tickets shortly after the stroke with no idea what my mobility would be like. She had bought tickets in the handicapped row, which meant that I needed to ride in the wheelchair. Being back in the wheelchair for the first time in a month triggered all sorts of feelings. I again felt the awkward gaze of strangers I knew pitied me, and the feelings of fraud on my part, that I was taking the seat of someone who might have needed it more.

During my first week home, Kirstin and I began laying the groundwork for my return to work. This meant having a neuropsychological evaluation, which the university required strokees to have before returning to the bureaucratic salt mines.

Kirstin drove me to a nondescript office building. At the end of a long windowless hallway, we found the suite and slowly cracked the door. A tall, bald man with wire-framed glasses greeted us in the waiting room before we could sit down and invited us back to the testing room. Kirstin, whom he mistook for my daughter before being gently corrected, was not allowed to be present for the test, so she excused herself to run two and a half hours' worth of errands while the neuropsychologist put me through a battery of exercises and tasks, most of which felt familiar from my numerous "speech" evals. The one part that stood out was a section that seemed to simply measure acquired knowledge, Trivial Pursuit-style questions that didn't require math or spatial reasoning or any such in-the-moment performance; you either knew he answers or you didn't. "The two tropics are the Tropic of Capricorn and the Tropic of . . ."

"Cancer."

"Yes. About when was the fall of the Roman Empire?"

"476."

"Very good. About how long does it take the light of the sun to reach Earth?"

"I want to say seven minutes."

"Good," he said (though it is actually eight and change). He sat back in his chair. "Have you ever thought about going on *Jeopardy*?" ("Oh, I bet you say that to all your clients with brain damage!")

A month later, it was time to hear the results of the evaluation. As Kirstin and I again made our way down the narrow hallway of the psychologist's office building, his door opened, and I was suddenly face-to-face with a fellow patient from Dripping Springs, there with her husband and daughter. They had just finished getting her results from the same doctor. We smiled at each other, and I gave her a big hug. "What's goin' on?" I asked her cheerfully.

"I had a stroke," she responded, not remembering that was the entire reason I knew her at all. Her husband gently tried to correct her. She was embarrassed and tried to move on, smiling and waving and saying how good it was to see me. The lapse was sobering and caused me again to be grateful for what I had left. Glass half full. Glass half full.

In the office, the doctor greeted us, presented me with a four-page, single-spaced report, and prefaced it with a well-worn caveat—that there were multiple dimensions to IQ tests, and therefore anyone who referred to a single IQ number didn't really know what they were talking about. I had done very well on some parts of the test and not so great on others, which I had figured, and which certainly would have been the case even before the stroke.

The report began: "Mr. Avrel Seale is a fifty-one-year-old married, right-handed, Caucasian man with a history of a cerebrovascular accident (CVA) who is participating in a neuropsychological evaluation . . . When asked about current cognitive difficulties, Mr. Seale was unable to articulate any problems." Let's just pause right there. Was his point that I had no problems, or was it that I obviously had problems, so much so that I couldn't even articulate them? And did I still beat my wife?

It was the start of a long and florid document, one in which nearly everything was science-ized with inflated clinical jargon. "Mr. Seale ambulates with a trekking pole." Why on earth would anyone want to just "walk" if he could instead "ambulate"?

"He denied any difficulty with basic self-care tasks such as bathing, dressing, grooming, or hygiene." The report was full, not of "opinions," or simply thoughts, but of *denials*. "He denied consumption of alcohol in the past 16 years . . . Mr. Seale categorically denied any current or past use of illicit drugs or tobacco products, and he denied any misuse of prescription medications . . . He denied ever being terminated from a job . . . Criminal history is denied." As I read the report, I felt I was about to be sent up the river for perjury at any moment.

"His daughter, who accompanied him to the evaluation and provided collateral information, reported mild forgetfulness in him, but stated that his overall cognition appears to be close to his pre-CVA baseline."

I found this passage particularly entertaining, because you will recall that when we had first shown up at his office for the evaluation, he asked if Kirstin was my daughter. I told him no, that she was my wife, and, embarrassed, he corrected himself and we moved on. He then proceeded to write up the report referring to her multiple times as my daughter, and in a paragraph in which he was sitting in judgment of *my* memory. I was also amused at the notion that a "pre-CVA baseline" even existed for me to be "close to."

The report continued: "He has three offspring, ages 16, 14, and 11." (And apparently, a daughter, age forty-five, sired when he was a precocious and virile five-year-old.) Why have children when you can have "offspring," like an antelope or a mole rat? Now, when I introduce my kids, I no longer use boring words like "children," even if that does convey their humanness; instead I opt for, "This is Andrew, our senior-most offspring. Meet Cameron, the penultimate of our issue. And this is Ian, our terminal spawn. They all deny criminality."

"Mr. Seale arrived on time to the evaluation, transported and accompanied by his daughter. He presented as a well-nourished Caucasian man who appeared his stated age." (The phrase "well-nourished Caucasian man" has entered our family's lexicon in a big way, as in, "How are you doing this morning, honey?" "I'm one well-nourished Caucasian man, appearing my stated age! Thanks for asking!")

The term "presenting as"—in contrast to the far more boring term "is"—has gotten a lot of play around the house as well. "I'm presenting as a fifty-one-year-old right-handed Caucasian man. Who knew I'm actually a seventy-six-year-old left-handed South Asian woman." Like they say, presentation is everything.

Then we got down to the good stuff, the test results: "Intellectual abilities. (Gulp.) Global intellectual functioning was estimated to be in the high average range: 84th percentile." It was uncanny that thirty-five years after my high school graduation, I was still nailing a B average. "However, significant variability was observed across intellectual domains, thus rendering the full-scale IQ an unreliable indicator of overall ability. Verbal comprehension (98th percentile) and perceptional reasoning (94th percentile) were both estimated to be in the superior range and emerged as relative intellectual strengths. Working memory was average (50th percentile). Processing speed was low-average and emerged as a relative intellectual weakness (18th percentile)."

This last piece was no great surprise. I long ago accepted the judgment of my first-grade teacher, Mrs. Gime, who told me multiple times, and I quote, "Avrel, you are as slow as molasses in January." I might be as slow as molasses in January, Mrs. Gime, but one thing I am good at is remembering, and boy, do I remember you—your polyester pantsuits that smelled of cigarettes, your white hair piled high atop your head, the Catalina glasses that framed your cold, militaristic stare, your threats to make boys wear petticoats if they accidentally got in the girls' line, the punishment that eventually came to us all: five minutes standing "nose-and-toes" against the classroom wall, arranging us with a new seating chart every week—smartest in the front row, dumbest in the back, the phrase you used on my friend Stephen: "I may have to drive a railroad spike into the back of your head so I can pour some sense into it." Anyway, you were absolutely right, Mrs. Gime—I was slower than average to turn in assignments.

I suppose I was always more concerned with being right than with being fast, and as a result, I did not excel on exams. While my classmates were flying through their standardized tests, darkening bubbles as fast as their No. 2 pencils would travel, I was internally arguing both sides of any awkwardly phrased question or premise that was the least bit subjective, wondering about the people who had written these questions and what they were *really* asking, looking out the window and pondering the full implications of a question taken to its logical extreme—as a white-tailed dove preened on a mesquite branch. Time's up! Pencils down!

The neuropsych report contained this gem of a sentence under the heading "Language Functions": "There was no evidence of ideomotor, buccofacial or ideational apraxia." I don't know that I had ever encountered an eleven-word sentence in which I had to look up four words, but here are the fruits of my labor:

- Apraxia—the inability to perform particular purposive actions, as a result of brain damage.
- Ideomotor apraxia—a neurological disorder characterized by the inability to correctly imitate hand gestures and voluntarily mime tool use, e.g. pretend to brush your hair.
- Buccofacial apraxia—the inability to imitate facial movements such as blowing out a match or sucking through a straw. One with buccofacial apraxia can usually perform normally when presented with a real match or straw.
- Ideational apraxia—the loss of ability to conceptualize, plan, and execute the complex sequences of motor actions involved in the use of tools or otherwise interacting with objects in everyday life.

Once I read all of these definitions and examples, I could remember him testing me on these things. "Pretend you're blowing out a match," he'd say. "Good. Now, pretend you've just woken up and are getting ready for work. Describe how you would do that."

If I were to translate the sentence, "There was no evidence of ideomotor, buccofacial or ideational apraxia," into the *English* language, it would read: "The survivor can mime and act, maybe community theater, but certainly nothing Oscar-worthy. Also, he knows that you have to wipe *after* you go potty." Perhaps there is a reason I have never been hired to write for medical journals. But hey, you knew what I was talking about.

"Generally intact cognitive functioning was observed, with average or better performance in most domains assessed." Oh, do go on! "The lone weakness observed was in right-sided fine motor speed and dexterity, which is due to hemiparesis. Overall, Mr. Seale appeared to be making a remarkable recovery from his CVA. Given that he is less than 3 months status-post his injury, further recovery is certainly possible. His overall recovery will be optimized by ongoing rehabilitation efforts."

It had been less than forty-eight hours since the therapy that would have facilitated those rehabilitation efforts had been denied by my insurance company, once again, by someone who had never laid eyes on me. It fell to my new neurologist to fight to get me the therapy I clearly still needed.

Despite this quickly accruing history of insurance as a pain in my ass, and in Kirstin's ass, I did my best to try to see my situation from all sides. After all, when is a stroke "over"? Cancer is generally over when you get the six-month all-clear check. Heart disease is something to be managed long-term—diet, exercise, medication—but is not helped by intensive therapy.

But a stroke is never over; to say it is shuts the door on the possibility of further return, and some strokees report amazing new returns years after their insult. That being the case, how long should insurance companies be expected to write these very large checks? I'm not an unreasonable person. I do appreciate that this is an incredibly complex game, and that money isn't unlimited. And I understand cause and effect, and that me being on the dole means that everyone's premiums will rise, and therefore that at some level, it becomes a zero-sum game, that insurance paying my claims equals insurance denying the claims of someone else.

The morning after our rehab case manager called with the news that "re-auth" had been denied, Kirstin and I spent one hour forty-five minutes on the phone with my insurance company. At one point we were transferred into the phone tree to a place from which there were no valid options, forcing us to hang up and start all over by dialing the customer service number on the back of my insurance card.

When I say we were on the phone for an hour and forty-five minutes, I don't mean to imply we were talking to people for that long. We were mostly listening to the two songs that alternately made up their on-hold music. The two songs in rotation were both instrumentals, each about three minutes, and each terribly distorted.

The first was an easy andante, quarter note = 60, with a I, vi, IV, V chord progression in the verse and a chorus with a rising, sort of inspiring sequence that returned us to the spacious, syncopated groove of the verse. Think "Summer Breeze" without any royalties being paid to Seals and Crofts.

The second song was an upbeat jazzy number featuring a clarinet and chord changes that invoked game shows of the 1960s. When this song came on, I would say, "Welcome back to . . . *Authorized or Denied!*" When it was over, we circled back to the heavily distorted easy-listening soft rock.

It's not entirely fair to single out the health care sector for things that are endemic in every part of society. Back in November, two months before the stroke, I had excitedly bought tickets to a concert in Austin, a double bill featuring two of my favorite bands, the Doobie Brothers and Steely Dan. I had bought three tickets—for me, my son Andrew, and David. The show was for May 27, Memorial Day weekend.

Then, I had a stroke.

The concert was at an amphitheater adjacent to Austin's relatively new Formula One race track. After my experience at *Wait Wait . . . Don't Tell Me*, I thought the prudent thing would be to check with the venue to see if I could get mobility-impaired seating. I called the venue, told the young lady about the timing of the ticket purchase and the subsequent stroke, and asked her if an exchange was possible. "I'm so sorry to hear about that," she said sweetly. "I'm sure that's something that can be done. Unfortunately, all of that has to be handled by Ticketmaster. I have the number right here for you," she said helpfully.

Since I already had the tickets up on my screen for reference, I simply went to the Ticketmaster website, and there was invited to chat live with a representative. I typed in my question, restating everything I had told the woman at the venue, and hit enter. "You are number 35 in the queue," the robot responded. No problem, I thought. I'll just check Facebook and my email. In about fifteen minutes "Alicia" answered me. "Yes, we can absolutely do that. Unfortunately, that has to be done with a phone call to the 800 number."

"Okay," I responded. "Should I ask for you?"

"I am sorry, no, I am a chat agent and do not handle calls. Any agent will be more than happy to assist you . . ."

My skin had been thickened and my perseverance starched by innumerable calls to the insurance company and doctors' offices. I would see this through. Dutifully, I called the 800 number, and after a short time on hold I was conversing with another pleasant agent. The answer to my question was, yes, my tickets could be exchanged for mobility-impaired seating. There was a space in the handicap row and two companion seats with it. However, mobility-impaired seating was not available at the price of our current tickets. Despite the fact that I had already spent more than $200 for our three tickets, I was now informed that it would be another $20 per ticket to get mobility-impaired seats.

"I don't think I want to do that," I said. "You know, our seats right now are on the very last row, and this is an amphitheater, so does that mean that those are at ground level, because that would be just fine if they were. But if I have to climb a hundred steps to get to my seat, that would be bad."

"I'm sorry, sir, that's something you would have to ask the venue about."

"Well, they told me to call you."

With a flurry of I'm-so-sorrys he was gone, and I was right back where I started. Just as with insurance and doctors, there did not seem to be one person who could see the whole picture and therefore help me. Everything that possibly could be outsourced was, and non-integrated automation seemed to be the common denominators between the health care sector and every other customer service issue in our mega-state society. First-world problems, to be sure, but problems nonetheless. Moreover, why was I, someone already spending more than $200 for the farthest possible seats, being up-sold on the basis of having had a hemorrhagic stroke? That seemed unjust.

I received a phone call from the Stroke Institute at the Dell Medical School. Would I mind answering a few questions? "If there was a magic pill that could return all of your function tomorrow, and there was a zero percent chance you would die from it, would you take the pill?"

There was a long silence while I tried to figure out what the downside to this arrangement was. Finding none, I finally said, "Sure, let's take it."

Then she proceeded. "If there was a magic pill that could return all of your function tomorrow and there was a ninety-eight percent chance you would survive, but two out of a hundred people die in their sleep, would you take the pill?"

"Aha!" I said, "I see what you're doing. Hmm. Let's see. Hmm. Okay, yeah, I'd take it."

Then she raised the stakes again. "If there was a magic pill that could return all of your function tomorrow, but four out of a hundred people would die in their sleep from taking it, would you take it?"

A beat, and I said, "I think I'm out."

"Okay well, Mr. Seale, thank you so much for taking the time to participate in our survey."

"You're most welcome," I replied, "and good luck with that magic pill."

CHAPTER 17

All I Ever Need Is You

On the first Saturday in May, I decided to take a walk, not the six-block out-and-back I normally did, but the hike-and-bike trail loop, which, including the walk from my house to the trailhead, totaled 1.6 miles. I made the decision to do that loop about five minutes after I left the house. Had I made it before I left the house, I would not have worn a black shirt, and I would have taken half a bottle of water, but c'est la vie.

As I strode down the sidewalk toward the trailhead, I met a man coming the other direction who greeted me warmly and, without me saying anything about my condition, started telling me in a thick Chinese accent about his stroke. "I walk every morning," he said, "and now, eighteen years later, I can hold a bowl!" he said excitedly, as he awkwardly lifted his left hand up into a claw shape. I thought about the right-hand coordination required to play Jerry Reed's "Stump Water" or "Swingin' 69," and how excited he was to hold a bowl *after eighteen years*. "Great!" I said with an enthusiastic smile, but I was sobered.

He also said he was here visiting his sister. He had moved to Southern California years earlier, because after the stroke, when he was forty-eight, he could not handle cold weather. His limbs hurt. All that said, he looked otherwise healthy and happy, in fact, young for sixty-five.

On May 8, I sat at my desk at home and was interviewed for the *Shattered Reality!* podcast I was preparing to do when the stroke struck. Interestingly, the stroke didn't come up at all. It was refreshing to be doing something, anything, that had no relation to the stroke. For an hour and a half, I lived my old life, only occasionally stuttering or searching a moment too long for just the right word. A month later, I did a phone interview about *Monster Hike* with a talk radio host in Kansas City.

Monday was to be my first day back at work, but I had started the process of wrangling forms too late; human resources had not yet given me the green light, so Monday was another day home alone. I hastily texted my therapists, Anna and Debbie, to see if they wanted to work with me Monday morning. One could and one could not. After PT, I spent forty-five minutes on the phone with HR and my neurologist's office trying to get the two to communicate so that I could go back to work.

Now, I had the rest of the morning to fill. I had been wanting to do something special for Kirstin for some time but had not yet gotten the momentum to do it. Mother's Day, the previous week, would have been the ideal time to do it, but I had not acted. Perhaps late was better than never.

There was a jewelry store about a mile away, but it wasn't just any mile; it was six blocks to get out of the neighborhood, then another third of a mile along and across Ranch Road 620, a busy state highway that fluctuated between four and six lanes, across a Fuddruckers parking lot, across the Lakeline Mall entrance, and into the store. I could have just called for a Lyft, but there was something about walking there to accomplish it that I hoped would make it more meaningful to me and to her, maybe the way pilgrims walked on their knees as penance for their sins.

I was half a block away from the house when my trekking pole began collapsing, telescoping down little by little until it was fit to support only a small child. As I could not re-extend it or lock it down, I turned around and hastily returned to the house to get the other one of the pair, then set out again on the long journey to escape our subdivision. As the crow flies, it would have been less than a fifteen-minute walk to the store, but I am not a crow, and so I girded my loins for an hour-long trek.

In about twenty-five minutes, I reached the traffic light that marked the exit from our neighborhood. There, cars whizzed along Highway 620. A large yellow diamond-shaped sign across the intersection showed a stylized man walking, the kind with the perfectly round head and no feet or hands, and a large "busters" symbol through it. Could there be a more perfect symbol of our car-dependent society than a sign actually prohibiting walking?

This was my last chance to call a ride-share service, because if I went any farther, a car would not be able to pick me up unless it spotted me on the side of the road. It was fourth and long, but I decided to go for it—to turn right and make the foolhardy journey along Highway 620.

I would find the most level ground I could in the grassy easement between the asphalt and the half-mile stone wall that defined the neighborhood. I had gambled and left the house without a hat because a hat holds in heat, and it was quite cloudy outside. Now, of course, the clouds parted, and the sun beat down on me mercilessly.

I thought long and hard about jaywalking, as taking the hypotenuse of this right triangle I was tracing would have shaved ten minutes, but I considered my wife and children, and thought better of it, and set my sights on the traffic signal at Pecan Park Blvd. At last, I arrived at the intersection. Before me lay five lanes of eastbound traffic, a median about forty yards wide, then two wide lanes of westbound traffic, and on the other side, like a beacon, yon Fuddruckers.

As I hobbled into the jewelry store with my black AFO around my calf outside my pants, leaning on my pole and bathed in sweat, I sensed alarm moving through the sales staff. (Angels and ministers of grace! Who is this guy and what is wrong with him?!) Understandably, it didn't even occur to them I might be a customer. A salesman moved toward me quickly and asked if I'd like to take a seat. I enthusiastically accepted. He then disappeared to the back and returned moments later with a bottle of cold water before asking how he could help me. At length, after finishing the bottle of water, I got K a bracelet, then called a Lyft for the ninety-second ride home.

The following day, I lay in the hammock, on a beautiful spring afternoon, completely miserable. Although I had made much progress, it seemed undeniable that I would never really be the same again. It's one thing to know it in theory; it's another to know it in your bones. Alone with my thoughts of hopelessness, I went down a deep rabbit hole, mentally cataloguing all the many things I probably would never do again.

But after about fifteen minutes, something inside me snapped. I struggled to sitting, got up, and put on my AFO. I then proceeded to mow the yard for the first time, front and back. To do this, I used Lefty to rig a short bungee cord that would hold the handle-mounted throttle down so the motor would not shut off if I lost my grip. Soon, all three boys appeared in the yard, dispatched by their mother to see if they could siphon away some of the work. But my newfound help only stoked the fires of my ambition, and I directed the boys to collect sticks and yard trash, and I asked Ian to put them in the fire pit and burn them.

For more than three hours that day, I worked in the yard. I was hitting back against the stroke, winning back a piece of my old self. As I began to wrap up the yard party, I felt alive, sweaty, and the kind of good tired you feel after a day well spent outdoors. I was glad I had mowed, because dark clouds were closing in. I banged on Cameron's bedroom door and asked him to come help me again in the front yard for a minute, coiling up the extension cord and getting yard tools back in the garage. I was coming back up the sidewalk toward the porch when my entire field of vision went white as lightning struck less than a quarter mile away. I thought a bolt of lightning had succeeded in inducing a seizure, even as the EEG a few weeks earlier had failed. One second later, a deafening thunderclap nearly startled me off my feet, and my right arm shot up in a wild fit of clonus tremors.

When I told my PT, Anna, about the episode, concern spread across her face, and she felt compelled to give me some sort of professional advice. "Well . . . I guess I would say, don't put yourself in a situation like an electrical storm," said the woman twenty years my junior.

"Okay," I said with a belly laugh. "I'll try to remember that!"

Even as I hit back against the stroke, it was an uncomfortable balancing act— doing therapy, doing things to help around the house to pull my weight, and doing things I actually liked—things that kept my soul alive and my spirits up. I didn't always get that mix right.

On the one hand, all the conventional wisdom held that the earliest rehab paid the largest dividends, and since life was a zero-sum game, every minute I spent on something other than prescribed therapy, like working in the yard or taking out the trash, was a minute I was not doing prescribed therapy. Kirstin established a family mantra, which was, "Dad's recovery is our family's highest priority." The boys bought into this to a large degree, but they were still boys, and the fact of my stroke did not miraculously give them adult perception about what needed to be done to keep our house and yard respectable, and I did not want to just reflexively start asking them to do chores every time they came into view; that would have colored my relationship with them permanently, and not in a good way. Nor did I want Kirstin to feel like she always needed to be the heavy. So I tried to pull my weight in the home, even when Kirstin clearly would have preferred me doing what looked more like therapy instead.

On the other hand, it was largely a matter of an old dog and new tricks. I never liked working out for its own sake, ever. I could count on one hand the times I had been to a gym before the stroke. I wasn't a jogger. Not a yoga practitioner. I enjoyed being active if there was some point to it other than a health benefit. I could hike a hundred miles in a week if I was looking for something, or even just to see some sights. I could spend fourteen hours a day working on a home improvement project or building a raft. But I simply could not muster the will to spend hours a week for many months on end doing something both exhausting and soul-crushingly boring. It wasn't in me.

All that notwithstanding, I was trying, and judging from the reaction of my therapists, trying much harder than most neuro patients. Nonetheless, I always fell short of the prescribed amount of therapy homework, always carried the guilt of doing two sets instead of three, or forgetting a whole set of exercises, or missing a day altogether. Guilt piled on top of grief.

It was hard enough mustering the will to work on things that *were* coming back, such as my walking and range of motion in my shoulder. What I could not muster any excitement for was spending hours a week on therapy for things that showed no signs of improvement.

Which brings us to Pancho. The most vexing part of recovery continued to be extending the fingers of my right hand. If there had been any progress there, even a scintilla, then I would have done it. But there was zero progress on this front. Maybe that part of my motor strip was just gone and never coming back, underwater too long. My neurosurgeon told me that there was as much brain matter devoted to the leg and foot as to pointing and curling just the index finger. This started to explain why I had been walking for some time but Pancho was still mighty quiet. One therapist after another spoke of my hand being "next," as if its comeback was inevitable, and offered the comfort that recovery progressed from the core to the shoulder, then down the arm to the hand and, finally, fingers. But as the months wore on with no sign of life in my hand, it grew harder and harder to keep driving down what appeared to be a dead-end street.

My principal attempt to revive my hand was a spring-loaded glove introduced to me by OT Debbie. The best way to describe both the device and the experience of using it is to explain the donning, the process of putting it on:

Picture a Roman soldier. Now zoom in on his forearm. You know the guard that extends from the wrist to the elbow? Make that blue plastic and cut a large slot all the way down its length, then force your arm through the slot and into the arm guard. Reach with your hand all the way to the outer edge of the piece and thread two large Velcro straps through buckles, pull taut, then secure them by doubling them back on themselves. Breathe deeply and remember that you asked for this device. At this point the rest of the apparatus will be dangling loosely around your hand.

Next, place the five plastic thimbles called DigiCaps on each fingertip. Debbie called this portion of the donning "Wrestlemania," because Pancho no want to go quietly into DigiCaps. DigiCaps bad. Pancho want do something else—anything but this. At this point, I always stood and breathed deeply as this would relax Pancho enough to give Debbie a fighting chance. Once each finger had donned its own sporty plastic helmet, each and every one was strapped in with its own Velcro chin strap. Next? You guessed it, more Velcro: one strap went across my palm, through a buckle, then back on itself to snug my hand against the plastic back piece. Another strap went down the inside edge of the forearm piece, made a loop around my thumb, then crossed beneath my wrist and up to a waiting square of Velcro near my pinky knuckle.

When all of this was done, I lifted a spring and hooked it onto a C screw. The bottom end of the spring was attached to five metallic bead lines that had to be adjusted every few uses. The bead lines attached to what appeared to be deep-sea fishing line that ran through metal eyes on the back-of-the-hand piece before angling down to attach to the DigiCaps. Finally, a smaller spring pulled up the thumb, tethering it to the Roman forearm guard.

If you're exhausted from reading that, well, now it's time to get to work! And that means "poof balls." The object of this exercise was to grasp one of the four-inch balls with the glove, move my arm over a bucket on the floor, then relax and let the spring-loaded glove pull my fingers open releasing the ball, then do it another ninety-nine times.

Each ball was two colors, which reminded me of sports teams, so I narrated with a nonstop stream of sports references. First time through the set of six balls would be a simple recitation of the teams each ball represented to me: Rockets, Spurs, Raiders, Clemson Tigers, Broncos, Seahawks. The next time through, it was a player from each team, often separated by decades: James Harden, David Robinson, Peyton Manning, DeShaun Watson. The next bucket might be play-by-play commentary: "Harden draws the foul—plus one." "Ginobli from the corner!" ... "Elway looking deep ... " ... "Kenny Stabler scrambling" ... "Tony Parker—downtown *for the discount!*" When a poof ball would get away from me, which was often, a "loose ball foul" was called by me on myself. And every time we emptied the six balls out of the bucket back to a box on the table, Ian or Kirstin would make another hash mark on a little chalkboard. Seventeen buckets was the goal.

I had high hopes for the glove. I'm sure it has worked for some, perhaps many people. Maybe had I done tens of thousands of reps instead of merely thousands, it would have made a real difference, but I can't say it did, at least not as of this writing. It did provide some nice family time, though.

May was the month of awards, and as we prepared to go to Cameron's eighth-grade academic awards, I slowly dressed myself, and, having spent more than ten minutes trying to button my shirt, I finally asked for K's help getting the last button. Then her bra hook had come loose, and she, in turn, now needed my help getting it fastened. "Hmm," I mumbled, "I've never had to get one of these *on* with one hand before." She laughed.

Mid-May is also fully summer in Texas, and I decided to do a couple of summer-related things I had not attempted since the stroke. The first was to wear a pair of flip-flops. This might not sound ambitious, but getting a flip-flop on a mostly paralyzed foot takes the patience of a Zen master. Once it was on, though, I managed to keep it on surprisingly well.

The second goal was to go swimming. It was not my first time in a pool; I had been four times during rehab in February. But it was my first time with any exercise of free will. We chose a neighborhood pool that had a gradual "beach" entry, and I used a bamboo trekking pole to steady myself. Andrew, by then a Red Cross-certified lifeguard, stayed within arms' reach of me at all times.

As I set the pole near the pool's edge, Andrew held up the strand of buoys that divides the shallow end from the deep, and I passed under. I took a deep breath and fell forward into the water, stroking, as it were, with my left arm, my right arm limply dragging through the water. I had set my sights on a point at the opposite edge of the pool, but, of course, immediately began curving sharply. I was reminded of the sea turtles we visited periodically at the rescue center on South Padre Island, many of which had lost a flipper or two and therefore could only swim in a circle. For some of those turtles, they had designed an ingenious rudder that strapped to their shells. Perhaps they could design one for me too.

After a few failed attempts at this, I tried backstroking, which worked quite well. I could breathe at will and could hold my line surprisingly well. I quickly decided that the backstroke would be my go-to stroke if I ever willingly or unwillingly went swimming.

At four months and five days post-stroke, I decided to enter the back-to-driving program I had learned about when I was at Dripping Springs. There was only one return-to-driving program in all Central Texas, and it was located at St. David's Hospital, just north of the university campus. Like all things, it started with an evaluation.

Enrolling in this program meant that I was entering a whole new hospital system. The gentle reader will recall that I had my stroke five minutes from three different hospitals. Two of those hospitals were in the Seton group, and I had been multiple times to both of those, both on the day of the stroke and for follow-ups and CT scans. Now I was turning the hat trick by applying for therapy in the third and unrelated hospital.

As Kirstin drove us downtown to St. David's, I called my mother and put her on speaker. She had been trying to get ahold of me for some reason or another and was headed to the airport later that day to visit friends in California. We had chatted for fifteen minutes about this and that before she took a deep breath and said, "Well, you might have already guessed this, but John and I are getting married. It'll be here in McAllen, around Thanksgiving." I had not guessed that but was happy for them. He was kind to his core, the embodiment of a gentleman. It would be a good Thanksgiving.

We were told to arrive thirty minutes early for our 9 a.m. appointment to fill out paperwork, and boy was there ever paperwork. I was starting all over. No one knew me from Adam. The receptionist handed me a clipboard *and* an iPad, then told me how to go about scrolling through each of the disclaimers and waivers totaling well in excess of a thousand words, initialing some pages, signing others with my finger, hitting the "next" button. The first question after my name and birthdate and insurance, was "What brings you in for therapy today?"

"A stroke," I scrawled with my left hand.

"What are your therapy goals?"

"To drive," I wrote in jagged print, summoning all of my patience. In a room near the lobby, I met Jennifer, my instructor. Near my feet, she arranged a mock set of driving pedals. She told me to hit the gas with my right foot and then timed my reaction for braking. There would be no return to normal driving for me, at least not now.

Fortunately, there was adaptive equipment that allowed people like me with hemiparesis to drive with their left foot. We proceeded outside and loaded into a small SUV. She drove us to a nearby strip center, where we switched places. I took to driving with my left foot much quicker than I expected to. After nearly five months of not driving, cruising through a parking lot at ten miles per hour felt as freeing as piloting a fighter jet. I did well enough that she asked me to drive us back to the hospital via neighborhood side streets. There, we made plans for three more sessions to complete my training.

On Saturday morning, I awoke at first light and decided to walk to see Andrew compete at a swim meet at our neighborhood pool a little less than a mile away. When I got there, the meet had been delayed because of a Code Brown. Yes, that means that someone, hopefully one of the youngest swimmers, had pooped in the pool. After the swim coaches applied gigantic scoops of chlorine to the area of the pool in question, the meet got underway.

I had three goals that day. The first was to walk to the pool. The second was to see Andrew swim. And the third was to carry my hiking chair there in a backpack, set it up, sit in it, *get out of it*, pack it up, and walk back home.

A children's swim meet at a neighborhood pool would have been rated an advanced community mobility outing at the neuro-rehab center—hundreds of people crammed into a fence-enclosed area, excited children without a care in the world darting in front of you while laughing with friends. Uneven surfaces including grass and wet concrete. Pop-up tents. Loud pumping music, a deafening PA announcer and starting buzzers that can scare the life out of you, indiscriminate screaming and squealing. There are many good reasons it is not where one would expect a recent stroke survivor to be spending the morning.

There were a number of volunteer positions that saintly parents like Kirstin filled to make these meets run. There were lane timers, of which she was one. There were concessions volunteers. Some manned the check-in table, some organized the ready bench, and some were stroke judges, whose job was to disqualify any swimmer whose stroke departed from acceptable standards. When I got to the pool, I asked Kirstin if I could be a stroke judge, as I was now eminently qualified. "Good one!" she shouted from her lane-timer position.

Keeping my forced-function therapy goals in mind, I retrieved my hiking chair out of my backpack and at length was able to stretch the canvas seat over the frame. I carried the chair and my trekking pole with Lefty to a grassy spot between the ready-bench and a high chain-link fence. I squatted carefully over the chair and eased into it. When I had made contact with the seat, I relaxed my legs and went all the way back, then kept going and kept going and in one and a half seconds was sprawled on the grass. The soft, wet ground had put up no resistance to the chair's back legs. In any other setting, there would have been three or four alarmed Good Samaritans attempting to help a crippled man up off the ground. Here, in this sweet chaos, no one thought twice; I was just one more person sprawled on the grass, as "Happy" blared over the PA speakers.

I used the chain-link fence to struggle to my feet, then bought a breakfast taco and a cup of coffee and sat in the camp chair Kirstin had brought as I broke down the hiking chair and tried to get the mud off its legs. When I had watched Andrew swim his first race, I decided it was time to get home before the sun got any higher in the late May sky. As an added therapy challenge, I decided I would try to carry my empty Dunkin Donuts coffee cup with Pancho all the way home.

About a block from the pool, an old man I had never met saw me hobbling along with my cane and came shooting out to the sidewalk to share the story of his quadruple bypass fifteen years earlier. After telling him multiple times how great he looked for eighty-nine and how great his yard looked, I finally just had to excuse myself. I had to get home, I said, and sit down in some air conditioning. "I'm retired military," he continued undeterred, "thirty-five years in the Marine Corps. Retired as sergeant—"

"That's great," I assured him and hobbled away as briskly as I could. "See ya soon, John!"

I dropped the empty coffee cup about seven times on the walk. Finally, I figured out that if I gripped it upside down I had a better chance of holding onto it if my arm hung by my side. One especially unfortunate outcome of the stroke was that Pancho, if I wasn't actively doing something else with him, gravitated directly to my crotch. This was a cruel irony, because I had always loathed the crotch-grabbing habit increasingly common among hip-hop and pop stars, and now I defaulted to it everywhere I went. With my newfound technique of holding the coffee cup, I now looked like the Michelin Man who had shed all of his costume except his bright white codpiece.

When my six-week authorization for therapy ran out in mid-May, we figured that my insurance company would deny our request for further therapy, and indeed it did. The rehab provider appealed the decision without our even requesting it. When I called my neurologist to ask about something else, his assistant said he had just finished another peer-to-peer conference. They were now denying treatment options Kirstin and I were not even requesting, as if for sport. Moments after I hung up with my neurologist, my insurance "telephonic case worker" cheerily rang in. How was I doing? Apparently, I *sounded great!*

I asked if she could clarify who had requested the therapy that was being denied? The form she was seeing didn't show the provider.

"What?!" I asked. She went on to explain that she was limited in what she could see, and that the people who could "see more" and might be able to answer our questions were in Utilization Management.

I don't mean to seem unkind—to a person, to a company, or to an industry. But there was something about this particular situation that seemed intentional. That a company would ask us to form a relationship with someone who then could not speak for that company seemed like a colossal distraction, a deliberate attempt to placate me while doing nothing to address my real concerns. We could send a probe beyond Pluto, but information within a single company was so cumbersome and siloed as to be unnavigable. It seemed like no more than a cynical attempt to run out the clock, to make me deal with so many individuals and so many departments that I would finally just give up rather than fight. It was unmistakably their business model, and although I'm sure all of the individual players were perfectly nice people just trying to feed their own families, the system itself seemed sinister. Someone in some conference room had decided this was the most profitable way to deal with patients.

St. David's had tried to get preauthorization to cover my driving sessions, and those too were denied. It would be seventy dollars per session out of pocket, but if I could get back to driving, that would be the best money I ever spent.

About three weeks into my stroke, I had asked Kirstin to bring my guitar to the rehab hospital. From there, it had made the trip with me to Dripping Springs. But the three or four times during all those weeks I had picked it up were desperately sad occasions—a few spastic bashes of the guitar's body with Pancho as I tried to even position the instrument under my arm, and that was about it.

Now at home, and with my mental and physical stamina steadily returning, I figured I was ready to give it another shot. For half an hour, I tried everything I could think of. Standing, sitting, with a strap, without a strap, with thumb-pick, flat-pick, no pick, with a wrist brace, without a wrist brace. Nothing worked. Nothing would even allow my arm to get into a position to begin to strum the guitar. When my right-hand fingers did contact the strings, they only deadened them, as if to make the point even more emphatically: this part of my life, one of the biggest parts, was over.

As I lay on the bed, tears began to spill down my temples as the realization began to sink in, and within a minute, I was weeping like a man in physical pain. My chest heaved. "Oh God!" I cried out, "I just want to play! . . . Oh God! I just want to play!" I cried for thirty minutes, then rose, donned my spring-loaded therapy glove, and transferred a hundred poof balls from their box to the bucket. Then I collapsed with my head on the table and heaved sobs in front of the whole family. This was followed by a shower, where I continued crying for twenty more minutes.

That night, I dreamt I had spontaneously begun playing the solo to "All I Ever Need is You," a Ray Charles song covered by Jerry Reed and Chet Atkins. In the dream, I knew I had had a stroke, and was astonished and overjoyed that I was now playing my guitar as if nothing had ever changed. I was back, baby! Then I awoke, and, of course, nothing had changed. I could not figure out if dreams like these were gifts—brief bursts of virtual reality—or a form of torture; the realization that they were only dreams was almost too much to bear.

I had the thought that perhaps in the afterlife I would be able to play normally again. This thought frightened me, for I was having a hard enough time struggling through each day in this world without something like that beckoning me toward the next. I would not say I ever became suicidal after the stroke. I knew I could never go through with it. Apart and aside from what it might mean for the state of my soul, it would be the worst thing I could do to everyone I loved. But I came to understand the temptation as I never had before, the temptation to no longer wake up to sadness.

But I could not stay away from the guitar.

At my desk, and now through my amplifier, I started to once again pry some music out of its six strings with only Lefty. On May 3, I posted the first video to Facebook of me playing guitar, with the caption, "Just trying stuff." I used my electric guitar, the butterscotch Telecaster, and just played a random assortment of blues licks and single-string jams.

A few days later, I arrived home after an errand to find an Amazon box on the front porch. Ed had bought me a new looping pedal for my guitar. Looping pedals are a little like multitrack recorders you can perform with; you can play a section of a song, then press the pedal with your foot and the section will repeat, allowing you to play over it, adding layer upon layer. I tried a few songs with it, including a signature riff from *Jesus Christ Superstar*, Yes's "Owner of a Lonely Heart," and Chicago's "25 or 6 to 4," and got a take that was far from perfect but good enough to post.

Then I had a powerful realization: If someone had told me in the moment of the stroke that I was about to lose one of my hands and asked me which one I wanted to sacrifice, I would have picked the left, of course. I was right-handed. Now, months later, I realized how lucky I had been. Sure, my handwriting looked worse than a first grader's, but I could still play guitar. Had the stroke taken Lefty instead, Pancho could have fingerpicked the most fantastic patterns ever heard, but it would be all the same open chord, and how do you make a song out of that?

I guess I would have taken up the one-handed harp.

CHAPTER 18

Working Man

On May 15, just less than four months after the stroke, I returned to work half-time. This meant full days on Mondays and Wednesdays and a half day on Fridays. But first I would need to get there.

Getting to work started with Kirstin dropping me at the bus stop, as I could not drive yet. The first difference I noticed in my routine was how often I would miss the bus, usually by just seconds. For one thing, before the stroke I frequently would jog from my truck to the bus or from the office to the bus to make certain that I caught the very next one. Had I walked, I would have missed a number of them back then as well. In the old days, if I had just missed my homebound bus on campus, I sometimes would sprint full-out the three blocks to the next stop and catch the very same bus. Whereas before if I was thirty feet from a bus, I could make up that ground in five seconds. Now, the same thirty feet could take thirty seconds, and try as I might, I could not walk any faster than the most leisurely stroll of the able-bodied.

For another thing, each bus stop served numerous routes, and if a rider wasn't moving toward a bus with purpose, the driver assumed they were waiting on another bus. At this point I was moving so slowly, and without a cane or other visual cue, that drivers just assumed I was pacing, waiting on the next bus. Like Gracie, they didn't even recognize my walking as walking. Time and again, buses would pull away as I approached, sometimes from forty feet away, sometimes fifteen feet from the door. Over time I learned that waving my arms would help, although since I couldn't wave both arms, I think they sometimes read my wave as "Bye-bye!" "Drive safely!"

For the first three months at least, each time I narrowly missed the bus I threw a full-blown temper tantrum. "Shit!" I would curse as the bus pulled away. "*Shiiiiiit!!!*" Sometimes this was accompanied by flinging my baseball cap to the ground, then struggling mightily to bend over and pick it back up.

This would be followed by moodiness, and occasionally, outright tears of rage or frustration.

At long last, as a simple matter of emotional survival, I made a conscious decision not to worry anymore about catching a given bus. If one pulled away, I would be all right. There was always another coming. Eight, thirteen, twenty-one minutes—who cared? Like everyone else, I could while away hours if need be, cruising the internet on my phone, or heaven forfend, I could just stand there and think about life for a while.

Two kinds of buses drove my route, the flat bus and the coach. I had ridden both of these types for years but could not have articulated the differences. I sure could now. The flat buses were highly accessible. They "kneeled" with the front-right wheel to minimize your step in and out, and once aboard, there was a nice wide aisle to a section of handicap seats. The other buses, the coaches, did not kneel, had Angkor Wat-like flight of stairs just to get into them, and an aisle about eight inches wide that was cut like a trough in the floor. In the coach, the handicap seat was the front seat.

Each and every day, I learned to negotiate the emotionally loaded issue of who was entitled to sit where. Though there were multiple signs notifying passengers that the front two rows of seats must be given up for seniors or those with mobility impairments, in either type of bus, many people seemed unclear on the definition of those classes. At the same time, I learned to tread lightly with my own assumptions. I'm sure many people did not take me for a disabled man if I was just sitting there at rest. I had no cane, certainly no wheelchair, not always an ankle brace. It was not until I tried to rise to standing that I could read their thought bubbles, their silent exclamations of, "Whoa! That guy's crippled as hell!"

So, not wanting to make the same faulty assumptions about others that some no doubt made about me, I would not ask, "May I please sit there?" Rather, I would ask, "Do you require handicap seating?" at which point ninety-nine of one hundred would realize where they were, what I needed, and would disappear in a scramble of apologies.

I had been a man with plenty of flaws before the stroke, but one virtue I did have was that I was very deferential on a bus. For years, I had taken the next-to-last seat. Now I had to sit at the front. And I was rather old fashioned in that I would usually allow ladies to board first. Now they waited for the crippled man to board. Time was, if it was an especially full bus and people had to stand, I would offer my seat to a lady or to an older man and stand for the forty-minute ride home. Now, standing with one arm to steady me on a speeding, swerving, hard-braking bus would make me a top candidate for a Darwin Award.

Whereas I used to sit in the back of the bus and was usually the last to get off, now I sat in the front of the bus, but still waited for everyone to get off before I teetered my way to the door. This created an odd situation as I watched the same people parade past me day after day. Over time, I got to know them and they me, and so at the end of each day as we pulled back into the park-and-ride, I would remain seated and watch as they all filed past me, and I would nod goodbye to each one. I was like the Capital Metro flight attendant bidding everyone a pleasant stay at their destination. "Goodnight. . . . See ya . . . Bye now . . . Take good care . . . Have a great weekend . . . So long . . . Thanks for choosing Capital Metro."

When everyone was off, I labored to standing and picked up my backpack. Often, the driver would assume everyone was off and as soon as he or she closed the door I would urgently call out, "One more!" before the bus began to move again.

I mentioned the lack of a cane. A cane or walking stick was a great visual cue to those around me that I might need a little extra space and a little help here and there. Going without it put me in a no man's land, a twilight zone between abled and disabled. So why didn't I just use one? It was primarily riding the bus that made me give it up. Having one useless hand meant that every time I held a cane with my good hand I could do almost nothing else. It was difficult to grab the handle on the bus door and pull myself aboard while also holding a stick, and to reach for the rail when it was time to descend the steep stairs of the coach. Nor could I do much else once I was off the bus with a stick in my one good hand, like opening a door or carrying a cup of coffee or a plate from the kitchen to my desk.

One day, on my way from the bus stop to my office, I passed a man shoveling dirt on the opposite side of a chain-link construction fence, next to a storied campus bar called The Hole in the Wall. Bald, shirtless, the color of black coffee, in rolled jeans, heavily muscled not from a gym but from long days of old-fashioned work, he could have been an extra in *The Green Mile* or *Cool Hand Luke*. Our eyes met, and he walked toward me, taking a breather. "Where's your walkin' cane at?!" asked the stranger through the fence, almost scolding me.

"Don't need one," I called back, without breaking my wobbly stride. He raised his eyebrows as if to say, "If you say so," and went back to shoveling.

After my return to work, I had run into the dean of the medical school, reintroduced myself, and explained to him what had happened to me. I showed him my CT scan on my phone. "Wow," he said, "that's really high up. You're walking great for it being in that location! Lucky to be walking at all." So see, construction worker? The dean says I'm walking great!

In the few months I had been gone, the great urban scooter craze had descended on the campus, and getting from the bus to the office now had a whole new dimension of unpredictability and danger. Enabled by the convergence of apps, GPS, and credit cards, startup companies had dropped hundreds of scooters along sidewalks around campus and downtown literally overnight, and it was a high-tech Wild West. Students sped merrily along sidewalks, sometimes glancing up to see me at the last moment before swerving around me as I stood frozen with fear. And there being no consequence for leaving them in an inconvenient place, the worst of young-adult human nature was often on display: scooters parked across the sidewalk, requiring circumnavigation, scooters blocking front doors of offices. It was quite a scene to step off the bus and see. I felt like Rip Van Winkle awakening after twenty years. Flying hoverboards would have scarcely been more shocking.

Once, when I encountered a scooter blocking the sidewalk, I lifted it up with my left hand and heaved it off the sidewalk into a mulched bed. I got as much height on the toss as I could, and it landed with an incredibly satisfying crash.

Another interesting difference I noted in my return to the campus area was that the beggars now left me alone. Whereas before I would be solicited at least once on any walk along the western edge of campus known as the Drag, now street people would no longer even meet my gaze. I don't think they had any idea what was wrong with me, they just knew something was. ("I can't hit that guy up for beer money—he can barely walk.")

I sometimes wondered what I would think my issue was if I'd encountered my future self a year earlier. At a distance, I might just suspect extreme old age—probably somewhere between 105 and 110 years old. Close up, I likely would have assumed cerebral palsy or some other birth defect that caused my arm to curl up. I suppose in the final analysis I did have a birth defect—it was just one that took fifty-one years to manifest.

But my feeble condition could only hold the Drag's hot mess of humanity at bay for so long, and within a few months I again was being accosted by mentally ill homeless people and other folks who had decided to take a walk on the wild side. One poor woman, sunburned and wild-eyed, accosted me at eight o'clock one morning—"Can you spare a coupla dollars?!"—as I was trying to safely step off the bus. A young man smoking a cigarette and wearing a backwards baseball cap walked right up to me, looked me in the eye, and asked, "Can you spare a grand?" I tried to maneuver around him. "What if I told you that for two thousand dollars you could go to the Scientology building right there and be cured of your disability?" he asked, with a sinister, sneering tone I could not fathom.

"You don't know what my disability is," I said, adding, in the understatement of the decade, "and I'd rather not talk to you right now," at which point he moved off to shout mad ravings at someone else. I've never hit anyone, either in anger or self-defense, but situations like that made me wonder if I could even if I wanted to. If he had laid a hand on me, I would have certainly wound up on the ground, but not before I had gotten in the left hook of a lifetime.

Most work mornings I was utterly exhausted by the time I got to my desk. But within an hour, after some coffee and some sitting, I would perk up a bit.

I spent the first week attending meetings, explaining the basics of neurological recovery to colleagues in the staff kitchen, and deleting email that was long irrelevant. Everyone was exceedingly careful to not give me too much work too soon. For my part, I tried my best to dot my i's and cross my t's, in short, to prove to them I still had what it took to write for the communications office of a Tier One research university. I knew I was coming out of the woods on this front when they dismissed a freelancer who had been working on our homepage messaging and gave the project to me.

My experiments with adaptive technology were short lived. The Dragon speech-recognition software they had bought for me was buggy on my Mac, and I didn't have the perseverance to get it sorted out. I had used Google's "voice typing" tool, but it required so many style corrections that I found it easier to just hack it out with my left hand, as I did writing this book.

Meanwhile, I was becoming thoroughly accustomed to this part-time thing. Work never got old at twenty hours a week. And at any rate, at this point in time, going to work was really *practicing* going to work—getting there and back, getting into the bathroom stall and getting out of the restroom with my zipper up, staying awake and upright for hours at a time, and figuring out how to carry a full coffee cup from the staff kitchen to my desk forty feet away.

Coworkers could not have been nicer. Several times, colleagues who were feeling nervous or awkward asked me in a private moment, perhaps when everyone else had left a meeting, if I ever wanted help—not help writing, but just with logistical things. Did I like it when people held doors open for me or scooted chairs out of my way? Or did I *not* like that—resent it because it implied that I couldn't do it myself?

It was a minefield first navigated by my family, then my friends, and now my coworkers. My answer was always first and foremost to thank them for asking. I knew it was awkward, and so I appreciated the ones who just came out with it and cleared the air. The answer to the core question was that I would always ask for help when I truly needed it, and I did. More than once I had to break down and ask for one of them to roll up my left sleeve, which I could no more do myself than dunk a basketball from the free-throw line. It was an odd sensation—having a coworker do that for me, but not as odd as it had been two months earlier when my friend Stephen came to Dripping Springs to take me to dinner and had to button my pants for me before we left for the restaurant. At work, at least it was just upper-body stuff.

I struggled with the question of when to practice fierce independence and when to graciously accept help from others, because there is virtue in both, and, if carried too far, there is vice in both as well. Too fiercely independent and you become an ornery old cuss that people walk on eggshells around all the time. Accept help from everyone all the time and you come to expect it, and become soft, and resent when it doesn't happen. What I decided I absolutely could do, should do, and would do is be gracious. I decided I would rather live in a world where people held doors for other people than a world where they didn't—whether those other people needed the door held or not.

As I was struggling to get my burrito into the microwave in the staff kitchen, my cell phone rang. It was Hannah from Rehab Without Walls, and she was wondering if now would be a good time to ask a few follow-up questions.

As I had yet to hit the start button on the microwave and did not want to deal with a call-back, I acquiesced. "On a scale from zero to seven," Hannah began, "how satisfied are you with your life?" Wow. That was some cold open! I thought about Kirstin and the boys. That's a solid seven out of seven. But then, I was left by bus drivers three times yesterday because I couldn't walk fast enough to get on. That's a two. But at least I could walk, right? And don't get me started on how lame it is to not be playing guitar, one. But at least I've got my left hand, so that becomes a four.

She read on from the script: "On a scale from zero to seven, zero being, 'I would change almost everything about my life,' seven being, 'I would change almost nothing,' how much would you change about your life?"

Well, I would have drunk less in my twenties, in fact, not drunk at all. And there were some fashion trends I would steer clear of if I had it all to do again. But what does any of that have to do with how I'm recovering from my stroke?

I couldn't go anywhere or do anything anymore without being pestered to take a survey. The previous Saturday morning, I had gone to Whataburger for a cup of coffee and a pancake platter. The cashier handed me a receipt—no exaggeration—more than a foot long. Of course, it was that long because it was effectively a coupon for a free burger *if* I would take a quick survey about my experience. I wished everybody would take their surveys and their one-to-five Likert scales and stick them where the cross-tabulated data points don't shine.

It was good to see and hear from other colleagues across campus as well. A few had not heard the news of the stroke at all. When one acquaintance saw me walking through the student union, he said, "So it looks like you might have had a stroke."

"Yeah, I sure did."

"I'm so sorry to hear that. You're looking good!"

"Thanks—it's a little bit better every day," I felt obliged to say, even if that no longer felt true.

"Have you read *My Stroke of Insight* by Jill Bolte Taylor?"

"Have not read that yet," I said. "Heard a lot about it, though, a lot."

By the end of a work day, even a short one, I was spent. It did not help matters that I had to wait for the bus home in the direct late-afternoon Texas summer sun because that's where the bench was. The heat wrung any remaining energy out of me, and at day's end when Kirstin drove up to get me at the park-and-ride, she often found me lying on a brick wall, nothing left.

Mind you, those were just Mondays, Wednesdays, and half of Fridays.

Tuesdays and Thursdays were filled with outpatient therapy at St. David's and with doctor's appointments. At St. David's, I had a vast array of therapists, all in navy polo shirts and khakis, a look that suggested airline gate agents. One-Armed Bob, whom I had met while on a field trip during my Dripping Springs stay, was there. I usually had three hours booked—PT, OT, and pool.

When the schedulers could not get me a solid block, I would make my way to the hospital commissary, which, in a flourish of needless branding, was designated as The Café at Barclay Park.

One new twist in this therapy was the addition of biofeedback. A PT hooked me up to sensors that would show me on a monitor the effort I was expending. A yellow line might show the output of my triceps and a blue line of my biceps, and I was asked to try to make them cross back and forth as I flexed different muscles. The theory behind biofeedback therapy was that seeing the results of my effort on a screen would reinforce that effort neurologically and accelerate the recovery. It was the kind of thing that probably would be very effective if done two hours a day for five months, but five sessions of forty-five minutes spaced out over two months—I wasn't so sure. We seemed to be trying a little bit of everything and hoping something clicked.

The big takeaway from biofeedback was that the PT told me I was getting about 25 percent signal to the affected muscles. This made good sense to me, because when Pancho picked something up, it did feel about four times heavier than it should have. A recycling bin with no more than two pounds of empty cartons, cans, and bottles felt like eight pounds as I tried to carry it from the kitchen to the driveway.

Another new therapy exercise was pushing a shopping cart full of miscellaneous crap—ankle weights, even an old jam box from the nineties—up a fifty-foot carpeted ramp near the St. David's waiting room and then backing it down without falling and being run over by it. Therapists called the ramp Mount St. David's. Good training for my future ventures in homelessness.

One day during a therapy session, One-Armed Bob interrupted my workout and asked if I might be interested in participating in a joint study being conducted by St. David's and the University of Texas mechanical engineering department. The study was testing robotic exoskeletons as therapy devices for people recovering from right-sided strokes. I said I would be. Thus, I entered a six-week study that took place just next door, at the top of Mount St. David's. Two grad students—one from Brazil, one from Idaho—sat with me at a conference table and explained how the study would work. Then Bob took my vitals and they all took me in to meet the robot, HARMONY.

HARMONY conjured up a dozen different science fiction and fantasy references all at once: an Imperial Stormtrooper from *Star Wars*, Iron Man's suit, the robotic suit Ripley wore when she battled her nemesis in *Aliens*. In the middle of the room sat a black seat about the size and shape of a tractor seat. When I was on it, Idaho Kevin strapped in Lefty, and Bob, ever skillful with the one arm he had, lifted Pancho into position, then secured both limbs to the robot's arms with Velcro—palms, wrists, forearms, upper arms. Though there existed in the hospital other robotic aids for legs—I sometimes would hear motors whirring while in the gym and look up to see a man plodding through with an astonishing pair of black plastic robotic pants—this device worked solely on the arms and was mainly of white plastic segments suggesting a Stormtrooper to someone of my demographic.

After a few technical exchanges that sounded like a preflight check between Kevin and Ana, the Brazilian PhD candidate who sat at a nearby computer, Ana asked me if I was ready. "Never been so ready," I said. With her keystroke, the robot slackened, like someone had just punched it in the gut, then it held my arms up, as if I were in water. This was its zero-gravity setting, in which the machine supported its own weight plus the weight of my arms. With Lefty, I moved HARMONY's left arm about with ease, her tiny motors in each joint whining and whirring as I changed position. Now Kevin and Bob placed a horizontal aluminum rack in front of me with orange, green, and purple tennis balls mounted on it left to right. "When you're ready, touch the orange ball," Ana would say. Above me was an array of motion-sensor cameras picking up sensors attached to the robot. I would try to touch the tennis ball but would usually miss by a few inches.

After recording my successes and failures with the tennis balls, we would run through a series of motions with Pancho. To make it more interesting and help me remember the motions, I made up my own terms for them. What they called "scaption," in which I would keep my arm straight and move it up and down in front of me, I called "Milk the Giant Cow." Their "diagonal" I called "Night Fever." Their "across" I called "Greased Lightning." (Wow! Two Travolta references for just six arm motions.) We would run through ten reps of each motion in passive mode, to help my arm remember that motion, then Ana would hit a key, and we would go into "assisted mode," in which I would initiate the movement and, if I initiated it in precisely the right direction, HARMONY would kick on and help me complete it. If I wasn't precise, it would lock up, imprisoning me for five or so seconds before automatically taking me through the motion again.

When I walked in on my twelfth and final day with the HARMONY team, Bob was grinning ear-to-ear. He had a surprise for me.

Once my vitals were taken, I was strapped in, all the preflight checks were out of the way, and he made sure that Kirstin was rolling video, Ana struck a combination of keys and the robot went into "mirror mode." Suddenly, everything I could do with Lefty I effortlessly could do with Pancho. Almost immediately, I began conducting a very slow opening to Beethoven's Fifth, then said, "This one's for you, Dad."

I had such mixed emotions. On one hand (so to speak), it was a great experience! I could have done it all day and into the night. It was freeing, giving me symmetrical sensations I had not had since the stroke. And it was glorious to take myself through ranges of motion—delicious stretches—that had been next to impossible. On the other hand, why, in the name of all that is right and holy, did they keep this from me until our final meeting?! As I critiqued the program days later, I told an entrepreneur who was partnering with the research program, "Mirror mode is it. That's the whole thing! All you would need for this to be fully effective is one switch, Mirror Mode, and one knob, which would let you dial back the assist a tiny bit every day. Or maybe you could program it to dial back the assist automatically by half a percent every day. That's recovery."

Of course, such a regimen would require access to the machine most of the day every day, in other words, in homes. When I asked the researchers what HARMONY would retail for if I wanted to buy one, they just chuckled. That was too far down the road then for them to even venture a guess, but they did say over $100,000. The first market would be rehab hospitals, because they had the money. But while an hour a day would certainly be better than nothing, it was clear to me from all my other experiences with rehab that this amount wouldn't be enough for recovery. Until HARMONY was in every patient's room, it, like biofeedback, would just be one more thing that was cool and interesting and perhaps helpful in some imperceptible degree.

The HARMONY study was not a game changer for me; I did not expect it to be. Nevertheless, I was glad to have been through it merely as an exercise in scientific altruism. This is how science works. And how business works. Therapeutic devices do not appear whole cloth, sprung full-grown from the head of Zeus. They appear little by little, thanks to engineers and doctors and entrepreneurs and lots and lots of lab rats like me.

A year later, I returned to HARMONY for a follow-up. Ana and Kevin were gone, and a new PhD candidate sat at the controls. As we chatted, she said, "There is this book about stroke that's really interesting, because it was written by a neurologist who describes what was happening to her, as a neurologist!"

I stared at her with a close-lipped smile. "*My Stroke of Insight,*" I said in almost a whisper. "It's called *My Stroke of Insight* . . . Jill Bolte Tay—" my voice trailed off.

So what *did* made the biggest difference in my recovery? By far, it was two pieces of equipment. The first Kirstin bought from a guy she found on Craigslist. She had gone to his house to look at a dining room table when she spotted something tucked away in his garage. It was a children's tumbling mat, the blue vinyl kind about two inches thick that folded out to four by eight feet. She asked him if he'd take twenty-five dollars for it, and he did.

This allowed me to get on the floor and develop core strength and better coordination, practicing the stretches and exercises my forty different therapists had taught me. Chief among those was simply getting onto my hands and knees, "quadruped." I also spent many hours stretching and strength building on our king-sized mattress. After doing every sort of downward-facing stretch I could manage, I slowly and carefully lay on my back, then would work on "bridging," or lifting my hips off the mat, and then lifting my arms symmetrically, learning to lift Pancho at every angle, then lower him slowly to the mat.

The second piece of equipment key to my recovery was the smart speaker Ed and Elaine bought for me way back in the rehab hospital days. As my mat was stationed right in front of the TV, it would have been easy enough to have it on. But I found that keeping it off was the key to keeping me working. TV lobotomizes you in a way music does not. For long hours I would stretch and lift while Alexa and Spotify entertained me. "Alexa, what was the fifth studio album by the Doobie Brothers?" I would ask, straining to lift my right leg off the mat.

"The fifth studio album by the Doobie Brothers was *Stampede.*"

"Alexa, play the album *Stampede* by the Doobie Brothers."

"Playing *Stampede* by the Doobie Brothers."

And just like that, I was good for another forty minutes. I would go through musical phases during my mat workouts. For about three weeks I listened to nothing but The Band. There was the Allman Brothers phase. The ELO phase. The Vulfpeck phase. The Meters phase. The Alan Parsons phase, and so on. When I wanted more interaction, I played trivia games with the speaker. This was something I could point to with no hesitation as a true game changer in my recovery, because it kept me on the mat.

One significant milestone I crossed due to this mat work was the ability to get off the floor by myself, to stand up without even the aid of furniture. A rickety and inflexible fifty-one, I scarcely could do this before the stroke. I didn't need a $100,000 exoskeleton, though it would have helped. I didn't even need a weight machine. The two most important pieces of equipment were a used children's tumbling mat and a modern-day juke box with enough music to keep me on the floor.

CHAPTER 19

Somebody That I Used To Know

By mid-June, I had been home as long as I had been gone. The hammock in the front yard had been up continuously since the last day of March, so long that the tarp that hung over it had faded from olive to brown.

June 21, the longest day of the year, lived up to billing. The summer solstice started with an 8:30 appointment at St. David's for physical therapy. At 9:40, we raced from downtown north to Pflugerville to get my truck adapted at virtually the only business in Central Texas that provided this service. I heard that lawsuits had forced many such companies out of business nationally. If that was the case, I was doubly grateful that this one was still around.

As we waited, I roamed the showroom, which, in addition to a minivan with the latest in chair-lift technology, featured an antique wicker-and-wood wheelchair in one corner of the office, a nod to adaptive technologies of the past and an exact match of the chair my great-grandfather had used after his stroke. I said a silent prayer of thanks that I lived in an age that, whatever else could be said about it, did have a recovery mentality—where a stroke survivor wasn't just set out on the porch and made comfortable for the one or two years he or she had left.

The left-foot accelerator they installed was surprisingly low-tech. First, they bolted a plate to my floorboard. Onto this plate, the driver clicked a pedal assembly into place. The pedal assembly was a simple affair, in which a roller rested against the regular gas pedal and a horizontal bar ran beneath the brake and connected to a left-foot pedal. That was it. It took about ten seconds of grunting to put the pedal in. Pull a switch, and the pedal came right out so the car could be driven normally. Installation took two hours and cost about six hundred dollars, parts and labor. And to the everlasting credit of the Texas legislature (a phrase I don't think I've ever used before), there is no sales tax charged on new cars for disabled people, a fact that almost always makes the adaptive pedals a wash.

It was go time. My very first drive in my own truck would be out of the parking lot and onto the frontage road of I-35 on a stretch between Dallas and San Antonio that is notorious as one of the most congested interstate highways in America. Kirstin was a trooper to let me, on my virgin voyage, take on I-35 and then the seventy-five-mile-per-hour toll road that led to our neighborhood.

We reached the house safely, but I did not want to stop driving. So I dropped her off and began a series of errands to assert my independence and my helpfulness. First, I took Cameron to band camp. Then I went to Whataburger, which had become a strange but potent symbol of everyday independence. "Sometimes you just want to go to Whataburger," became a stock phrase in my explanation to people of how great driving would feel once I could do it again.

Then I picked up Andrew, sixteen, who was taking a summer class at Austin Community College. Then we went to the grocery store to get my prescriptions refilled and buy a few household cleaners before finally going home. But I wasn't through. I took Cameron to Baskin Robbins. When I was finally out of errands, I drove to David's house. This was a historical echo, because I'm pretty sure the first place I had driven when I got my license at sixteen was David's house. We talked about the new mixes on our record as Cameron listened patiently.

On the drive home, I jokingly floated the idea of driving to El Paso that night, just because I could. (El Paso is nearly six hundred miles from Austin.) Cameron suggested using the e-stim unit on my eyelids to stay awake.

As I had been driving on busy highways from the very moment I got my new pedal installed, there was no reason I could not make longer drives, and within two weeks I drove Andrew to a swim meet in College Station two hours away. It felt good to be able to at least begin to take a few parenting duties off Kirstin's shoulders.

Driving again represented a significant step back to normal, while the left-foot accelerator that made driving a reality represented a significant surrender. My return to life was a collage of ten thousand such contradictions and decisions—when to hold out for further progress and when to give something up in order to get on with living.

Fifteen years earlier, my mother-in-law brought us a curious piece of cutlery back from an Alaskan cruise. It had a curved blade about four inches long and a wooden handle right in the middle of the top edge. The Inuit used the "ulu" to clean seals. It was a novelty we had kept in the cupboard but had not used much. But I recognized the design now as the same as the "rocker knives" I had used in Dripping Springs. Now, I used it all the time, so much so it stayed at my place at our table. The toughest piece of steak melted under the awesome power of the ulu.

Many adjustments were run-of-the-mill, like getting left-handed scissors. Others were equally low-cost but more geared toward my one-handedness than my new left-handedness, like a small pair of scissors I carried everywhere I went—much more useful now than a pocketknife. I used them ten times a day to open protein bars, crackers, chips, candy bars, and my daily frozen burrito lunch. Okay— when I say it like that, I guess I ate a lot of prepackaged food.

There were tasks I had never even wondered about before, like how do you floss with one hand? Kirstin came home from Walgreens with a bag of a hundred "Flossups," which looked like tiny plastic coping saws, or goal posts with a half-inch of floss tied between the uprights. These were probably no more designed for people with hemiparesis than the ulu, but I was certainly glad they existed.

The six-month mark looms large in the mind of a stroke survivor. Every prognosis, every chestnut of conventional wisdom, starts with the unequivocal importance of gaining back everything you can within the first six months, with the other milestones being a year and eighteen months, multiples of six months.

It was my semiversary, or, if you like, my hemi-semiversary. And now I began to notice an odd thing in myself. I began to dissociate from my old self, the person I had been for the first fifty-one years of life. I vacillated between desperately wanting that person back and an indifference to that person, almost an estrangement. I saw him as someone who didn't know how I felt, who had no idea how lucky he really was, someone not grateful enough for what he had, not thoughtful enough of others. As I say, it was a feeling more than anything I could build a rational case for. I think I had been a fairly good person—far from perfect, but at a minimum a loving husband and father. But as I watched old home movies of me jogging or playing guitar or walking smoothly or doing anything at all with my right arm or with two hands, the voice in my head would start: "That guy . . . that guy didn't know jack. Who even is that?" He seemed like somebody that I used to know, to paraphrase the song, let alone somebody that I used to be.

At the same time, the exact opposite also was true. Each day as I walked down the Drag toward work, I would catch a glimpse of my reflection in a storefront window and could scarcely believe that rickety old man was me. Once, my PT shot a video of me walking to try to help me analyze my gait. After the walk, we sat at the kitchen table and she played it back for me. "What do you think?" she asked, thinking only of the mechanics.

My eyes brimmed with tears. "I hate it," I said softly. Quickly she realized her question had landed in a place completely different from where she intended. "That's not me."

In these days—perhaps in all days—one has to look for silver linings everywhere one can. And one silver lining to a catastrophic health event is that it is a little like attending your own funeral, as Tom Sawyer did. That is, you get to hear people say nice things about you while you're still here. And it is more pronounced when it is a sudden catastrophic event like a stroke or a cancer diagnosis than with a gradual, degenerative catastrophe. I don't know that my father, who died after a twenty-year struggle with Parkinson's, ever really had the Tom Sawyer funeral I had.

One such moment for me came when I volunteered to give a Sunday morning talk at the Bahá'í center. These talks were something I enjoyed doing and had probably done twenty-five times in the sixteen years from my joining the faith until my stroke. But this one was unique in several ways. It was the first time many of my Bahá'í friends had seen me since the stroke. And it also was a talk about me and my experience, whereas the others were about abstract ideas, theology, history, and so on.

I don't remember a lot of what I said during that hour—something about not putting off things that you have thought about doing for no good reason. I think I might have disappointed some people with my rather ho-hum, glass-half-full spiritual insights. Like the archetype of the blind man being able to "see" more than others, I think some may have thought that the man who'd had a brain injury now might think more with his *heart*. If that was the case, I probably disappointed, as I was as cerebral and irreverent as I'd ever been.

Nor did I hold any greater insights on the world to come despite having been so near death. There were no tunnels or approaching lights for me, no conversations with spiritual guides or relatives who had already passed over. I had simply fainted on a gurney and, seemingly the next moment, woken up with forty staples in my scalp and orange hair. Sorry, folks. Wish I had more for ya.

The most memorable part of the talk for me came when my friend Brian raised his hand. When I called on him, he said my story reminded him of the story of Job, the point of which was that the only thing we are promised in this life is suffering, and the only thing expected of us is to transcend that suffering. "It's a big ask, but a good way to look at things, because then, all the good things are bonuses and all the bad things are part of the deal," he noted.

Part of having a catastrophic medical event while still gainfully employed is that you generally use all of your sick time and vacation time during the recovery. As a result, we had not had any sort of appreciable vacation that summer with the boys. But we did have one day while I was still working part-time and going to therapy to squeeze in a short road trip and make this year—as different as it had been in every way—a little more like years past. It was the third Friday in July, and as soon as I was done with therapy at noon, I would drive home, then to a routine neurology appointment. Next we'd grab the kids and take them somewhere they had never been, take them to a foreign country, Louisiana.

On the way home from therapy at St. David's, I exited the highway and slowed to turn at the light. I was cruising around forty miles per hour in an open lane with a huge line of cars to my right sitting still, backed up at the light. Suddenly a blue car darted out into my lane. I stomped the brakes and yanked the steering wheel to avoid it but hit it forcefully with the front right corner of my pickup, ramming it into another car. I jumped the curb up onto the grass before rolling back onto the road. My engine was off and the crash site was now 150 feet behind me.

I had been driving about a month, and this was my first accident in thirty-five years of driving. Pure coincidence? Well—yes. There was nothing I could have done to prevent it, and there was never any question but that it was the other driver's fault. Twenty years old and guileless, he came fast-walking toward me shouting, "I'm so sorry! I'm an idiot!" The police arrived, and he got the ticket. Rattled, I called Kirstin, and she arrived within five minutes. My truck was hauled to a nearby lot to be assessed. None of the three drivers or their passengers was hurt.

We had planned to take the family car to New Orleans anyway, and since I was fine, there was really nothing we could accomplish by staying in Austin. So Kirstin took me to the neurologist appointment, then we went home, got the kids, and headed east. We spent that night in Houston and pressed on the next morning.

In New Orleans, we walked four miles through the French Quarter in heat and humidity that could only be achieved in July and below sea level. We toured the Quarter in a mule-drawn carriage, listened to a jazz duo in Jackson Square, waited forty minutes for some beignets, and found a place for dinner.

It turned out to be more of a bar that served food than a restaurant. This legal distinction meant that, because the boys were with us, we had to go upstairs so that they would not be "in a bar." Because of good therapy, I was normally not scared of stairs, but this was no normal staircase. A historic building constructed long before building codes even existed, it was three flights long with no landings. I had not attempted a stairway like that since back when they allowed tourists to ascend El Castillo at Chichén Itzá. When we reached the upper room, we were amused that this was the space designated for minors, as the entire room was decorated with perhaps twenty-five large prints and paintings of nude women. Ah, New Orleans, must you be so predictable?

To pass the time on the drive back to Austin, we decided to count the number of billboards for personal injury lawyers. We charged Ian with counting them and keeping score with tally marks. The results: Gordon McKernan - 61 billboards, Morris Bart - 39 billboards, and a smattering of others for a total of 113 billboards for personal injury attorneys on I-10 between New Orleans and the Texas state line. ("Why does health care cost so much?!") As a result of these billboards, several new "isms" entered our family's lexicon, including "Put the Womack on 'em!" "One Call, That's All!" and "One Click, That's It!"

Back home now, I needed my own wheels, and auto insurance covered my rental. Of course, not just any car would do. I required a left-foot accelerator.

"A pedal extension," the overworked rental car agent said.

"Yes, that's right," I responded.

I showed up the next day to pick up the car, and he pointed to it in the lot and handed me the keys. When I reached the car and lowered myself down into it, I found that they had modified it not with a left-foot accelerator but with extensions upward for the brake and accelerator, as if for a midget. Did I mention I am six two? I could barely fit into the low-slung sedan *without* the mods. They put a rush on the correct modification, and the next day the car—the very same car—was correctly configured.

The other driver's insurance company accepted liability, and my truck was deemed a total loss. Meanwhile, Kirstin bought a new car—something that had been coming for a while, and I drove the old family car for a few weeks before buying a new truck. All told, my stroke was a windfall for the pedal installation company, as we wound up modifying four vehicles in the space of three months.

Our dealings with auto insurance were as maddening as they had been with health insurance, but they were resolvable. The more enduring mystery of my back-to-driving saga was the story of my license.

Let me preface this by saying that the state of Texas is a wonderful place. It boasts an incredible range of ecosystems and landscapes, a rich history rivaled by few other regions, and a famous warmth of spirit and can-do attitude. However, I do not understand the inner workings of its Department of Public Safety.

After the stroke, there was no automatic revocation of my driver's license, as you might think there would have been for someone who had a massive seizure and lost the use of a foot and a hand. This was an alarming realization, just from a citizen's perspective. I would have thought that there would be some automatic reporting mechanism linking the first hospital that admitted me to the Department of Public Safety, but apparently not. If I had been ornery enough to drive myself home from the ICU, perhaps using my left foot for both pedals, perhaps even left foot on the gas, my left hand on the brake and holding the steering wheel in my mouth, I would have had that legal right.

But I was not so ornery, and on the strong advice of various occupational therapists, I enrolled in the back-to-driving program mentioned earlier. After completing that program there, I was to present a letter from the hospital to the DMV, which then would retest me. The motive for doing all of this was that it would help insulate me from a lawsuit over driving with a disability if I got in an accident for which I was at fault.

I presented the letter to the DMV as instructed, and a confused scene ensued with the staff member studying the letter and consulting a variety of supervisors, none of whom seemed to know what this was. At last the clerk, after five straight minutes of typing and tabbing between fields, cut the corner off my license, threw it in his trash can, and issued me a temporary paper license with the phrase "with necessary modifications" on it. Odd that there was no test spoken of, as I thought that was the whole point.

Next, I received my new license in the mail. A few weeks later I received a letter, telling me to apply to retest within sixty days. The letter got buried on my desk, and, since I'd already received what seemed like a perfectly legitimate license in the mail with new restrictions on it, I sort of felt that the matter had been resolved. The next letter I got was a Notice of Revocation, stating that my license would be revoked in thirty days unless I scheduled a court hearing.

With this, I flew into a tizzy of phone calls, faxes, and emails, trying to connect my neurologist—who held my life in his hands—the Texas Department of Public Safety, and now, an entirely new entity, the State Medical Advisory Board, which was housed inside the Department of State Health Services. Was the hearing that I needed to schedule in order to not lose my license with the Department of Public Safety or the Department of State Health Services, or both? Which form on whose website did I need to print out for my neurologist? And to whom did that need to be faxed? Had the Medical Board ever gotten the original letter from the hospital way back when saying I'd completed my training? The faxes ran to twelve and fifteen pages.

Finally, the week before the deadline, the Medical Advisory Board, which met every other week, kicked my case back to DPS without fanfare, and a new deadline was given me for testing. The next day, I called the number on the DMV website thirteen times and never got an answer or a way to leave a message. So I took a half day of vacation time—since I had used all my sick time on therapy—drove to the DMV, and sat with the great unwashed masses for an hour. Taking vacation time to go sit at the DMV has to rate as one of the lowest moments in the entire saga of my stroke. Only the fear of God and of losing my driver's license could have compelled such a sacrificial perversion of the natural order.

I handed my new letter to the clerk on duty, who puzzled over it with the same confused expression as the clerk five months earlier. He photocopied it, scribbled my cell phone number on the back of it, and solemnly promised to have his supervisor, who was out that day, call me to schedule a test.

I had not taken a driving test since the day I turned sixteen in 1983, but nothing had changed; it was still parallel parking that gave me the sweats. Just two weeks earlier I had gone through all this with Andrew, coaching him on the finer points of when and how much to cut the wheel. Now I was having to do it myself.

At length, the supervisor called me back, and we scheduled the test for that Thursday. We had never met in person, but she knew me by my gait, and said "Mr. Seale?" as soon as I passed through the front door. I was a little early, as was my habit, and she asked me to have a seat. When my appointment time had arrived after fifteen minutes of sitting idle, she handed me a clipboard with a stack of forms to fill out with my non-dominant hand. Then it was finally time for the test.

I was not only on my best, most law-abiding behavior, but went on an all-out charm offensive, just to seal the deal, making pleasant conversation with funny asides, doing everything short of complimenting her on her hair. Usually in these situations, the testing officer does not stray from the script, nor ask a lot of questions that might distract you from the task at hand. So I was amused when, no sooner than we had backed out of my space, she began asking about the details of my stroke. "Oh-gay," she said with a stopped-up nose. "Pull arou'd right here a'd I'll test you od parallel pargeeg first. So, cad you feel your arb?"

"Yes, I never lost sensation in my—"

"Pull over right here!" she interrupted. I complied, and silently awaited the next set of instructions.

"So adyway, what were you sayi'g? You devver lost feeleeg id your arb?"

"No, I never did. I was fortunate in—"

"At this stob sign, we're goi'g to go left do the highway."

And so it went for the next twenty minutes, me never quite sure if the medical line of questioning was somehow related to the driving test or if it was just small talk. When at last we pulled back into the DMV, she had some encouraging words for me, indicating she saw nothing in my driving that concerned her. Good thing, as I had been driving just that way for six months already.

It felt good to have checked the final box in this long and tortured process, and it was time to get to campus. As I pulled into the bus stop park-and-ride, my cell phone rang. It was her, again. "Bister Seale, I'b so sorry, but I deed you to side od the back of the card I gave you od the clipboard. I'b so sorry I did't poi't that out. If you wa't to come in before we close at five, I can keep it for you here at the desk."

"No, no!" I said, "I'll come back now. It's fine! I'll be there in ten minutes. See ya then!" I chirped. I had not come this far to have this drag on one more day, one more letter, fax, or email.

"I'b so sorry!" she said again.

"No, it's fine," I insisted.

"You're just being dice to be!" she said. I felt sorry for her. DMV workers must rank quite low on any given popularity scale.

When I returned, she brought the clipboard out to me, and, still sheepish about the oversight and the extra hoops I was jumping through, she even showed me her marked-up scorecard with me passing with flying colors. "You'll get somethi'g id a few days," she said. As of this writing, more than a year has passed. I have received nothing to indicate I passed the test or that I ever even took one.

CHAPTER 20

I Saw the Light(s)

There are four things you need to know about Duke Soto:

    1. He loves eighties rock, and I mean really loves it. I think he might love it more now than in the eighties themselves.

    2. He loves pop culture generally and sci-fi specifically. He named his middle child after a secondary character on *Star Trek: Deep Space 9*. Perhaps the reverence for TV and film is genetic; after all, Duke's own parents named him after John Wayne.

    3. Unless at work doing IT support, you will find him wearing Vibram FiveFinger shoes at all times. These are the shoes for which every toe has its own compartment, looking like rubberized versions of those toe socks popular in the seventies. He is not a runner but just loves Vibram FiveFingers, the wilder the colors, the better.

    4. He loves a good road trip and doesn't need a lot of arm-twisting to go halfway across the country. A dark-skinned man of Mexican extraction, he will readily tell you tales of being the darkest person in Branson, Missouri, and being duly disturbed by the racist pall that hangs over much of the South. But he is undeterred by this and travels somewhere in Dixie at least annually. He loves a road trip.

I met Duke in 1982 in our high school radio and TV class. He carried the banner of that curious era more enthusiastically than anyone else we knew. He wore bandanas and parachute pants to class as if he were taking the stage at a Loverboy concert at any moment. And he excitedly brought new LPs into classrooms from bands we had never heard of, such as Mötley Crüe, bands that employed disturbing amounts of makeup and hairspray.

Like many high school buds, we had drifted in separate directions before reconnecting at the dawn of the Facebook era. Since then, he had been a stalwart friend, a profoundly supportive friend, especially when it came to my music. When I was doing solo acoustic gigs at a coffee shop, many were the nights I played to a handful of disinterested strangers—many on their laptops, some even with headphones on—then I would look over, and there was Duke, beaming, recording video with his phone, there for the umpteenth time hearing the same setlist.

When I had my stroke, Duke was among the first to visit me in the rehab hospital. He had lost his father to a stroke a year earlier, and news of my stroke brought back a wave of grief in him that had barely had time to subside. He was alone that day in late January when he showed up in his Vibram FiveFingers in Room 307 at Central Texas Rehab, and so was I. He cried when he saw me. That meant more than any words or gifts could have.

If you are Facebook friends with Duke Soto, you know road trips are a big part of his general *joie de vivre*. They are as numerous as they are refreshingly random. He does not post from the Empire State Building or the Las Vegas Strip. In addition to Memphis and Branson, he is in Fouke, Arkansas, of Boggy Creek/bigfoot infamy. Now he is making a pilgrimage to Johnny Cash's boyhood home. Now he is driving his son fourteen hours to Birmingham, Alabama, to see the touring clown act known as Puddles Pity Party. He welcomes comparisons to Clark Griswold. And, combining passions Nos. One and Four, he makes numerous road trips to see Night Ranger at this rodeo or Def Leppard at that festival, perhaps sharing a bill with Poison or White Snake.

I'm an active Facebooker as well, and for better or for worse, I long had posted performances of my playing. (The temptation to the performer to perform, no matter how small the audience or how flawed the performance, is mighty, and in this, post-stroke Avrel was no different from pre-stroke Avrel.) After Ed had gifted me with a looping pedal, I worked with it a couple of days and then posted a sloppy instrumental version of Chicago's 1971 track "25 or 6 to 4."

When Duke saw it, he messaged me asking permission to download the video and email it to "some friends of his." Within a few hours, Duke texted me a screenshot of an email response from Vivian Campbell. Campbell had first made a name for himself as the guitarist for the heavy metal band Dio in its heyday, but for the past twenty-six years had been a member of Def Leppard. "That's amazing!" Campbell wrote, generously. "Music is good for the soul and it will no doubt help his recovery that he continues to play."

A few hours later Duke texted me another screenshot, this one from Joe Elliott, Def Leppard's creator and front man: "Aw, bless him, Duke, he's a trooper," wrote the British rocker. "Hopefully he keeps on improving!! PS, Great song choice!"

Duke had posted plenty of pics of himself and his kids with these guys at fan meet-and-greets, so I knew he had met them. What I did not know is that over many years he had made himself so available to them as a Mac support expert that they were in more or less constant, casual contact. Who'da thought, these arena gods of the 1980s had just as many issues with their laptops as you or me? Duke Soto, that's who.

So it was that Duke had trained me to read his texts right away, and a few weeks later, a new one came in over the transom: "I think I know what the answer is, but would you want to go to Marfa next weekend?" Becky and their kids had gone to North Dakota, and, as I knew, he was not one to just sit around the house.

I checked our calendar. It was clear. I thought about it for about seven seconds, then wrote back, "Let's do it!"

Marfa is about seven hours west of Austin. Named for a Russian character in a Jules Verne novel, Marfa was long just a military outpost and ranching crossroads in the high desert of the Big Bend country. In the past twenty-odd years it had become a haven for self-aware hipsters, an ironic arts enclave, a sort of extension of South Austin that you had to pass through a wormhole for seven hours to reach. One artifact of this irony is a $120,000 art installation built in 2005 to resemble a Prada store, not in Marfa but twenty-six miles outside Marfa, in other words, the absolute middle of nowhere.

Duke wanted to get an early start. My alarm went off at 4:45, and his black Dodge Charger was idling in our driveway at five.

Six a.m. found us barreling west through the Hill Country. He was proud of a newly acquired dash cam that recorded video continuously to an old cell phone. It would record about an hour's worth of video at a time, and unless the operator intervened, it would record over the video in a loop. The point was, if you saw something remarkable, you could stop at your next convenience, play the footage back, and see if you caught it on camera. "Most people just don't get the value in this sort of thing," he said in disbelief.

By first light, we were in Llano, passing barbecue temples, ranch supply stores, and antique malls, and by eight, we had reached Junction, where the dark greens of the Texas Hill Country give way to pale green mesas and the fifty-mile views of the Edwards Plateau. Here we joined America's underline, the artery stretching from Jacksonville, Florida, to Santa Monica, California, I-10. Sonora, Ozona, Fort Stockton, Marathon. Now the pale greens of the Edwards Plateau gave way to the tan and rust of the Trans-Pecos, the high desert, with volcanic outcroppings lining every horizon.

As we bore south from Marathon, Duke glanced at his phone. "We're 3.5 miles away," he said. He was trying to remain calm, but I could sense him seething with excitement.

"From what?" I asked.

"You'll see . . . three miles now." He glanced back and forth from his phone to the road. "It'll be on the left," he said smiling, barely containing his glee. He was Clark Griswold. It wasn't an exaggeration—he absolutely loved this stuff. The Charger slowed near what appeared to be a small, cinder block structure near some train tracks, an abandoned rail depot of some kind.

"For those who don't want to make the drive to the Marfa Prada, I give you . . ."—and now the Charger slowed to a stop—". . . the Marathon Target!" Someone had affixed large black wooden letters and a Target logo to the abandoned shack and had furnished a red shopping cart to complete the experience. Well, if we didn't see anything else on this fourteen-hour round trip, this would have made it worth every mile.

We proceeded to Alpine, but our hotel room wasn't ready, so we pressed on the final twenty miles to Marfa. The first order of business was lunch, and, ever the planner, Duke had done some online sleuthing and found a food truck with excellent reviews. Duke and I raised the average age of the self-aware clientele of Food Shark a good decade.

After lunch, in the town square, we spotted an aging hippie selling straw hats in the shade of a lonely tree. The Anglo Fort Worth native introduced himself as "Miguel," a marketing ploy so transparent as to be endearing. Most of the hats were sold unshaped, and, with the crowns perfectly domed and the brims perfectly flat, they all appeared to be women's sun hats. I found one with about a three-inch brim. "Could you shape this into an open road?" I asked.

"Sure," said Miguel, "I'll just go ahead and make one, and if you don't like it, no problem." He dunked it in a tin bucket of cool water, and with a few masterful bends and dents, it emerged from baptism blocked and born again and bursting with character. Delighted, I told Miguel I had been in the market for an open road-style hat for some time, but shared nothing else about myself. "Yeah," he said, "I sell a lot of these to musicians in Austin." I had never felt so predictable and conformist in my life.

The open road's Guatemalan palm weave dried almost immediately in the desert air, and soon I was hobbling away from the town square eighty dollars poorer but now in full vacation mode. As Duke and I left, I heard Miguel on his cell phone—"Hey, just sold a three-inch [brim] as an open road. A full-on LBJ . . . looks great."

Back in Alpine, the hotel room Duke had generously reserved was ready. However, he had not thought to ask for a handicap room, and I, of course, had not thought to mention it to him. This traveling with a disabled guy was new to both of us.

In most respects, the room worked fine. There was no shower chair, but this was remedied with a trip to the front desk and a staff member stealing one from a handicap room whose occupants didn't need it. Two things I will mention for any bathroom designers who might be reading: First, the toilet paper dispenser was much too far back to my right to reach with my left hand. I somehow managed, but I cannot recall how, and that's just as well. Nor, when I showered, could I reach the soap or shampoo dispensers from the shower seat because the whole dispensing affair was bolted to the wall squarely behind me. Sometimes necessity is the mother of invention, but other times necessity is the mother of progress, and so I will always remember the Marfa trip as the first time post-stroke I stood while showering. Of course, sometimes necessity is simply a mother.

At four o'clock, the Alpine Cowboys would face off against the Trinidad (Colorado) Triggers in a Pecos League doubleheader. So after thirty minutes with our feet up, we were off to the ball field that Sul Ross State University shared with Alpine's minor league team. As a local country diva sang-shouted the National Anthem, there were thirty-seven people in attendance, including Duke and me. The players and coaches, standing along the first-base line, far outnumbered the spectators.

The afternoon was fun. The small-town diamond had no stands in the outfield and instead was blessed with a majestic backdrop of mountains. The dry, relatively cool desert air, even in summer, made one flirt with the idea that living with this remoteness might not be such a sacrifice after all. The most lasting memory of that day, however, would be the brisket nachos. They were five dollars and simply epic, more than any one person should eat at a full sit-down meal. I crossed my right leg over my left to create a table, balanced the large cardboard boat on my AFO, and over the next forty-five minutes systematically ingested what was probably three pounds of brisket, nacho chips, and processed cheese. And to think we had almost opted to go to a restaurant.

Now the summer sun had sunk low, the home team had prevailed in game one, and it was time to clip this doubleheader in half and head out to try and see that for which we had really come all this way.

The Marfa Lights were first reported in 1883 by Robert Reed Ellison, a young cowboy who speculated they were Apache campfires. The Apaches themselves said they were stars that had fallen to Earth. Since those early years, mainstream scientists and paranormal investigators have all taken cracks at explaining them: alien craft, the ghosts of conquistadors, ranch house lights, swamp gas, moonlight shining on veins of mica, headlights on US Highway 67. Maybe, probably not, nope, what swamp? no, and no.

The lights had become such a regular draw for the area that the Texas Highway Department had built a first-class rest stop from which to observe them. Duke helped me wrestle my reclining camp chair out of the Charger, and we walked around the bathrooms and set the chair up on the observation deck. About twenty-five people, spread out in twos and threes along the railing, peered with us south into the dusk toward the Chinati Mountains.

I had been there nearly twenty years earlier but had spotted nothing. Duke had been there once before with his kids. But, even were he a novice, his inner Griswold was well-read on the site and fully up to speed on when and where to look. He told me to look in the general vicinity of a radio tower with a red beacon light flashing on it. In less than three minutes, the first white light showed itself near the beacon.

We saw the lights almost continuously for more than an hour. They did not move, as headlights would, but were always perfectly still, seeming to hover at different heights though all relatively close to the ground. Now, off to the right and down near the sage brush, a lone one blazes with the luminosity and approximate size of Jupiter. It is easy to see how Apaches might have thought the stars or planets had fallen. Now this one remains, but another joins above the beacon, a duet, before the first blinks out. Is the new light ten yards above the beacon and five hundred yards away? Or is it one thousand yards above the beacon and fifty miles away? Could be either, or anything in between. Looking at them through binoculars makes them appear brighter and closer but does not make them any clearer or bring me any closer to understanding. Now three form an Orion's Belt grouping, like a trio of backup singers shimmering in sequined outfits, but rock steady. Now, one by one, they all blink out but are replaced by two others far to the left.

Are the sources of the light simply moving when "off," or is there a virtually infinite array of sources that turn on and off in place? The most we see at once is five.

Watching them for more than an hour, I did not get a feeling they were sentient or directed by a sentient being. Alien craft or conquistador ghosts should not be so confined to this area for more than a century, nor visible only from this vantage point. They struck me as naturalistic mystery, a reminder that we don't understand everything about even the physical world, let alone the others.

As the clock struck ten and darkness finally fell completely on Marfa, distant lightning flashed sporadically on all sides of us. It reminded me of "the valley of the midnight lightning," that recurring dream I had during the first few nights after my stroke of a lightning storm at midnight, somewhere in the desert Southwest—the dream that stoked my hopes that an electrical storm in my neural system was even then reconnecting my brain to my arm and leg.

The Marfa Lights had not disappointed. But we could have watched them another hour or eight hours and not been any closer to understanding. We headed back to Alpine and hurried to our beds. It had been a long, full day by any measure, one that had started at four that morning. The AC was cold, the mattresses firm, and Duke and I were both dog-tired.

So it was disappointing to say the least when at 1:30 a.m. I was awoken by muffled shouting in the room next to ours. This is an abridged version of what I heard. To render an accurate transcript, simply insert the adjective form of the F-word between every word that appears here: "That's it! I'm done with you!"

I rose out of bed and immediately began shivering in the frigid air conditioning. This, along with a huge jolt of adrenaline, made my right arm and leg both spasm as I teetered around stiff-legged, trying to pinpoint the source of the shouting. Earlier that day on the drive between Marfa and Alpine I had noted Border Patrol SUVs idling along a railroad track, checking culverts for undocumented visitors who might be hiding both from them and from the summer sun. Now, visions of cartel violence drifted through my semi-conscious brain, as the man continued to shout, "You hear me?! I'm done with this!" *Smack!*

Duke was peacefully sleeping, but something had to be done. "Dude!" I said in a stage whisper, "I think someone's getting the shit beaten out of them right next door!"

Duke sat up in his bed.

I sat down on my bed and clawed the covers back over me to avoid hypothermia. "I think we should call the police," I whispered, now keenly aware of just how thin the walls were.

A man of action, Duke grabbed the phone and dialed the front desk as I convulsed with adrenaline under the covers. "We're in Room 112, and there's some sort of fight going on right next door to us. You might want to get the police involved," he said.

Apparently, they took Duke seriously, because in four minutes there was a loud rap on our door. He cracked it to find eight police officers in the hallway. He once again directed them to the room *next door!* We were told the next morning that every officer on duty in the city of Alpine responded to the call.

The *Breaking Bad* torture scene I had envisioned turned out to be an instance of spousal abuse. The wife refused to press charges, so the cops relocated the husband to another room. As we sat at breakfast the next morning, I saw the woman getting ice from the machine in the hallway before retreating to her room. I figured she was icing her face.

The whole thing unsettled me, not least because it highlighted a new vulnerability. I had never been a confrontational person, but it unnerved me to feel like I no longer even had that option. Not only was I unable to insert myself into a harrowing situation to make a positive difference, I really couldn't even run away from one either. I had entered sitting-duck status. Oh well.

We headed into the rising sun back toward Austin and saw it all in reverse: Marathon, Fort Stockton, Ozona, Sonora. We were back into the Hill Country, less than two hours from home, and were climbing a gentle rise when out of nowhere a whitetail doe dashed into the road from left to right. Duke could do nothing but brace for impact. My right arm flailed wildly as we hit the poor creature and sent it sailing into the grassy easement in an airborne barrel roll.

At the top of the hill, Duke pulled to the shoulder and slowed to a stop. He asked if I was okay, and we both got out to assess the damage. Thankfully the doe was no match for the Dodge. Within an hour of the impact, Duke had uploaded a photo from his phone to his auto insurance company. For good measure and as bonus documentation, he also sent them twelve seconds of—wait for it—dashcam video.

It had been an eventful thirty-six hours—a day and a half that stretched me to new levels of community mobility, from bathrooms to ballparks. It had underscored new vulnerabilities in a still-scary world. It reminded me of the difference one thoughtful friend can make in life. And it showed me that ours is still a mysterious world. At that moment in time, the existence of mysterious power gave me hope—precious hope.

CHAPTER 21

Kinvarra's Child

At long last our CD came out, ten months after David and I had recorded it in Dripping Springs. We had gotten six original songs mixed and mastered, and my brother Erren had designed the cover. During the big rollout, we sold one (1) copy, which was purchased by David's Aunt Mary Ann. But it was done, we had set a goal and achieved it. And it was on Spotify, so when I was on my exercise mat, I could listen to our songs just by asking the device and earn back a few hundredths of a penny each time it played.

On the music front, the more important happening by far was that I was developing a new technique for playing with just my left hand. In August, I posted a video of me playing the Stevie Ray Vaughan classic "Cold Shot," and within a couple of days more than two thousand people had watched it.

The technique involved three ways of getting the instrument to sound with only the fingers of my left hand. The first was called "hammering on" and occurred when I hit the string with enough force that it sounded at whichever fret was hit. If a chord had a simple enough shape, I occasionally could get a whole chord to sound by hammering on notes together.

The second was the pull-off, in which, after hammering on a note I would pull my finger off the string in such a way as to pluck it, which would sound the open string or a note I was holding down below it. For example, I could hammer on at the fifth fret of any given string with my ring finger, then pull my ring finger off to pluck the string, which I was already holding down with my index finger at the third fret, then pull that finger off, plucking the open string. Hammer-ons and pull-offs were popularized by heavy metal guitarists in the eighties but were done with both left and right hands together creating rapid-fire arpeggios often up and down a single string. (This is also known as tapping. Nerds can argue over who was the first to do it, but it was Eddie Van Halen who popularized it.)

The third technique I used could be called a flick, in which I used any available finger to pluck an open string just before or after using that finger on an adjacent string. While the other two techniques are common among virtually all guitarists, the flick would only be adopted out of necessity.

Some songs, including our originals, were coming together nicely, though I had to invent new chord shapes to get the critical notes of each chord to sound. Before the stroke, open strings, which are strings plucked without the left hand fretting any note, were wonderfully useful and could be exploited in all sorts of ways. Now, open strings were the enemy, because plucking them meant I could not simultaneously hit any other notes in a chord.

But enough of all that. The important thing was I was making music, in fact a whole lot more than I thought I would.

I noticed that I was somewhat more emotional than before. It was not just that I had more reasons to cry, though I certainly did; my emotional shell was simply thinning. I cried for ten minutes at the end of the movie *La La Land*, and it was the second time I had seen it. It was so unfair that Mia and Sebastian couldn't get together! Why couldn't he have his jazz club and she her acting career at the same time? Why?! I just didn't understand!

Music was especially potent in bringing out feelings in me, which helps explain why the musical affected me. Growing up, there was a man in our church choir who had a steep decline due to Parkinson's and had no emotional shell. I remember him weeping openly in front of the whole congregation whensoever he was moved by the chorus of a hymn or a beautiful turn of phrase in scripture or the sermon. I wondered if I had a mild case of the same phenomenon.

In the 1990s, my friend Stephen insisted I go with him to a small club on the UT campus to hear a British guitarist named Adrian Legg. A middle-aged man with a buzz cut, round glasses, and an odd-looking Ovation guitar took the stage, and the gates of heaven opened to me. Nominally, he was playing an acoustic guitar, but a rich, cathedral-like sound filled the room through an artful combination of effects. His songs were hard to categorize, but often evoked the same feelings of awe as the great classical and romantic composers —achingly beautiful; other times they were more virtuosic country or avant-garde. I would see him many more times, buy practically his entire catalogue, and with the help of tablature books and instructional videos, learn many of his songs over thousands of hours.

Legg had ceased to include Austin in his tours, so it had been many years since Stephen or I had seen him in concert. But the fall after my stroke, Stephen kidnapped me for an all-expenses-paid overnight road trip to Houston. Steve and I checked into the hotel, dined on tacos of grilled grasshoppers in blue corn tortillas, and headed to the bar in the Montrose district for the show.

We were shocked and a little saddened that, at a performance of one of the greatest guitarists of our time, in the fourth-largest city in America, we were among just twenty-three people in attendance. On the bright side, we had great seats, sitting quite literally at the master's knee. But something was wrong, he didn't feel well, and long about the fifth song he said he'd better take a break. I figured he had gone backstage to lie down and perhaps put a cold rag over his face, so I wandered to the lobby to see if he had any wares for sale. And there he was, gamely chatting with patrons and selling and signing CDs. I introduced myself, asked him to autograph my songbook, and told him that I was learning to play with just my left hand because the stroke had taken my right.

A pained expression crossed his face. "Isn't there anything that can be done?" he asked softly in a British accent.

"I'm still trying to get it back," I said, "definitely still trying, but even if I get some back, I doubt it will ever be the same."

He told me that when he was touring with Joe Satriani, he noticed Joe would barely contact the string with his pick because the gain on his electric guitar was so high. (Gain is the amplification of the signal, sort of like volume, but not exactly.) It was a thoughtful tip that I filed away. We continued chatting for twenty minutes until the bar owner gently asked if he could begin playing again; a few people had started to move toward the exit. I had planned, in an audacious move, to ask if I could play one of his songs with him, "Kinvarra's Child," as he was the only one I knew who could play the right hand as I played the left. But he was sick, already despondent over the quality of his performance, and my nerve failed me.

Each outing was a stretch beyond the previous one in terms of both stamina and what the neuro-rehab center would have called "community mobility." Marfa had been my first night away since getting home. New Orleans had been its own brand of crazy, walking crowded streets and sidewalks in 160 percent humidity. But I'd been a mere passenger on those. Andrew's swim meet in College Station was a long day trip with me at the helm, but College Station was nothing compared to the highways of Austin.

At the end of August, I drove Andrew to Houston to attend the first NFL game for either of us, Cowboys at Texans in the final game of the preseason. I navigated the Houston freeways well enough to get our Honda Pilot to the massive parking lot. NRG Stadium stood on the horizon, across the freeway and next to the eighth wonder of the world, the Astrodome. We made our way to a train platform and herded into the cars, where we sat next to a gentleman wearing an outfit that traced the entire history of the franchise, a Houston Oilers hat, Tennessee Titans jersey, and Texans jacket, lest anyone be unsure of which side he was on.

From the train, my hobbling gait drew the attention of a courtesy bus driver who helped me aboard for a four-block ride. Now to the stadium, we started a long, long ascent, first up a series of ramps, then escalators, then up in a service elevator. Convinced we could go no higher without oxygen, we entered the stadium, turned, and beheld a long stairway up to where our seats were. As we reached our row, I stood paralyzed, flummoxed at which foot to lead with now that it was time to let go of the railing that had gotten me this far.

The state of the art in stadium-building nowadays is all about getting as many people as close to the action as possible. This means steep bleachers and vanishingly thin ledges of concrete on which to balance as you sidestep to your seat like a sure-footed mountain goat. Just as I began to make my move, a large lady wearing a Cowboys jersey and lots of gold jewelry had seen enough and decided to take matters into her own hands. "Let go, baby!" she shouted over the din of music and the chatter of fifty thousand fans. "Just let go! I gotcha!" and with that, grabbed me with both arms and fell backward into her seat.

When I had thanked her for tackling me and somehow left her matronly embrace and settled into my own seat, I realized our seats were three rows from the ceiling, which I should have considered more when instinctively selecting the cheapest tickets; I could practically reach out and touch the roof from which Lady Gaga leapt during Super Bowl halftime the year before.

The preseason game itself was largely boring—third stringers who couldn't throw or catch the ball on either side. But we had a good time, met some great characters, and saw some famous athletes avoiding injuries on the sidelines.

Summer was over, and so was my part-time work status. It was time to take the next step toward the new normal.

Part Four

First visit home three weeks post-stroke, with Andrew, Cameron, and Ian.

Horace Bradford Seale (1877–1929), my great-grandfather, post-stroke in wheelchair, Athens, Texas. Note dropped left shoulder and swollen left hand.

CHAPTER 22

September

In September, about eight months after the stroke, I returned to work full-time. The boys headed back to school and Kirstin to her job substitute teaching in addition to keeping the books for Catfish Parlour. Once again, Gracie would spend her weekdays napping in quiet solitude.

To return to work full-time, I found it helpful to simplify my routine in every way I could. For one thing, I now wore the same shoes every day, the ones with the Zubits magnets. Almost as soon as I returned home from Dripping Springs, Kirstin had taken me to get a pair of long pants that I could get on and off one-handed, owing to a small bit of elastic in the waistband. They were fishing pants from the sporting goods store, which meant they were lightweight and had an extra pocket on the side of my left thigh where I could keep my wallet and my small pair of scissors, while my phone and keys rode in my upper left pocket. They were fast drying, zipped off to become shorts, and, critically, had a black belt of webbing I could cinch with one hand, and with inches marked on the inside, so that if I hauled in a speckled trout on my way to the office, I could remove the belt and be certain it was of legal size before filleting it on the bus. The first pair I got worked so splendidly that I returned and bought three more, one in every color they sold. To this day, 99 percent of my waking hours are spent in these pants.

I looked for efficiencies everywhere I could. For example, Monday night was Boy Scouts night, so Monday morning I put on the green fishing pants because those met the Scout uniform requirement, and therefore I would only have to change shirts when I got home and not shirts and pants. This saved me three minutes of physical struggle, but this level of minute planning comes with its own cost in mental exhaustion. I also simplified lunch, every day taking a frozen rice and bean burrito in my backpack. Having something compact, relatively light, non-spillable, and that represented a decision I did not have to make was a win all the way around.

Even with those efficiencies, reporting to work every day was hard. I was utterly exhausted by the time I reached my desk each morning. I worked in a public space, and sometimes I became so tired and frustrated I had to retreat to the stall in the men's room to cry in private. Many times, I felt like I had reached the end of me and simply couldn't go on. As I've said, I never wanted to kill myself; I just wanted to stop doing the things required to live. I thought about just not going into the office, just stopping doing anything.

I imagined how it would unfold—the initial gentle inquiries via Slack of my whereabouts: "We weren't aware you were off today," then an email or two, then a text, then a phone call. These would be followed by putting me on a "performance plan," which would lay the groundwork for my termination if I did not start doing things, which, of course, I would not, as I no longer did anything. In light of my nearly thirty years of service to the university, my prompt firing would be messaged to coworkers as me "exploring new opportunities" and would be accompanied by an awkward happy hour. I would cash out my 401(k) from my previous job, take whatever prorated retirement was due me, and limp along for a year, maybe two, before the bank foreclosed on the house and evicted me ninety days later. I'd slide by for another year or so on the remaining generosity of old friends and family members, but my pride would not allow that indefinitely, and in time I would opt for living on the street, maybe down on the Drag, as that seemed to be the preferred place to do this sort of thing, sleeping in doorways, urinating behind dumpsters, and accosting people who were getting off the bus for a few dollars so I could get a 7-Eleven hot dog and forty-ounce malt liquor for breakfast. I would grow an epic beard, and my thinning hair would become long and greasy like Gollum's, and I'd get skin cancer from the constant sunburn and walk up and down the sidewalk shirtless, shouting to no one in particular about the CIA and Jesus and Julian Assange and the apocalypse, until the cancer spread to my kidneys, and one morning I didn't wake up. The End. Epitaph: "AVREL SEALE, 1967–2023. He tried . . . for a while."

Then, after that daydream, I'd remember that I was married and had three kids. The next morning, reality would dawn before the sun, duty would call, and I would struggle out of bed and go to work again.

On a weekend in mid-September, I was invited to an event called Footstock. It was a bigfoot researchers-only campout in Sam Houston National Forest. I did not really consider myself a "researcher," but I had written an entire book on the subject, so—I guess if the big shoe fits . . . As with the podcasts and talk-radio interviews I had done since the stroke, it felt delicious to be doing anything completely unrelated to the stroke, something to do with the person I was before the Great Interruption.

We arrived after dark, and Wade—God bless him—helped me string my hammock. I had lain in the hammock plenty since the stroke, and even napped a good bit in it. So I was surprised and profoundly disappointed in the result of my first night back in the woods. It was my worst night's sleep, maybe ever, and that includes all the nights spent with three newborn babies. There were loud, rum-fueled conversations at three in the morning at the next campsite over. There was cartoon snoring in a tent near me. It was hot, still, and impossibly humid. I imagined this was what Vietnam felt like in summer. I was so desperately uncomfortable that I limped in the dark to my car and dozed a few minutes in the driver's seat. But it took about twenty seconds for the mosquitoes to find me, which meant rolling up the windows, which meant turning on the engine for air. Despite it all, the next day I stood in my AFO on the low stage of the park lodge and gave a forty-five-minute talk as the forest was drenched in a violent downpour.

Every doctor or therapist whose care I was under had encouraged me to think about Botox injections to control my spasticity. Every little movement we make is controlled by an incredibly complex blend of signals to muscles. And in every pair of muscles that work to move limbs in opposite directions, like the biceps and triceps, or the quads and hamstrings, there is always one muscle that is stronger than the other. Without cortical control, this results in pointless flexing of limbs in the direction of the naturally stronger muscle. In the arm, it results in "chicken wing" because the biceps is naturally stronger. The theory behind Botox therapy is that by injecting this neurotoxin into the stronger muscle of the pair, you give the weaker muscle a chance to do its thing. Staying with the arm example, injections in the biceps would then allow you to more readily fire your triceps and straighten your arm. It is a temporary therapy and is out of your system in three months.

So I went for an eval at the Physical Medicine and Neurotoxin Institute and was presented with a fresh stack of intake forms asking about the referring physician, current medications, allergies, and so on. Not only were they the questions I had answered dozens of times before, but half of the questions on the second page were the same as on the first. I resolved I would no longer answer the same question multiple times for the same doctor. I simply but nicely declined, and lo and behold, they admitted me anyway. I encourage everyone to do this from now on.

I sat in the waiting room with a gentleman reclined in a motorized wheelchair, his thin arms and legs twisted into grotesque positions I couldn't get into if I tried, feet curled into unusable vestiges, hands like the stiff talons of a dead raptor. Here was someone who would have given anything to be in my shoes, to be in any shoes.

The PA began the eval, and something she said got my attention right away: "Keppra is suppressing your neural system, so—" She was on her way to making a point, but I didn't hear anything after that. I had never thought of it that way, and it made me question anew whether the anti-seizure drug was really necessary for me and whether by taking it I was somehow violating the Hippocratic oath to "first, do no harm."

When the doctor came in and examined me—lift your arm this way, take off your shoes and walk down the hallway and back—he said, "You're definitely one of the more complicated cases we've seen."

It wasn't until this point, nearly eight months post, that I truly began to understand that I was not just dealing with one problem called "stroke." Rather, the stroke was simply the cause of multiple problems, some of which were related, others of which were completely unrelated. By my back-of-the-envelope calculations, I was not dealing with one problem, but with nine. There were five neuromuscular problems related to stroke and four emotional problems that were common to many catastrophic injuries or diseases.

Within the neuromuscular category, the first was the problem of initiation, or more accurately, failure to intentionally fire muscles. A completely separate issue was spasticity—the unintentional firing of muscles. These first two problems are basically opposite sides of the same coin—either the muscles won't fire on time or else they all fire at once—famine or feast—often with the same result: getting nowhere fast.

The third problem was weakness, what feels in the beginning like paralysis. This weakness, resulting in weeks and months of partial immobility, leads to inflexibility—frozen shoulder, subluxation of the shoulder, stiffness, hip problems, back problems, and the like. In turn this leads to pain. You basically have to work this chain reaction backward. Flexibility, range of motion, must come first, then you can try to regain strength.

On the emotional side there was frustration, grief, and, if left unchecked, depression. In my case, any of these three could trigger the other two. The gateway between the two realms—physical and emotional problems—was fatigue.

Two weeks later I reported for Botox injections. I quizzed the doctor and his PA about the origins of what they were about to inject me with. I was expecting an answer like the Netherlands, or San Jose. But he took the question of origin to mean origin of botulism. Turns out the discovery was made in Germany in the 1820s, when people began dying from tainted sausage.

Three vials of botulinum, the approximate amount the doctor had in mind for me, cost $1,500. But the pharmaceutical company had an arrangement whereby all we would be responsible for was the doctor's copay. So, for the expenditure in energy of signing my name, which in those days was not insignificant, I could basically have the rotten sausage poison for free. I wondered what the catch was. Was this like the playground crack dealer giving you your first bag for free? Would this stuff be so good I'd come crawling back for more in three months, willing to pay any price? So far, no such sinister scheme has emerged.

They rolled in a sonogram machine with a laptop display. This would be the first sonogram since voiding my bladder into the urine hat for the last time in the rehab hospital. The assistant held my hand outstretched while the doctor studied the screen closely and injected the neurotoxin into my arm in five places and my calf in four places. Then I was off to work, like I hadn't just been injected with one of the most lethal toxins known to man.

My physical therapist during this period was Ukrainian and had quite the accent. When I returned to PT, she asked me how my buttocks injection had gone. I gave her a long, puzzled stare, "Oh, *Bo-tox!*" I said. After we got straight what we were talking about and exactly where the injections had been, she tested me on a range of tasks, of which the maximum score was 28.

When I started at St. David's in June, I was a 15. That day, I scored 22. So big picture, that felt like progress. In six minutes, with no brace or cane, I could walk 1,055 feet. I could step over two stacked shoe boxes without breaking stride, stand for thirty seconds with my feet together and eyes closed, rise from a chair and walk while counting down from ninety-nine by threes. Things I still could *not* do included balancing on my right leg and raising up on my right-foot toes (plantar flexion). Of course, this was all just PT. OT was a whole other ball of wax and not as encouraging, but it was nice to get this snapshot.

On October 24, I broke twenty minutes on my walk for the first time, recording a time of 19:47. I had found the key to a better gait and improved speed was a more pronounced swing of my left arm as I stepped with my right foot. When I thought about that, it was like hitting a turbo charge switch, meaning I could for short spurts walk half as fast as an able-bodied person instead of one-tenth as fast. But it also made me feel as if I were striding the stage in a jaunty Broadway number. Every time I began to swing my left arm dramatically out and slightly across my body, I would spontaneously begin humming "Surrey with the Fringe on Top" from *Oklahoma!* Whatever it takes.

On November 17, my time dropped to 16:04. I did the walk again later that day and got the same time, to the second.

About five months after leaving Dripping Springs, I received a denial of coverage for my final week there. They dismiss you if you don't make enough progress. They deny you if you make too much. It was interesting to read the letter cataloguing all of my accomplishments in a cold, litigious, even accusatory tone:

> March 14, 2018, it was documented that the member was ambulating for 15 minutes without a quad cane. (I think that means me and not my member.) He was able to stand 20 minutes without a rest break. On March 27, 2018, it is noted he has sustained attention skills for completion of increasing complex visual targets independently. He also demonstrated decreased neurocognitive fatigue following completion of sustained complex tasks. There is no documentation why the member required an acute inpatient rehab stay. Do not allow acute inpatient rehabilitation stay for dates of service March 26 through March 30, 2018, for diagnosis codes 169 non-traumatic intracranial hemorrhage, unspecified.
>
> There was no documentation of the member needing close physician involvement for active medical issues. He was safely ambulating and his cognition status did not show deficits which could not be treated on an outpatient setting as residual rehab needs could be met in the outpatient setting.
>
> Your doctor ordered a stay in a rehab hospital. Could have been done at an outside facility.

Well, insurance may have denied my final week in Dripping Springs, but at least I had outpatient therapy at St. David's, which I continued enthusiastically.

But there was a problem here too. Apparently, the hospital had been leaning on therapists to shed their long-term patients—something about it recently becoming a Medicare facility and needing to be dealing only with worse cases than mine. One day, my lead OT broached the subject with me in a conversation that felt very much like a breakup talk with a girlfriend: "You're back to work! You're driving! You're at the top of the pyramid! You're where all these people are trying to get," she said in a hushed tone, gesturing to other patients in the rehab gym. "Your right side is never going to be like your left. I mean—you'll continue to get some back, but it's never gonna be a hundred percent!" The implication was that it would be greedy of me to keep pursuing therapy when so many needed so much more.

If I had been getting the same message from all of my therapists, that would have been one thing. But others had told me that we were about to double down on therapy because of my Botox injections. I was confused, but this therapist was the one in charge, and St. David's was breaking up with me, no two ways about it.

"All right," I said with tears in my eyes, for I had just been told by an expert that I had done most of the improving I was going to. "I guess I'll go to Scheduling on my way out and cancel the sessions on the calendar."

"Good," she said. "Just keep doing all your exercises at home."

Over the long Columbus Day weekend, we decided it was past time to give the boys the Texas State Fair experience. We would arise early Sunday and arrive late morning, go to the fair, then drive north to Plano, and spend the night in a hotel. On Monday, we would drive on to Sherman, near the Oklahoma state line, so Andrew could visit a college there he was interested in.

When we got to Dallas and finally were parked, I donned my AFO, shouldered my collapsible stool, and we took the trolley from the enormous parking lot to the fairgrounds entrance.

We passed a pen with a small crowd gathered around. As we approached, we glimpsed in the gaps between the assembled a seven-foot-long, eighteen-inch-high mass of lightly haired pink flesh. Signage revealed we were in the presence of "Boris," a domesticated hog who tipped the scales at 1,150 pounds. Boris lay on a bed of fresh wood shavings, his back to a guffawing audience with naught visible but testicles the size of cantaloupes. Having no modesty, I wondered if he too was freshly discharged from a hospital. There was also a fresh pile of excrement between himself and us, size: large, texture: medium.

We walked along a midway, me waddling along in the lead, Kirstin subtly directing the boys to stay close to me in case I lost my balance. At dozens of booths, people queued up in the hundreds for deep-fried atrocities of every description, not simply corn dogs and other fare you might find frozen in a grocery store, but deep-fried shepherd's pie, deep-fried bacon on a stick, deep-fried ice cream, deep-fried Dr Pepper, and the fattiest thing ever conceived by the mind of man—the fat beyond which there exists nothing fattier—deep-fried butter. It was a Saturnalia of heart disease and diabetes in which Texans gleefully thumbed their noses at medical science, nutritional do-gooders, and even dietary common sense. I could envision a time in which this aspect of a fair really added to the novelty. But to modern eyes, it seemed instead like a day only marginally more decadent than any other.

After a quick lunch of Fletcher's corn dogs at a dirty picnic table, we hurried across the way and into an arena, where men in overalls and with wireless mics staged pig races. Sitting on the front row due to my handicap, I got an adrenaline rush when one of the larger specimens being paraded around before the races nearly crossed the flimsy chain that separated us from the action and sent me and the stool into the wood shavings.

We made our way around the Cotton Bowl football stadium to Big Tex, the State Fair mascot. The State Fair was the "driver's ed film" of community mobility for a disabled person. And I was now at the point in my recovery when I was in some sense at my most vulnerable. Had I been in a wheelchair, most of the crowd would have parted like the Red Sea. Had I been using a cane, revelers would have gotten the visual cue "this man is handicapped" and would have given me wide berth. But such was not the case, and, in the "concert crowd" atmosphere, the able-bodied darted in front of me willy-nilly, maneuvering baby strollers, staring at their phones, laughing and talking to friends behind them. What's more, there was rarely a level surface on the ancient fairgrounds, much of it laid out for the state's centennial in 1936, its decades of potholes repaired to "good enough for a fairground."

Big Tex is a fifty-five-foot cowboy, of the dandy 1940s variety, who welcomes visitors to the fair. His unpolished, almost improvised quality—in a day and age when he could be made perfect, including the poorly proportioned body and terrifying visage—somehow added to his charm. It was as if a ninety-year-old whittling enthusiast with glaucoma created the model, and a high school shop class with access to oil field equipment executed his vision.

We headed to the Ferris wheel, where we snaked through a line with twenty switchbacks and one that never paused quite long enough to set up the stool.

After getting me up a flight of stairs and across a gap into the swinging, caged gondola, we nervously enjoyed the ride high over Dallas.

At the Birthing Barn, goats and sheep quietly strained to lighten their loads. From a stand near the entrance we spent the balance of our food tickets on a piece of fried chicken paired with waffles with syrup and powdered sugar, awkwardly shared it, and, just like that, we were back in line for the trolley, then back to our car.

At our hotel in Plano, we showered off the day's grime, ordered pizza, and dozed off to the regular-season football matchup of Dallas at Houston playing on three different TVs throughout the suite, the height of American excess.

I awoke in the middle of the night and after a few minutes began crying quietly. The shaking of the bed woke Kirstin. She thought it was stroke grief, but instead, I was heaving and sniffling because sunrise would mark the beginning of the end—the day we began looking in earnest at colleges, the beginning of the end of the five of us living as a happy nation, a happy, crazy, silly, noisy nation under one roof.

In the morning, we drove to Sherman. I dropped Andrew and Kirstin at the campus and headed out to find an adventure for Cameron, Ian, and myself. Just an exit or two up the highway was Dennison, birthplace of Dwight Eisenhower. Alas, the boyhood home of our thirty-fourth president and Supreme Commander of Allied Forces in Europe was closed, because, Mondays. So we cast about for another way to burn two hours.

We found it in the form of the Grayson County Frontier Village, a collection of old homes and cabins that had been brought from all over the county and plopped down in an oval just off the main highway. After making my way through leaf litter and across uneven ground to each house, I would struggle up the porch's rickety steps, and Cameron would lead the way in. Each home featured a living room with low-slung ceiling, lit only by windows, and almost all with an out-of-tune piano. Ian would improvise a creepy tune on the untuned piano, we'd study an old photo or a piece of Victorian technology that had made it all the way out here, then move to the next house. At length, we left behind North Texas's largest collection of untuned pianos and headed back to Sherman. We caught up to Andrew and K and got an abbreviated campus tour.

When we got back in the car to head home to Austin, I hit refresh on my phone's health app. Since leaving Austin, I had walked more than eleven miles. It felt like I had passed a milestone.

At my nine-month follow-up with my neurologist, he agreed to let me come off Prozac. By contrast, he also proclaimed I'd probably be on Keppra for life. "On January 19 there was a fire on your motherboard," he said. "When we did the EEG, I saw the zip-zip-zip. We might do another EEG in a year or two, but I see no reason to reduce the dosage now. There's still a zip-zip-zip." Then he went back through the setback a seizure would mean: no driving for three months.

This visit, and the life sentence of Keppra, made me wonder what the future of stroke treatment will look like. It seemed people of the future are as likely to look at current practices with as much amusement as I felt reading *Vitalogy*, with its talk of large heads and short necks as risk factors and its prescription of ligatures and cayenne pepper-infused baths.

What will be the accepted protocol for stroke in a hundred years, in five hundred years, in ten thousand years? I imagine something *Star Trek*-inspired, the waving of some sort of light-wand over a patient's scalp and immediate healing. Maybe having a stroke will mean you just knock off a little early for the day, as you would for a headache, but then are back, good as new, the next day:

"What's up, Jim? Why'd you miss our two o'clock huddle on the Johnson account yesterday?"

"Yeah, sorry about that. Had a stroke. Anyway, what decision did you come to?"

With strokes, the punishment simply doesn't seem to fit the crime. So there's a few tablespoons of blood on your brain for ten minutes, or a blockage. Why does that equate to a lifetime of giving up something you love, like guitar, or something you need, like language? Like the ability to walk? Like the ability to use your dominant hand? When you accidentally drop your cell phone into a toilet, you put it in a bag of rice for twelve hours and it's as good as new. If the brain is the cell phone, then what is the rice? We seem to be making progress on ischemic strokes. But what is the quick fix for a little blood on the brain?

Additionally, it seems to me there is a time element to this that is not fully being taken into account. Workplaces have defibrillators now, because we recognize that time is everything when it comes to a heart attack. But in a "brain attack," is time any less critical?

At a bare minimum, it seems there are logistical things that should have been worked out by now, such as forcing someone who is having a stroke to think about which hospitals in his city are "in network," then sending him to a second hospital because it has a better neurology team. I often think about the fact that it was four hours from my stroke to my surgery, and I wonder what I might still be able to do if it had been three hours, or two hours, or one hour.

CHAPTER 23

Today Is Mine

...the trials which beset our every step, all our sorrow, pain, shame, and grief, are born in the world of matter; whereas the spiritual Kingdom never causes sadness. A man living with his thoughts in this Kingdom knows perpetual joy. The ills all flesh is heir to do not pass him by, but they only touch the surface of his life; the depths are calm and serene.

–Abdu'l-Bahá, *Paris Talks*

In November, my coworkers and I moved from a four-story building on the northwest edge of campus to the twenty-seventh floor of the UT Tower, the architectural symbol of the university. Moving to the highest floor of a skyscraper when you're coming off Prozac is a dicey proposition. Alarm bells should have been clanging the moment my workout playlist started including Pink Floyd.

The UT Tower is infamous as the site of the first mass shooting in US history. On August 1, 1966, an engineering student and ex-Marine rode the elevator to the twenty-seventh floor—my new floor—with a footlocker full of guns, ammo, and enough food and water to last several days. As he came out of the elevator, he made a right, went into the stairwell, and climbed the final flight of stairs to the observation deck. There, he was greeted by receptionist Edna Townsley, like me, fifty-one, whom he killed with the butt of his rifle so as not to waste any bullets on such an easy target. Over the next ninety-six minutes he terrorized the campus, taking sixteen lives. The story is well known, perhaps too well known, and I only recite these macabre facts to convey the vague unease I felt in the space, despite all its otherwise desirable traits: its iconic status, the walnut-paneled decor, large windows, and high ceilings.

In this office, I worked back-to-back with Von. It is hard to pinpoint the most interesting thing about Von. Was it the nomadic nature of his early adulthood? Was it his newfound interest, at age fifty-four, in calligraphy? The fact that he changed his last name to his first name, then took a girlfriend's surname as his own? Was it the fact that he was forced into buying a car because he needed a way to transport his new harp, or the fact that he had once studied the ancient craft of cobbling?

I was chiefly a writer. Von was a production designer and a frequent proofreader, and so he and I could have long conversations about Associated Press style versus Chicago style, especially around commas and capitalization. He told me he wanted to write a book and, knowing that I had written a few, picked my brain about the process.

About a month after the move, I arrived at work at an impressive 8:15, impressive because getting myself out of bed at all was a significant feat requiring dogged determination, then there was dressing, remembering my meds, feeding Gracie, navigating traffic, climbing on and off the bus, and staggering uphill to the soaring UT Tower as the state song, "Texas, Our Texas," rang out from its carillon. Entering the dark ground-floor hallway, I turned down the gray-tiled corridor with its low ceiling that led to the Tower's elevators. I called the elevators and waited patiently to see which of the two would arrive first. The west one did, and I rode alone in it, swiping my ID on the sensor and punching "27."

The doors between the elevator lobby and the office were locked, as we all had agreed they should stay, in this iconic office that seemed to be something of a magnet for crazy people, and I was still fumbling with my keys when a beeping alarm began to sound. Having worked in the building once before, I knew instantly what it meant.

The beeping was followed by a recording of a calm but stern woman, the kind that's in all futuristic movies when the powers that be want people to be calm and compliant, usually in the context of something sinister: "An emergency situation has been detected in the building. Please evacuate immediately using the stairwells. Do NOT use the elevator."

Oh no. For the love of all that is good and right, please let me have heard that wrong. But again, I knew it was happening, that which was inevitable. Not knowing if I would be coming back that day or if we might just be dispatched back home, I kept my backpack on and the open-road straw hat from Marfa on my head. By the time I had made it to the stairwell, my colleagues who were already at their desks were following me down the first flight. Twenty-six, twenty-five . . . I have not even had a chance to get my coffee. Twenty-four . . . twenty-three . . . The alarm is still going off, and the dystopian lady is still warning of an emergency situation detected. Twenty-two . . . twenty-one . . . I encourage my colleagues to go on and get out of the building. I do not want to be the cause of their death by smoke inhalation or a gunman, but they decline to go ahead. By the twentieth floor, I am sucking wind. I am holding tight to the old polished wooden handrail with Lefty and stepping down reciprocally to try to make time as my coworkers amble down the flights with ease, joking and laughing and going at most half the speed they would have if they were serious about evacuating a building. Nineteen . . . oh good, we're in the teens . . . Eighteen . . . damn, that announcement is loud on this floor . . . Seventeen . . . sixteen . . .

At about the fifteenth floor, three of the four decide to go ahead, in case there is an actual emergency and our department head is looking for us. Robin, who has been my boss for only three weeks, refuses to go ahead. "If you think I'm gonna leave you in the stairwell, you don't know me very well," she says with a laugh. I search for any way to convince her to go on. "Well . . . I'd leave you!" is the best I can come up with. She laughs and continues on behind me. Fourteen . . . thirteen . . . twelve . . . At eleven, I have to stop and catch my breath. There is no more small talk, no more clever asides, and I stifle a sob.

At the eighth floor, the Tower stairwell ends and routes us twenty or so feet to a new stairwell, the one that would take us the balance of the journey through the Main Building that sits at the base of the Tower. We just have four flights to go, but they are twice the length of the others, meaning if I slip I will fall twice as far to the next landing. Three . . . Now jovial construction workers join Robin and me. Two . . . They too wave off my encouragement to pass me . . . One . . . a cruel false ending, as one is not the ground floor. With one final pivot and a final descent, I see the square sign, a white sans serif "G," on a black background, side-lit by a window in the door that leads outside. From that day forward, I would regard G as my favorite letter of the alphabet.

Outside, police cars and fire trucks clog the street behind the building. In less than a minute, a female firefighter who is walking away from the building with an ax, calls to the police, "All clear." We turn on our heels and take the elevator back up. Someone had likely burned the popcorn.

A few days later George H. W. Bush passed away. He had been president when I was a college student, and at that time I was not a fan. But adulthood had taken me all over the political spectrum, and maturity had allowed me to sort among the achievements of political leaders and to appreciate those achievements piecemeal. I paused to thank him that day, for it was he who signed the Americans with Disabilities Act. That afternoon, custodians came through the entire building with a diagram of which office lights to turn on and which windows to pull the blinds over. The result, when the Tower was darkened that night, was a twenty-seven-story "41."

Monday morning, we all received a Slack message from Von that just said he would not be at our morning meeting. When we returned from the meeting, Von was there but down. My coworker Thomas had seen him in the elevator lobby, seated at a table, rocking back and forth with his eyes closed and talking in what sounded like gibberish. "Are you okay?" Thomas asked.

"No," Von said.

Thomas proceeded tentatively. "Are you praying?"

"Yes." That was all he said.

When Thomas told me this, I said that made sense because he was Pentecostal, and "speaking in tongues" is one way they pray. At 10:32, Von Slacked the office that he was not feeling well and was going home. Tuesday morning, we got another one-sentence message: "I'll be in the hospital for several days." Hospitalization was not new or especially alarming. Shortly after I began working with him three years earlier, he had been out for two months with pneumonia, then another hospitalization a year or so later for Crohn's disease. Still, I had a sinking feeling this time.

The next day, I was in the men's room on the twenty-seventh floor, indisposed, when through the door's frosted glass window I saw the strobe light going off in the stairwell. Again the blaring recorded Orwellian announcement: "An emergency situation has been detected in the building. Please evacuate the building immediately. Take the stairwells. Do NOT take the elevator." Because I was in the restroom, everyone assumed I wasn't in the office and so went down without me. This was actually my preference. As I struggled to get my pants up and open the heavy door, I heard their footsteps and laughter fading into the depths below me.

Stair after stair, flight after flight, I coaxed my right leg to swing out straight, then planted my foot hard with a thud on the step below. Sweat began to bead on my brow and my lower back on about the tenth floor, and my breathing turned heavy. On the final flights I struggled past construction workers and first responders who seemed remarkably incurious about why there was still a crippled man in the stairwell more than ten minutes after the alarm had sounded. And yet again, as soon as I had made the entire descent and gotten outside, we were given the all clear.

I had had enough. The moment I returned to my desk I drafted an email to my two bosses asking for them to find another spot for me to perch, the sooner the better. Within an hour they had found a temporary space on the building's second floor, inside the graduate school office, and I began to gather my things.

Wednesday passed uneventfully as I found my way around the grad school office—the coffee machine, the bathroom, the Kleenex, and so on.

Thursday, I continued acclimating to life back on Earth. But reports about Von were becoming more frequent. The wording became more formal and there was a switch from Slack back to old-fashioned email. One email from Robin announced that "it was with great sadness" that she was "reporting Von's hospitalization," and she gave his ICU room number. On the bus ride home, my phone rang. He was on dialysis, and the end might be near. If I wanted to see Von again, the time was now. It was a shocking decline.

When I reached my truck at the park-and-ride, I raced home to check on the boys, as Kirstin was out of town. I then turned and raced against traffic, retracing the route I had just ridden on the bus. Von was at Seton Main, the same hospital I went to from the office when I had my stroke almost exactly a year earlier. In-bound traffic was light, and I now understood how Kirstin was able to reach Seton so quickly the day the call came.

My navigation app was taking me through the neighborhood a way I had never gone before, and in between her robotic interruptions, I brainstormed what I might say to him if he was awake. *Hey, Von, you've got this*— No, that wasn't right. It wasn't right because it wasn't true. He knew it. The doctors knew it. We all knew it. This was it. What's the good in pretending? —IN A QUARTER MILE, TURN RIGHT ONTO SHOAL CREEK AVENUE . . . *Whatever this is . . . you'll be ok.* That was better. That was truthful without being hopeless. He *would* be okay, even in death. I believed that, and I knew he did too. I kept searching for other talking points, better options: *This is just a transition*— IN ONE THOUSAND FEET, TURN RIGHT ONTO CRAWFORD RENFRO AVENUE. *You are loved.* Oh please, really? I'm going to use passive instead of active voice on a technical writer? He wouldn't like that even now. *There's a lot of love here.* Better, but still passive. *We love you.* True, but isn't that sort of passing the buck, first person plural? *I love you.* That was it. At the end of life, that was really all there was to say.

I reached the hospital at sundown, found a handicap spot, and tried to walk with long, steady strides. Following a helpful tech, I rode up an elevator to ICU. I turned and saw a group gathered at the end of an impossibly long hallway. But even at this nautical distance, I could tell they were my coworkers. As I approached them, there were hugs from former colleagues who had moved on to other work. Red eyes and tight, closed-lip smiles.

I went into Von's room and beheld him, thin and frail, unconscious with eyes barely open. A black beanie to cover his bald head. Tubes and tape all over him. I did not approach him, as I did not want to be in the way. I hoped that if his spirit had already left his body, he would see me from above, standing near the foot of his bed, tears streaming down my cheeks.

I had not been in this hospital in almost a year, and everything about it brought a flood of memories—the fluorescent lights I remembered strobing over me as I was wheeled through the hallways and swinging doors, the antiseptic smell, the hundreds of rolling stands, thousands of bags and plastic tubes, the beeping of automated machines.

At last I had to leave. There would be no conscious goodbyes, no words of comfort from me or him. It was too late for that. I passed the rest of the evening stretching on the tumbling mat, telling the boys goodnight one by one, and dozing in the recliner as pundits on CNN bemoaned the state of national and world affairs. I decided to go to bed. I checked my phone one last time, and just as I did, an email came in from Robin. Von was gone. He would never write his book. I turned out the lamp and went to sleep.

I woke in the dark the next morning and told Alexa to play Louis Armstrong in Von's honor, as he loved jazz. After a few songs, I reverted to the song I had her play every morning, "Today Is Mine" by Jerry Reed. Andante and uncharacteristically earnest, it spoke of how unimportant our troubles are compared with the opportunities each day presents.

Exactly a week later we were all together once more, this time with Von's family members, from Long Island to Spokane, to say our final goodbye. It was hard to pinpoint the most interesting thing about this most interesting of men. The nomadism, the calligraphy, the harp, the cobbling. These all contend for the title. But for my money the most interesting fact about Von was that, after studying Buddhism and wandering widely through the world of wisdom traditions, he found a spiritual home at Freedom Temple Pentecostal Church, a nearly all-black congregation in Austin. And Von was as white as I am, which is to say, completely.

And so to say the funeral was lively would be like calling a hurricane "moist." Kirstin and I went into the chapel wet-eyed and mopey and came out feeling like we'd just been to a rock concert. The Freedom Temple Praise

Team, with four female singers, keys, bass, and drums, praised God to within an inch of His life. And the congregants danced in the aisles, hands lifted as if warming their palms on a bitter winter night with the fire of God's love. His family and predominantly white coworkers smiled and clapped on beats one and three, square-dance style, as the Freedom Temple crowd held it steady on the two and the four.

Minister Joshua Edmond told us that Von would be dancing more fervently than anyone, were he able. In fact, he relayed a curious thing. He said that on Sunday, the day before Von went home sick from work, he danced at the church "for hours." "Brother Von just danced and danced and danced." Minister Edmond said he'd never seen anything quite like it.

Prayer (written 2012, four years prior)

That my life might be acceptable
That I mightn't have squandered too great a fraction of it
That I might have nudged one soul toward the cause of unity
That I might have stifled the critic within once or twice
That in the next life I might not be embodied in that ether at the height of
    my gluttony
That I might have loved
That I might have exerted some effort, risked anything, sacrificed
    something
That I might have put to some good use this oxygen, these animals and
    vegetables, this precious water, this spacetime real estate—that my matter
    had mattered
That I might have once put comedy second to reverence, cleverness beneath
    sincerity
That my spiritual armbuds and legbuds and embryonic eyes might have
    grown enough to serve me after that birth that is death
That I might be forgiven a debt or two
By those I loved imperfectly, such as You
That my life might be acceptable
That my life might be acceptable
That my life might be acceptable

CHAPTER 24

Nature Boy

Once, I actually Googled "camping with a stroke."

As you might imagine, there were not a tremendous number of hits. As a matter of fact, I got exactly one, an article about what sounded like a lovely camp run for stroke survivors. "During the weekend," it read, "the campers are treated to meals (served by volunteers) and a day of pampering, which includes massages, paraffin waxing, rides around the grounds or time to relax and chat with new friends." In other words, the exact opposite of camping.

A licensed psychologist could probably do a better job of explaining why going into wilderness areas and being able to survive a few days on my own is so important to me, but I was determined to get this part of my life back.

My attempt in September had been a spectacular failure, as I was unable to sleep more than fifteen minutes at a time in the hot and humid forest.

My next attempt was on the last night of November at Lake Georgetown, just north of Austin. It would be my return to Boy Scout camping. We arrived in darkness on that Friday night. With the batteries in my headlamp nearly dead, I had to negotiate a gravel slope multiple times to get my gear from my truck to the campsite. Another dad helped me set up my hammock.

The first night was a success, cool and comfortable. I even enjoyed a moment of cozy satisfaction as a squall line of storms moved across the lake and past us, with me high and dry in a tarp-covered hammock.

I awoke to a clear and windy morning. The day's agenda was geared around our eleven-year-old Ian's "grubmaster" requirements, which included preparing a meal in camp and cooking a meal during a hike of at least five miles. We got on the trail early since the boys were to eat breakfast at the farthest point of the hike.

I started down the trail at the rear of the patrol, with my sixteen-year-old, Andrew, hanging back to make sure I was okay. But within five minutes of camp I was stymied by a rocky slope. I told Andrew to go on ahead and stay with the group and that I would go back and hang out at camp. He did as I said, scampering down the limestone slope and disappearing around a bend in the trail, swallowed up by the cedar and live oak.

I turned around to head back to camp, but my feet would not move. Tears filled my eyes, then streamed down my face and soon my shoulders heaved with grief. This was not right. This was not how it could be. This was not how this was going to go down. For five minutes, I stood there and cried, and calculated the risk of going on. Then I turned back around and headed toward Walnut Springs, toward the boys. I wore high-top hiking boots, which offered good protection against the rocks and a slight bit of protection from rolling my ankle. I also used my trekking pole.

But even with those supports, the going was unbelievably slow, the ground treacherous. I studied every descent and incline and squeeze between rock formations with an eye not just for ease but for survival. In many places, the trail became entirely theoretical, dissolving into long stretches of karst, a limestone formation formed by the flow of water, thousands of years of which had not rounded the stone, as one might expect, but had made the edges sharp. Minerals that pool on the strangely shaped rocks over eons eat holes in them about the size of an eye socket, so that I felt I was climbing along a jagged mountain of human skulls, perhaps the bleached remains of all those who had tried to hike this trail in years past and had been found wanting.

After two and a half hours of carefully teetering my way along landscapes that alternated between jagged karst skull fields and long swaths of loose rock, I finally reached the flat, abandoned Jeep track that ran along the lakeshore to Walnut Springs. When at last I triumphantly entered the camp, the boys were nowhere to be found. They had reached the camp, eaten a meal, cleaned up, and moved on to explore farther afield in the time it took me to get there.

I sat in the campsite alone and pondered the events of the morning. There was no way around it—I had done a profoundly foolish thing, and for that, I did not deserve a triumphal entry. I had wanted to support the boys, but how much support had I been two miles behind them? Moreover, if I had fallen, alone on the trail, it would have meant a chaotic rescue that eventually would have consumed the remainder of the campout. If my attempt to make the hike had set an example of bravery and perseverance, then my attempting to go it alone had also provided a negative example, flouting a cardinal rule of Scouting, the buddy system.

When the boys arrived back at Walnut Springs, duly surprised to see me, I just took another bite of apple and said to Andrew, "I changed my mind."

Though the previous night in the hammock had been pleasant, our second night was miserably cold, so cold I got up at two in the morning, drove my truck to the other side of the park so as to not keep the boys awake, and slept in the driver's seat with the engine running for heat. Would every night camping from here on out be spent sitting in my truck, dozing for ten minutes at a time? I had changed. Maybe it was time to change strategies.

It was almost New Year's again, and therefore time for Wade's and my New Year's campout. Having had a terrible hammocking night less than a month earlier, I decided we should use a tent. But the dome tent's poles and clips proved impossible for me to manage, and Wade wound up doing all the setup. Nor was it easy to get off the old cot I had used when we had camped out here three weeks before the stroke.

The next day, I felt like trying a modest hike. We unknowingly picked a stretch of trail in which hundreds of magnolia trees sent their root nodules up and out of the sand like teeth out of gums. Every step was tentative, as I felt for the presence of these thumb-sized root structures hiding among the leaf litter, fearing my ankle would twist and my right foot would snap off at any second. The walk felt less like two friends out on a hike and more like something arranged by the Make-A-Wish Foundation as a last request, Wade patiently holding me by the elbow as I climbed up onto wobbly boardwalks and steadying me as I stepped down off them.

After an hour of hard going for me, we reached a waterfall and washed-out bridge about a mile away from camp. There, I unpacked my stool and feasted on the peanut butter and apple quesadillas I had made for the trip. I suggested we return to camp and then drive to another section of trail I was interested in. For the return hike, I dug my black plastic AFO brace out of my day pack and donned it while balancing precariously on the stool.

The difference was immediate and dramatic. While it had taken us an hour to get out there, I flew back to camp in fifteen minutes. As Wade had carefully gotten me out there, Malcolm Slade, the man who made my AFO, had gotten me back. As I ate up the trail with long, confident strides, I felt the beauty of this invention and the glory of his devoted craftsmanship, his divine calling in action. And I saw Malcolm's stoic face shining before me there in the darkening forest.

Clearly, the AFO would be key to any hiking for the foreseeable future, but the puzzle of a camping setup I could handle by myself persisted. It was no big deal for Wade to set up the simple tent, and he was more than happy to do it, but that was not the point. I had to have something I could manage all by myself.

Convinced that a return to tent camping was inevitable, when we returned to Austin, I went to REI ready to part with a significant amount of money for a tent that I could set up by myself. The young sales associate escorted me to a large classroom at the back of the store and cleared away a table and some chairs so I could try to put the tent up. Within three minutes, I knew it was no use. What's more, I couldn't get it back in the stuff sack, which is a problem equal to the inability to set it up. I left the classroom a mess and departed the store bitterly disappointed.

Then I realized I had succumbed to the siren of a false religion: technology. When most people are confounded by a problem, they reach for a high-tech solution. I am in a vanishingly small minority that, when confronted with a problem, seeks answers by going back toward the primitive. I'm famous in my circle of longtime friends for suggesting, after a long day of unsuccessful surf fishing, that we just eat the bait shrimp. We cooked it plain and dry over a driftwood campfire on the beach, and if memory serves, it wasn't bad. Throwing seafood away just because other seafood didn't want to eat it right then seemed exactly like throwing good money after bad. The high-tech solution would have been to go to a more specialized, complicated lure, and more expensive fishing setup. The primitive solution? Just eat the seafood you've already got.

When it came to camping, this meant forsaking the high-tech factory-forged origami masterpieces that packed up into stuff sacks the size of a deck of cards, with all of their shock-cord self-assembling fiberglass poles and plastic clips that held the spaceship-like structures taut. Before these high-tech tents, with their high price tags and California-mandated carcinogen warnings, before the high-tech hammocks that I had become such an evangelist for, there was ... the tarp. To be clear, there were tarps, and ropes, and poles. Hmm, I thought. A tarp, and a cot. What would be wrong with that?

Of course, for all my romanticizing of primitive solutions, I went straight back to REI and purchased a high-tech lightweight tarp, and then to Cabela's for a deluxe cot, taller, wider, and longer than my old one to accommodate my new needs. Then I got on YouTube and watched about three dozen tutorials on tarp camping. The A-frame pup tent, the arrowhead, the ridgeline diamond, the three-sided pyramid. I must say there was something extremely satisfying in rigging a ridgeline with a trucker's hitch and securing the guylines all with one hand and my teeth. On the Boy Scouts wilderness survival campout that next February, it didn't work perfectly, but it was thirty degrees and raining. I eventually tapped out and slept in the driver's seat of my truck . . . again. But the Scouts kept walking past my tarp, cot, and one-pole setup, intrigued by the anachronism.

The next campout was in the spring, and I was relatively successful, tying a ridgeline between a dead tree and a staked seven-foot pole, pitching the tarp in an A-frame, and setting up the deluxe cot below it. It suggested a scene from the Civil War. But this ground-based and open-air approach was not for sissies. There was nothing to prevent any insect in south central Texas from flying or climbing right into bed with me, nor reptiles, nor mammals, nor any living thing that flew or crawled upon the earth. And there were a lot of bugs, though it wasn't even summer yet. Once, overnight, I reached into my pants and pulled something off my thigh about the size of a June bug.

Despite my serial failures at hammock camping, my thoughts kept returning to its elegant solution to just about all of the problems I was trying to solve. I could string it at any height, so no struggling onto or off the ground. Being off the ground eliminated crawlers. My sewn-in bug net eliminated fliers. All the groovy tarp configs and knots I had learned during my tarp phase could still be used.

It was the temperature that presented the only remaining challenge. In the case of cold, the challenge was keeping my sleeping bag over me and at the same time not letting it tie me up and bind me in weird ways. After talking through it with Wade, I determined that I should abandon the sleeping bag altogether and simply sleep in insulated coveralls. That way, I would never have a freezing gap in coverage, and my arms and legs would always be free to push me into the next sleeping position. For warm weather, it had been unfair to judge the hammock a failure for the one night I had tried it, on the most humid and still weekend of the year, in the middle of a steamy forest. The key to that problem would be something I had used on previous summer trips—a battery-powered fan trained on my face.

And one more thing. By the time I tried the hammock again, I was stronger, steadier, more coordinated. The hammock had come back to me, and I had come back to the hammock.

What Grace Is (2014, four years prior)

Under ancient live oaks
My son and I hang in hammocks
Opposite edges of the campsite
Like fruit,
His small green hammock having ripened
Into my double-wide red one
As if a time-lapse split-screen.
Two-thirty a.m.
And the ash still invisibly exhales
A feeble tendril of smoke between us
The gentle rain,
Barely more than mist,
Begins to fall.
Silently—I cannot wake the scouts or other dads —
I rise to sitting
Slip my feet into hiking boots like house slippers
Shuffle clumsily to him.
I move the camp chair that holds his sneakers
Under his tarp.
Now they will be dry for him
When he stirs in five hours.
It hits me, maybe for the first time,
What grace is:
It is all that The Parent does for us
That we sleep right through,
Softly snoring sweet oblivion
Under rain-heavy clouds.
Being spared that which we never even knew
Was threatening.
Unknown unknowns.
Dry tennis shoes.

Pancho and Lefty

Administer an injection composed of a half pint of soapsuds with a half tablespoon of salt in a teaspoon full of cayenne pepper. The patient should be covered warmly, in order to excite perspiration. Hot bricks covered with clothes wet with vinegar may be applied to the extremities to assist in recalling the blood back to its original channels.

—Vitalogy, 1904

At Thanksgiving, we traveled to South Texas for my mother's wedding. She was seventy-nine and John, eighty. It was a sweet occasion, the families meeting for the first time, old friends of our family happy for Mom's autumn love.

It was my first trip back to my hometown since the stroke, and so most attendees of the wedding were seeing stroke-Avrel for the first time. Knowing that many would want to visit with me, Mom gave me the job of manning the register book in the lobby of the McAllen Country Club, so that each and every attendee at the wedding could offer niceties like, "You look great!" and, "So great to see you!" with me reciprocating over and over, "Well, it's great to be seen!"

I also had been asked to give the toast for our side of the family. When the ceremony had been sealed with a kiss and the chairs cleared off the dance floor, the deejay handed me the mic, and I stood alone on the darkened dance floor in a suit and tie and my AFO. I began:

"To paraphrase a great American proverb, if Mama ain't happy, ain't nobody happy. And I don't think I've ever seen Mom as happy as she is tonight. When Mom got Kirstin's text back in January that I had pulled this little stunt—this stunt being a nearly fatal brain hemorrhage, John could have been forgiven for just peeling off at that point and excusing himself for a few weeks. But as night fell, there he was, speeding up US 281 with Mom and Erren and Fernando. That's when I knew this thing was serious."

Winter marked the return of allergy season, and the newfound joy of sneezing when you have no cortical control over two of your limbs. Once, lying on my tumbling mat with my arm near my face, I sneezed and simultaneously punched myself square in the jaw. This made me the only person I had ever cold-cocked. I later developed a cough for the first time since the big day, and when I started up, my right leg would kick out so hard with every cough that I nearly threw myself to the ground numerous times a day. Lying in bed one night, miserable with the cough, I rested on my right shoulder with Pancho a few inches from my head. When I suddenly coughed, my hand flew off the mattress and into the air, then fell, deadweight, onto my eyeball. I screamed in pain as the shock to my optic nerve sent lightning flashing inside my closed eye. It was misery upon misery.

After the stroke, people overwhelmingly cut me slack. The goodness of civilized people and the forms of assistance put in place to help folks like me, such as handicapped parking and bathroom grab bars and extended sick leave, were lifesavers. But life itself was indifferent. Allergies still came just as they always had. Germs still circulated. Traffic accidents still happened.

For nearly a year, the stroke had been the central fact of my life—my personal "hinge of history," all life events being categorized as pre or post. All activity was seen through the filter of the stroke. Would the stroke allow me to do X? What would be different now because of the stroke? For some people, such a powerful event and the all-consuming focus required to survive it can reshape their identity permanently. I think many veterans of war are susceptible to this phenomenon. But I did not want the stroke to remain the central fact of my life. And as time wore on, I began to purposefully move the stroke away from the central position.

Whereas earlier in the struggle, I might have instinctively started to explain my disability to strangers, just assuming they would want to know why I was moving this way and be interested in the details, I now entered the need-to-know phase of information sharing. When I met faculty members or university administrators for the first time, they offered their right hand and I shook it with my left, pulled my chair out from the table and eased down to it. I was always happy to share with anyone who asked, but very few inquired after my condition except those who thought it was a temporary injury and were just trying to make small talk.

This increased whenever I wore my AFO. I was shopping one night at Office Max for printer paper when a woman noticed my brace and said in a loud jocular voice, "Well *that* doesn't look fun! Whadya do?!"

"I had a stroke," I replied, not knowing how else to put it. Then, trying to lighten the mood and ease her shocked embarrassment, I chuckled and added, "And no, it isn't fun."

The next day, David and I were eating supper at Dairy Queen when a sweet old woman approached our table and asked if we were military, because her husband (she motioned to the man standing patiently at the exit) had served in World War II. I'm sure she thought my leg was prosthetic, and while I probably could have used the misunderstanding to secure free Blizzards for both David and me, I resisted and said simply, "No—no we're not."

Winter also marked the return of Christmas decorations, so in early December, we went to Lowe's and bought a Christmas tree. We had the option of having them cut the bottom off, but I had always preferred to do that myself and saw this as an opportunity to score a new post-stroke first. When we arrived home, I had the boys drag it into the front yard and bring a couple of metal chairs off the porch to act as sawhorses. In the garage, I lifted the bow saw off its pegboard hook and teetered back to the yard.

Forcing the cold metal saw handle into Pancho, I grabbed the tree trunk with Lefty and managed to rest the teeth of the saw on the trunk. With lots of torso movement I managed to move the saw, but it merely scratched the bark before falling off. I tried again but still could not start a cut. And now, for good measure, I fell backward onto the lawn, letting go of the saw, breaking my fall with my left arm, and gradually collapsing into a roll. I was clearly not making a saw cut today.

As I turned to the house to ask Ian to make the cut, I decided instead to try with my left hand. The saw bit all right, but now I had a different problem. Every time I pushed or pulled the saw, the whole trunk would move with it. Finally, Pancho came forward and held the trunk in place. And we were off to the races.

At that moment I realized at a deep level two distinct things: First, I was now left-handed, and probably would be the rest of my life. And second, Pancho could not just check out; he had to help. Just as I would never have cut the trunk with my right hand, neither could I have cut it with my left alone.

The left hand would get the credit, but the support of the right was crucial. Pancho could help and would have to help in many ways going forward. He would be the wind beneath Lefty's wings.

I had pursued just about every kind of treatment I could think of, and a few I hadn't but that were suggested to me by others. Aside from conventional therapy, which included some forty-two different therapists in three different categories, I got a dozen or more acupuncture treatments, deep-tissue massages, and Botox injections.

One dear friend had been helped greatly in his recovery from cycling injuries by electromagnets. He brought some over, and I laid on the bed while he moved them over my arm, leg, and head. He then connected me with his own therapist, who spent three hours over two sessions dry-needling my arm and leg. For this, he sent acupuncture needles deep into my arm, then, attaching clips that looked like tiny jumper cables to those needles, sent electrical current from one deep needle to the other. He also performed extensive cupping, creating the circular bruises familiar to anyone who has watched Olympic swimmers on television, and he scraped my skin likewise to separate it from the underlying fascia and get me "unstuck." This did temporarily help my tone, and I found his methods an intriguing hybrid—at once thoroughly science-based and yet still maverick, outside establishment orthodoxy, and cash-only.

I visited one therapist who had seemingly worked wonders when Andrew had knee problems. With me, he spent about an hour pressing on different spots and holding my limbs in different positions while testing my strength with my good arm, seeing if I could resist his pushing down or pulling up on Lefty. As well as I could understand it, this muscle testing told him where the neural problems were, though that seemed sort of obvious. When my arm became fatigued, he switched to pushing on Kirstin's arm on the theory that her muscle strength would tell him something useful about my injury. I fancy myself open-minded; having authored a book on bigfoots, I hoped I no longer had anything to prove on that front. But this felt like a bridge too far even for me. He also spent a great deal of time focusing on a car wreck I was in at the age of eight, something I disclosed during our intake interview in response to a question about "ever" having "any" accidents. He was the nicest guy, and as I say, had great success with Andrew's knee, but a stroke just seemed out of his league. I was willing to try anything to further recovery, but there were only so many hours in a day and only so many dollars in the bank, and at one hundred dollars an hour and no noticeable change, this was one to which I didn't return. I had spent all of our "couldn't hurt!" money on acupuncture.

As my colleague Von lay dying, a friend of his I did not know approached me in the hospital waiting room and handed me her business card. "I'm not sure what your issue is," she began, "but I am pretty sure I could help you." The business card said MELT Method Hand and Foot Instructor and Hatha Yoga Teacher.

"Thank you," I said, and put the card in my shirt pocket, still trying to process Von's impending death. It seemed everywhere I turned, another healer had a new method I should try. If I had wanted to, I could have spent every spare minute going to appointments and every spare dollar chasing after recovery. But to a large extent, my body seemed to be on its own timetable of recovery, coldly indifferent to this parade of one-off, two-off, or twelve-off therapies.

There was one thing I still had not tried, though, and that was the original therapy, the only treatment my great-grandfather had available to him— mineral hot springs. I had thought of driving up to Mineral Wells, Texas, to see how close I could get to his experience, but Kirstin and I found one sooner than I could get there. It was our twentieth anniversary, and to celebrate we had traveled to Banff National Park in the Canadian Rockies.

When railway workers discovered hot springs near what today is Banff, a well-rehearsed cascade of developments ensued, including the building of a huge hotel nearby, then the largest in the world, so that wealthy patrons from the east could buy a rail ticket to Alberta and avail themselves of the presumed curative powers of the springs.

I wanted to "take the waters" at the Banff Upper Hot Springs, because (1) Who wouldn't? and (2) It would give me some reference point for Horace's stroke experience a century earlier. We found ourselves there mid-morning after a gondola ride up and down Sulphur Mountain, and I was just bemoaning the fact that I hadn't brought my swimsuit when Kirstin spotted a sign. "Oh, babe," she said, "hold . . . the . . . phone. This could be the play. Says here they'll rent you a historic swimsuit."

Moments later, Kirstin and I were closed into a changing room together, she helping me out of my clothes and into a polyester replica of a 1920s swimsuit. I spun the suit around and around with Lefty, trying to find the right leg hole. I couldn't even figure out which end was up. "You've clearly never worn a jumper before," she laughed.

The bathing suit resembled a navy-blue wrestling singlet with a thick white belt and something akin to a micro-miniskirt to veil whatever anatomical specificities might emerge in the snug garment. "Is this even for a man?" I wondered aloud, Kirstin doubled over with laughter at the whole scene. It did not help the overall look that I was about three inches too long in the torso for this particular suit.

At any rate, I finally donned the garment and made my way down a gradually sloping tiled pool entrance designed for invalids who had traveled there to take the waters. I could picture Horace being rolled in a wooden wheelchair down a ramp such as this.

The result of the therapy was relaxation and a good conversation with three retirees from Wales (one who had worked in a stroke ward), and a hilarious sunburn line from the historical suit. But there was a more significant takeaway.

When Horace left Mineral Wells a century earlier, they had done all for him they could. Two men carried him off the train at the depot in Athens on a stretcher and delivered him into the care of a sober and disappointed wife, and he lived out his few remaining years as an invalid. By contrast, Kirstin and I went upstairs to the hot springs cafe for a cheeseburger and a tuna salad sandwich. Then went back to the hotel for a nap before a fabulous meal and spa in one of the world's most beautiful resorts. This was a vacation we could afford because I had been able to return to work. And I had been able to return to work and to driving and to all manner of other things partially because of good fortune and partially because we as a society had developed a culture of recovery.

My life had become an indecipherable blend of good luck and bad luck: It was bad luck I had been born with an arteriovenous malformation, good luck I had been active and in relatively good shape. Bad luck that the AVM had ruptured, good luck that when it did, I was within five minutes of a hospital instead of twenty-five miles out on a trail. Bad luck that I had been taken to a suboptimal hospital first and that it took four hours to get me into surgery, good luck that the surgery was successful and I didn't die. Bad luck that I had largely lost the use of a hand, good luck that it was my right hand and so I could still play guitar. And good luck, such unspeakably good luck, that I had married Kirstin twenty years earlier.

New Year's came and went. The anniversary of my stroke approached, and Kirstin and I both struggled with what it meant. We could dwell on what was lost, but we thought the better choice was to use the occasion to thank all the people who had helped us. Kirstin consolidated various lists she had been keeping for a year of people who visited the hospital, folks who had brought meals, given to our Go Fund Me account, and more.

They had said prayers for us in churches and synagogues, in Bahá'í holy places and Scout meetings, and in their homes and their cars and anywhere they could. These thoughts of love prompted them to action. They visited me in the hospital in January and February. They stayed by my side, and by Kirstin's side. They sent thoughtful cards and letters. They brought Gracie to see me. They gave me a smart speaker and a Spotify account so I could pass long weeks in my hospital room listening to music that lifted my spirits.

In March, they visited me in my rehab dormitory in Dripping Springs, laughed with me and reminisced about old times, brought me barbecue, and busted me out for dinner. They made the two-hour round trip to bring me home and get me back again before curfew. They loaned me a television and a lamp, checked up on me, brought me to their home and spread a feast before me.

Within hours of the stroke, they set up a CaringBridge site and then a Go Fund Me account to make financial gifts possible. These gifts covered copays on doctor's visits and therapy sessions without number. And because of those, I was walking and working and driving and leading a life very different from the one I might have led after a stroke fifty years ago. Financial support helped us replace the carpet in our home with hard flooring that kept me from falling. In preparation for those new floors, they helped us move out furniture and, once the floors were in, they put it all back.

They gave Andrew, Cameron, and Ian rides when Kirstin was stretched thin. They brought meals to the "magic cooler" on our porch that kept giving week after week. They sent gift cards for meals. (The boys were never so spoiled in their lives.) David bought and installed grab bars in our restroom, and so I had not fallen. They changed light bulbs, helped us buy and move a new refrigerator when our old one gave out, and helped with a hundred other chores. Fellow Scout dads cleared our side yard of weeds and saplings and installed a new gate, and as a result, I did not die trying to do it myself.

As I improved, they spent time with me, helping me do the things I love— took me to East Texas and helped me string my hammock in the woods and took me on a West Texas road trip and to Houston to hear a longtime guitar hero.

Their support allowed me to get left-foot accelerators in our cars, and as a result, I could get myself to work and to Sunday school, or to Dallas for the State Fair, or Houston to see my first-ever NFL game, or McAllen for my mother's wedding.

To say that my stroke had been a life-altering event would be a vast understatement. I awoke each morning to the realization that the day ahead would be harder than when my brain fired on all cylinders and I had two good arms and two good legs. The struggle was real.

But what was equally real—and what was more powerful and more lasting—was the goodness Kirstin and I witnessed that year. January 19 would never again be just another winter day. It was my stroke-versary. It could not go unnoted. But instead of mourning what was lost that day, Kirstin and I chose instead to celebrate what was gained—and that was a deeper knowledge of the profound goodness that still exists in the world, the beautiful light that shone through our family and friends, be they lifelong compadres or people we had never even met. Hardships come and go, but those acts of love and generosity would live in our hearts forever and ever.

Additionally, Kirstin and I decided to throw a party. It was around my birthday, so it morphed into a birthday party of sorts, but it was more than that; it was a thanksgiving party for as many friends as we could manage to host. We would follow the same format of my fiftieth birthday party two years earlier. I would smoke a brisket; Kirstin would bake oatmeal-chocolate chip cookies and crock pot mac and cheese. Then David and I would lead a hootenanny.

On the eve of the party, the boys helped me trim the brisket. That could have gone a lot better, really. As the bag was pulled off the brisket, a half-pint of blood was dumped on Andrew's cell phone. But at great length, we managed to wrestle the ten-pound brisket out of its bag, onto its baking sheet, get the salt and pepper rub on it, and wrap it in foil for the morning.

My favorite touch of the party was Kirstin's idea. We put the ice chest for drinks on the front porch, as was our custom, but this time, the ice chest rested in the wheelchair, which otherwise stayed in the garage.

When it was music time, David and I started off with one from our early nineties playlist, Stevie Ray Vaughan's "Cold Shot." We had brought out a snare drum and one cymbal, and Ian held down the beat. We played as many songs off our record as I could. We played Pink Floyd's "Wish You Were Here," The Beatles' "Let it Be" and "One After 909," Glen Campbell's "Wichita Lineman," "Up on Cripple Creek" by The Band.

Honestly, as a performance, it wasn't great. Oh, there were moments of adequacy, moments when, if you closed your eyes, you could almost hear a normal guitarist playing. But, as Adrian Legg would say, there were plenty of "clams," forgotten lyrics, blown chord changes, poor improvisational choices. No one but me cared in the least what I sounded like; they were happy to see me happy, period. The delayed takeaway from Steve's and my road trip to see Adrian Legg became this: that if one of the world's greatest can have a few clams in the throes of a stomach virus, I could forgive myself for a few clams in the wake of a stroke. There would be time to make all that better. This was only a proof of concept. A guy with one working hand could still sort of play the guitar.

In the parking lot of the Methodist church where both the Cub Scouts and the Boy Scouts met, an old friend who was the den leader for the fifth-grade Webelos approached me one evening. He was nervous and tentative. "I don't know how to ask this, but would you say that you have a disability?"

We happened to be standing directly next to my truck, and I pointed to the license plate, the number of which led off with the handicap symbol. I had gotten my new license plates only a few weeks earlier, and doing so required me to check a box identifying myself as "Permanently Disabled." That was quite a sobering moment, and I wished they had offered some other option or wording, such as "Disabled for Now" or "In a Rough Stretch" or "Could Be Better, Could Be Worse" or "Good Days and Bad Days." But I supposed "Permanently Disabled" was what I now was in the eyes of the state.

At any rate, the Webelos were working on a unit called Aware and Care, and Adventure Requirement 7b was, "Invite an individual with a disability to visit your den and discuss what activities he or she currently finds challenging or found challenging in the past." Would I be willing?

A month later, I reported to the second floor of the Sunday school building and found the room where the Webelos were meeting. There were three boys attending that night and their dads.

"Mr. Seale agreed to come talk with y'all about disabilities, so take it away," said the den leader.

"Thanks, Mr. Holder. So who knows what a stroke is?" I asked.

The boys were not shy and spoke right up. "Isn't it when you can't move your legs or something like that?"

"Well, it's true that I have trouble with one of my legs, but a stroke is actually not a problem with your arms or legs—it's a problem with your brain." Thus, I explained the basics of cross-lateral hemiparesis, motor strips, bleeds versus clots, and so on, no doubt in way too much detail.

At this, the chubby blond boy mentioned that sometimes his leg fell asleep in class. The one with the rat-tail haircut was compelled to share that his grandfather had a heart attack a few years ago. Mr. Holder tried to steer the conversation back to the topic at hand and consulted the requirement in the handbook. "Is there anything you currently find challenging or found challenging in the past?" he asked.

I stifled a guffaw, thinking, "Only every second of every day!" then reeled it back in before answering: "Well, when the stroke first happened, I couldn't even sit up. Then I was in a wheelchair for what seemed like a long time. Then I used a quad cane. Who knows what 'quad' means?"

"Four!" one said.

"Very good! It has four little feet. Then I used a hiking stick for a long time, just like y'all use on your hikes. Now I don't have anything like that, but I still have a disability, which is one point I wanted to make. You can't always tell by looking who has a disability and who doesn't. If I were sitting in this chair just like this when all of you walked in, you would have no idea I have a disability. But if I try to get up and walk across the room, trust me, you'll know right away.

"I'm lucky to be alive, but it's hard. Some days, I don't know if I can do it." My eyes drifted, and I realized I was headed to a dark place that was not appropriate for Cub Scouts. "But—but, I just keep on trying, 'cause that's all any of us can do, right? What's the Cub Scout motto?"

"Do your best!" they chanted dutifully.

"That's right," I said, ". . . do your best."

Eighteen months and one day after my stroke, Kirstin, the boys, and I were on a summer vacation in the mountains. We decided to do a short hike Andrew had found in our guidebook, a two-mile round trip. It so happened that a park ranger was scheduled to lead a "walk and talk" just as we reached the trailhead, and he had no other takers.

As he was sizing up my family and introducing himself at the trailhead, I hobbled out of the restroom. He gestured to me with a vertical sweep of the hand that included my trekking pole and my AFO and asked, "And you are . . ." I think he was expecting an answer like "healing from a broken leg" or "mobility impaired," but after a long moment I answered, "Avrel."

"Avrel," he repeated, "glad you'll be joining us."

We chatted about the level of difficulty of the trail, the terrain and change in elevation. He announced that the theme of his talk was nature overcoming adversity—seeds that had to be opened by fire, trees growing on bare rock with little rain, things like that. *Adventure*, he said, was just the word for a journey with *adver*sity.

As we started down the trail, we could see in the distance the bare, gray granite dome we would be summiting. Ranger Dave talked about the wild cherry bushes the bears liked to feed on and the large rusty Jefferson pine that grew in the trail. Soon, the sandy path became a challenging obstacle course of granite nodules and steps up and steps down and squeezes. I did not want to slow the family down and twice suggested to Kirstin that I just sit down by the trail and let her and the boys go on ahead to the peak. I would be fine to just enjoy the afternoon scenery, but Kirstin resisted that suggestion. Scanning the trail ahead, she would say, "I really think you can make this next section," and forward we would go.

At one point the trail became so tough we spent five minutes strategizing with the ranger how to get me six feet farther. Kirstin and Ian blocked me from falling off the trail and down the mountain. Cameron took my right side. Andrew stayed in front giving me his hand so I could pull up with Lefty. I made it through, only to fall to my knees four steps later, my arms and legs curling up defensively with unbreakable muscle tone.

"Okay, Dad, we've got you," Andrew said. "Let's just lift." He and Cameron grabbed me under the arms as Ian and Kirstin steadied me from behind. "One . . . two . . . three." I was up.

"Tall and handsome!" Kirstin said, quoting my Dripping Springs PT to lighten the mood.

The path ahead of us flattened back out to dirt, and I hurried ahead, trying to make up for lost time. The granite soon returned and, in large flats, overtook the entire trail, and we were at the base of the dome, starting the final ascent. I could see to the top now, but the grade was steep and the uphill view daunting.

"I've got you," Kirstin said, "anything you want to do." The trekking pole no longer was enough, and I grabbed the back of her neck. She bore my full weight and spread her feet and crouched low for stability and went wherever I said I felt safest. We tried to tack widely around the dome, creating our own switchbacks on the granite and inching upward. I started and stopped, then started and stopped again.

At last, I could go no higher. It was simply too steep. I pointed to a tree thirty feet away and told Kirstin I wanted to sit next to it while she and the boys went to the top. She and Ranger Dave made sure I got to the tree, and I slowly sat on a low boulder. They receded behind me toward the summit.

Alone, in the windy quiet that envelopes mountaintops, I braced myself beside the old gnarled lodgepole pine, mildly fearful of the sloping rock before me and increasingly aware of how little there was keeping me on the mountain.

Across the valley to my left, the world's largest granite monolith, El Capitan, with its sheer face, two-thirds of a mile straight down. Low and to my left, a formation known as the Cathedral Spires. Back over my right shoulder, Half Dome. And directly before me across the steep valley, Yosemite Falls, spilling off a cliff and swirling into the air for hundreds of feet as a mist before re-aggregating on the rock and funneling into a second raging falls two thousand feet below.

As I removed my hat, I began to weep at the sight. But more. I wept in gratitude. I wept for all that day had meant, and all that the previous eighteen months had meant, and all that my life had meant.

I wept in gratitude for Kirstin, my biggest rock, my El Capitan, immovable and eternal in her love for me. I wept in gratitude for Andrew and Cameron and Ian, my Cathedral Spires, who had risen to the occasion of my stroke, who had grown up so fast, and who had shown me such loving kindness in getting me up that mountain, that day and every day. Finally, I wept in gratitude for the waterfall, something like the grace of God, the universe, life itself, raining down blessings like millions of droplets, the cast of characters that were my ancestors from ages past, my mother and father and brothers and in-laws, my golden, beloved friends and caring therapists and park rangers, and all who made life in this new body possible.

As for me, I suppose I was that tree right next to me growing on the bare granite, bent but still very much alive. And blessed with the finest view on this good earth.

Kirstin and me in Banff, seventeen months post-stroke.

Me (left) still improving at nineteen months, with director of therapy services, Gracie.

A Little Unsolicited Advice

Before I go, I'd like to speak directly to fellow survivors and offer a little advice. You've probably gotten a lot over the past weeks, months, or years, so just take what you want from this baker's dozen, and remember that all strokes are different, and I'm only an expert on my own.

1. Hold your head up. No—literally, hold it up. It's easy to look at the ground, and it feels safer, but you only need to look down occasionally. Your posture has a profound effect on your self-image—and your actual image, the image you present to others. Head-down means defeat. Head-up means dignity and pride and courage. Head-up and you are facing the world. Head-up and you're a survivor, and that's something to be proud of. It's a simple thing that can make a big difference.

2. You will find in time that you actually can do a huge percentage of the things you once did, but just more slowly. I can still get on and off the bus; I just do it much more slowly. And what is really lost by that? Is every moment of every day so jam-packed with life-affirming activities that spending forty percent more time on logistical things like getting dressed or making a sandwich represents such a tragedy? No. It only means that I have somewhat fewer minutes in the day to rot in front of the television or scroll past memes on Facebook. That's okay, and in the big picture, it's probably a blessing in disguise. The stroke has forced Zen upon you. "Accepting that which you cannot change," as the Serenity Prayer counsels, will make you more, well, serene.

3. That said, you will encounter numerous tasks every day that you will not be able to do the old way and might never again be able to do the

old way. But that doesn't mean you can't do them; it only means you can't do them the old way. If I had insisted on sawing the Christmas tree trunk with my right hand, I'd still be sawing today, more than a year later. The first time I tried to bowl after the stroke, I had to use my left hand, my feet firmly planted behind the scratch line, and rolled an abysmal 43, including a lot of gutter balls. But by the third game, in less than an hour, I was bowling over 100. It just took me a few minutes and patience. A little rebellious swagger can go a long way, too: "I'll show them!"

4. Beyond simply switching hands (if switch you must), you will face seemingly insurmountable challenges related to one-handedness. To the extent you can, gamify those challenges. Break problems and processes down into their basic components and face them one at a time. When your working hand is full of stuff and you can't open a door, stop. Take a deep breath. Then break the problem into its components and see if you can solve the first one first. Can you hold something under either of your arms and so free your hand to turn the knob? Is there something you can hold under your chin or carefully in your teeth? If not, then just set the items on the ground; picking them back up once the door is open will be good therapy. You'll likely get good at using found objects as tools, then using them for leverage, tearing, prying, twisting and all the thousand other things we do automatically with two hands. Get in touch with your primordial toolmaking self. One-handed guitar playing and one-handed knot tying are prime examples of this type of thinking in my story.

5. Don't put an end date on your recovery. You will hear three numbers thrown around a lot: six months, one year, and eighteen months. Every stroke is different, so depending on yours, you might be good as new in six months or you might still be making tiny improvements ten years post. Obviously, improvement is more gradual the farther away from the injury you are. Remember—I was flat on my back for the first few days, then in a wheelchair for a solid six weeks while I tried to get my legs back. When I finally got home, it took me nearly an hour to walk six blocks, but that time fell dramatically over the next three months.

Jill Bolte Taylor (yes, I finally read the book) writes that it took her seven years to consider herself "completely recovered." Her stroke was significantly different from mine, with much more cognitive impairment and much less motor impairment. All the same, the severity of her stroke and the totality of her recovery offers hope to all of us who are still in midstream.

6. Because recovery can still happen many years after a stroke, we would be foolish not to keep the option of full recovery open. Personally, I have no plans to stop improving, but that requires keeping my options open. Here is what I mean:

    All my therapists were unanimous in this: once your soft tissues— your muscles, tendons, and ligaments—shorten, especially in your forearms, it's game over. You cannot get that back, and therefore will never get full function back in your weak hand. There's certainly no guarantee that if you keep those tissues long the hand will come back; it might not. The only guarantee is that if you don't stretch and keep those muscles and other tissues long, then it doesn't matter if your nerves reconnect or not—you've foreclosed any chance of full recovery. Don't let your body atrophy. Don't let your arm shrivel or your hand retreat and curl into a claw. You have control over this, and Botox can help. And even if you don't get back function, there will be other benefits of keeping your range of motion, like the ability to get your hand open to get it clean or to cut your fingernails. Even if it's just for looks, it's worth staying flexible.

7. Remember what I said about a children's tumbling mat and smart speaker being the most useful tools in my recovery.

8. Of course, no matter how much you get back, you'll experience a tremendous amount of frustration in the meantime. But you can mitigate that a great deal by streamlining your logistical life and just avoiding some things altogether. I don't buy shirts any more that must be buttoned down at the corners. Those were stupid anyway! Am I now going to waste two minutes of precious life per button struggling to accomplish something that served no real purpose in the first place? I hope to have peppered these tips—those that save time, energy, and sanity—throughout this book, like shampoo from a pump bottle instead of a squeeze bottle, squirting toothpaste directly into your mouth, using a rocker knife at mealtime, and pants with cargo pockets

on your good side. If someone tells you cargo pants aren't cool, a.) They're wrong, b.) You tell them they can kiss your sweet, cargo-panted ass, or c.) Say "Oh, these aren't cargo pants—they're *tactical* pants . . ." then give them a long, disturbing stare.

Streamline and simplify. That's good advice for everyone. You've been wanting to simplify your life for a long time. Now's your chance.

9. Get a good pair of small scissors and take them with you everywhere except to bed and on airplanes. You'll use them all the time and avoid a lot of frustration. They should fit in the cargo pants.

10. Assume people's best intentions. Having a newly acquired disability presents a psychological minefield for you, your family, friends, coworkers, and strangers. Be gentle and generous with them as you all figure this out together.

11. Cry. It's OK. You've got a right. Something profoundly sad has happened to you. You'll feel a certain societal pressure to "be grateful for what you have left." And you should be. But just because it could have been worse (it can *always* be worse) doesn't mean you don't have a right to grieve. What's more, you have to. Experts agree that grieving is not really something that can be skipped or fast-forwarded through. It's okay to be pissed off about your stroke. I still am, two years on. And when you're ready to cry, go for it and don't hold anything back. Cry long and cry hard. I recommend the shower for this, as it washes all the tears and snot down the drain, and you generally come out feeling much better.

12. So you'll get frustrated, and you'll cry, but don't waste a lot of time brooding about all you can no longer do. That is ultimately a waste of time, and wasting time is wasting life. Once you start obsessing over that stuff, you are basically just waiting to die. Some people spend thirty or forty years just waiting to die when they could have been doing something interesting, something that made the world a better place. Focus on what you *can* do and try to do more of that. What can you still do? Do that.

13. Try new things to fill the voids in your life left by the stroke.

Wheelchair-bound? Well, that sucks bigtime. But maybe it's the universe's way of forcing you to fulfill your destiny as the next great writer or singer. Aphasia (loss of speech)? Then take up painting or photography or cooking. Life on Earth offers thousands of ways for us to engage with the universe and each other. What have you always thought you might try but have put off for some reason? The cliché that when one door closes another opens might sound unbearably cheesy right now, but it also happens to be true. Be open. Be adventurous. Why not?

—A.S., January 2020

Acknowledgments

I hope this book is itself an acknowledgements page, albeit a very long one. It is impossible to separate those who helped me survive and recover from those who helped with this book, because there could not be the latter without the former. And so to list all of the people who helped me would be much like reprinting the book, and that would be very inefficient indeed. That said, there are a few I would like to thank, in addition to those I have already named.

I would like to thank the following therapists, some of whose names I have changed in the book. Their real first names are: Ami, Amy, the other Amy, Anna, Audra, Bekah, Bob, the other Bob, Carrie, Cassie, Christine, Cindy, Cynthia, Debbie, Elise, Emily, Geralynn, Hannah, Heather, Irina, Janelle, Jennifer, the other Jennifer, Jimmy, Kathleen, Kathy, Kim, K.T., Lisa, Melissa, Meredith, Robert, Roni, Rose, Roxanne, Sarah, Susan, and Vicky. You've chosen a noble profession, and you got me to where I am.

I would also like to thank the early readers of my manuscript, especially my mother and the real writer of the family, Jan Seale, who provided sage editorial guidance in addition to giving me life. Also in this category are my wife, Kirstin, my big brothers Erren and Ansen Seale, and my friends Ed Cavazos, David McLeod, Wade Walker, and Rohit John Varghese.

Finally, I would like to thank TCU Press for giving me the chance to tell this story. Thank you, Dan Williams, Rebecca Allen, Melinda Esco, Molly Spain, Kathy Walton, and Ariel Zinkan.

Glossary

ABI—acquired brain injury. Strokes are one kind of ABI.

ADLs—activities of daily living. Brushing one's teeth and grocery shopping are ADLs.

AVM—arteriovenous malformation, a tangle of blood vessels in which arteries connect directly to veins without an organ separating the two.

balance billing—a practice common among city or county ambulance services, in which the ambulance services, typically monopolies, bill at a higher rate than insurance will cover and the patient is billed the balance.

brain attack—stroke, CVA.

central line—large-bore intravenous drug delivery line that uses jugular, femoral, or subclavian veins of the neck.

clonus—muscular spasm involving repeated, often rhythmic, contractions.

CVA—cerebrovascular accident, a stroke.

DCed meds—discontinued medications.

DME—durable medical equipment, e.g. a wheelchair or an AFO.

goniometer—angle finder in physical or occupational therapy.

intubation—the insertion of a tube into a patient's body, especially that of an artificial ventilation tube into the trachea.

on the floor—in nursing, to be on call at a hospital. Ex: "I transitioned into wound care because I was tired of being on the floor."

OT—occupational therapy, in stroke, mostly works to recover arm and hand function.

pre-auth—to be authorized by one's insurance company to receive a treatment before receiving it.

PRN—pro re nata, literally "for the thing born," "if the situation arises"; in medication, PRN indicates an optional drug such as a pain reliever or a vitamin supplement, ex: "That Zyrtec is PRN." In nursing, PRN most likely means a temporary gig, someone picking up a shift to supplement their permanent position, ex: "I work at HealthSouth, but I am PRN at St. David's."

prone—on one's belly, ex: POE = prone on elbows

PT—physical therapy, in stroke, works to recover gross motor function, most often standing, sitting, walking, etc.

subrogation—the attempt to avoid payment of a claim by searching for other parties that might be liable, such as an employer, or other insurance that might be "primary" under the circumstances.

supine—in supination, on your back; opposite of prone, or in pronation (on your belly).

TBI—traumatic brain injury, e.g. from a car accident, motorcycle crash, gunshot wound, snowboarding. Strokes are not TBIs, but rather ABIs, acquired brain injuries.

VFSE—video fluoroscopic swallowing exam.

About the Author

Avrel Seale lives in Austin, Texas, with his wife and three teenage sons. The author of nine books, he has been a newspaper reporter and columnist and has spent most of his career in writing and editing positions at the University of Texas at Austin. He is an Aquarius, blood type A-negative, and an INTP according to the Myers-Briggs Type Indicator. Fluent in Pig Latin, Seale holds the Jackson Elementary School record for the flexed-arm hang, and was champion of the 1982 Dungeons & Dragons tournament participated in by more than five adolescent males in McAllen, Texas. He was a keynote speaker at the Second Annual Southeast Texas Bigfoot Conference. Avrel Seale has shaken hands with Stevie Ray Vaughan and has built two working boats.